"A solid exposé that reads like a psychological detective thriller . . . this brilliant, meticulously researched book probes what many see as the failure of psychoanalysis to confront the real world." —*Publishers Weekly*

"His scholarship is impeccable."
—*Los Angeles Times*

"One need not follow Masson's rabid acceptance of a tightly construed [seduction] theory to regret, with him, Freud's emotional withdrawal from patients and his intellectual withdrawal from social criticism. . . . Jeffrey Masson has raised important historical questions." —*Washington Post Book World*

"A lavishly documented, carefully reasoned work, written in a straightforward, reasonable style."
—*The Nation*

"Newly revealed letters and long-secret documents offer further indications of Sigmund Freud's anguish over his first major theory, new evidence of efforts to cover up that anguish and provide new information about the life of the man himself."
—*The New York Times*

Other books by Jeffrey Moussaieff Masson

Final Analysis: The Making and Unmaking of a Psychoanalyst

Against Therapy: Emotional Tyranny and the Myth
of Psychological Healing

A Dark Science: Women, Sexuality and Psychiatry
in the Nineteenth Century

The Complete Letters of Sigmund Freud to Wilhelm Fliess, 1887–1904

The Oceanic Feeling: The Origins of Religious Sentiment
in Ancient India

The Assault on Truth

Freud's Suppression
of the Seduction
Theory

by *Jeffrey Moussaieff Masson*

HarperPerennial
A Division of HarperCollins*Publishers*

*I dedicate this edition to Catharine A. MacKinnon for the
seven years of friendship. For her example of an
uncompromising search for truth. For the courage to say it.
For finding new and powerful approaches to ending sexual abuse.
For the person she is.*

Grateful acknowledgment is made to Basic Books, Inc., for permission to reprint excerpts from *Collected Papers of Sigmund Freud*, vols. 1-5, copyright © 1959 by Basic Books, Inc., Publishers; from *The Origins of Psychoanalysis: Letters to Wilhelm Fliess* by Sigmund Freud, copyright © 1954 by Basic Books, Inc., Publishers; and from *The Life and Work of Sigmund Freud* by Ernest Jones, copyright © 1957 by Ernest Jones; to Judith Dupont for permission to quote from the letters and diaries of Sándor Ferenczi; to Mervyn Jones for permission to quote from the previously unpublished correspondence of his father, Ernest Jones; to Sigmund Freud Copyrights, Ltd., the Institute of Psycho-Analysis, and the Hogarth Press, London, for permission to quote from *The Standard Edition of the Complete Psychological Works of Sigmund Freud*, translated and edited by James Strachey; to Sigmund Freud Copyrights, Ltd., for their kind permission to quote from the previously unpublished correspondence of Sigmund Freud, copyright © 1984 by Sigmund Freud Copyrights, Ltd.

HarperCollins books may be purchased for educational, business, or sales promotional use. For information, please call or write: Special Markets Department, HarperCollins Publishers, Inc., 10 East 53rd Street, New York, NY 10022. Telephone: (212) 207-7528; Fax: (212) 207-7222.

First HarperPerennial edition published 1992.

LIBRARY OF CONGRESS CATALOG CARD NUMBER 91-50507

ISBN 0-06-097457-5

92 93 94 95 96 RRD 10 9 8 7 6 5 4 3 2 1

CONTENTS

ILLUSTRATIONS

ACKNOWLEDGMENTS

B ECAUSE of the controversial nature of this book, many of the people who helped me in various ways may well wish their names had been omitted here. I can only stress that no one mentioned is any way responsible for my views—they are mine and mine alone.

Without the generosity of K. R. Eissler, Anna Freud, and Muriel Gardiner, this book would not have been possible. Through them I was given access to a vast storehouse of otherwise unavailable documents. Because the conclusions I reached on the basis of these documents were not such that they could share them with me, our original collaboration unfortunately came to an end. I remain deeply grateful, however, for their many acts of kindness.

Many of the views expressed in this book are the result of long conversations with my former wife, Terri Alter. She has a remarkable ability to see into the depths of things, and I profited enormously from her moral courage and intellectual brilliance.

Marianne Loring has been associated for many years now with my forthcoming edition of Freud's letters to Fliess. We read through every document together and translated them jointly. Her dedication to research and her personal friendship were an inspiration in the writing of this book.

Robert Goldman read the entire manuscript in several versions and brought to bear his unusual gifts and incisive thinking and made many invaluable suggestions. Over the many years of our friendship, spanning Poona, Toronto, and Berkeley, we have had long and fruitful discussions that enriched my intellectual life.

Sally Sutherland read the final draft closely; I value her perspicacity.

Gerhard Fichtner prepared a reliable transcript of the German text of the Freud/Fliess letters and also gave me the benefit of his wide knowledge of the history of medicine.

Lottie Newman was responsible for the first draft of the translation of the Freud/Fliess letters and gave me excellent advice on further drafts.

Mark Paterson of Sigmund Freud Copyrights has remained friendly through difficult times.

Nancy Miller, at Farrar, Straus and Giroux, with tact and great understanding, has suggested innumerable improvements and her enthusiasm never flagged. The book would have been very different without her help, and I am deeply grateful.

Edith Schipper of the Bayerische Staatsbibliothek in Munich graciously searched for obscure articles on my behalf. The staff of the Lane Medical Library at Stanford University, especially Mrs. B. Vadeboncoeur, were unfailingly courteous. The staff of the Bibliothèque de la Morgue de Paris devoted an entire day to assisting me. Jill Duncan of the library at the London Institute of Psycho-Analysis was very helpful, as were the staff at the Health Sciences Library at Columbia University, where part of Freud's library is housed. For several years I borrowed many of Freud's books from the house in Maresfield Gardens, thanks to the generosity of Anna Freud. Hilde Lorentz was a superb and efficient typist.

I have received various grants for research on the forthcoming edition of the Freud/Fliess letters. Since the present book is a direct result of this research, I gratefully acknowledge the financial assistance I received from the New Land

Foundation, the National Endowment for the Humanities, the National Institutes of Health (National Library of Medicine), and the Fund for Psychoanalytic Research of the American Psychoanalytic Association.

Finally, for the joy they gave me while I was writing this book, I want to thank Karima and Denise, and most of all my daughter, Simone.

Jeffrey Moussaieff Masson

Berkeley, California
May 5, 1983

PREFACE TO THE
1985 EDITION

WHEN THIS book first appeared in hardcover, the many reviewers who wrote about it concentrated their criticism on the supposed character of the author. I was, in their words, "a vengeful outcast," "perpetually adolescent," "monumentally stupid," "an opportunist," "a charlatan," "a kid," and "a master of seduction." When reviewers did turn their attention to the book, it was not often to the arguments within, but to the volume's very existence. "All that the book and its author deserve is oblivion"; it is "a grave slander"; it is "comical and self-serving," "pathetic and mean-spirited." As one can see from these adjectives, unusual in the book pages, my book was generating considerable emotional response. My character was attacked, my motivation was attacked, but my arguments, and even more importantly, the new historical material I brought to light, were not adequately addressed.

The reason for this unusual response was the appearance, in December 1983, of two articles in *The New Yorker* by Janet Malcolm, entitled "Trouble in the Archives." These pieces recently appeared as a book, *In the Freud Archives* (Knopf, 1984). Most reviewers not only found her book delightful and instructive, but also concurred with her evaluation of me: I was, without question, "an intellectual terrorist," "a veritable Iago, papered over with charm yet filled with motiveless malignity." Christopher Lehmann-Haupt, reviewing the book in *The New York Times,* concedes that Freudians have been reluctant to acknowledge childhood rape, "but with predators like Jeffrey Masson lurking in their territory, one finds it difficult to blame them for perpetrating it [the cover-up]."

None of these reviewers ever stopped to ask whether this portrait of me was fair or accurate, how it was acquired, and what my role in it had been. In fact, Robert Coles in the *Boston Globe* went so far as to state that "it is not Janet Malcolm who calls him such: his own words reveal this psychological profile—a self-portrait offered to us through the efforts of an observer and listener who is, surely, as wise as any in the psychoanalytic profession." It is crucial to note, however, that Malcolm is not always the disinterested observer she claims to be, and that much of what she presents in her "profile" of me is colored by her interpretation of our conversations. Carlin Romano of *The Philadelphia Inquirer* learned, for example, that when Malcolm wrote "At no time during our acquaintance did Masson answer my question about what had brought on his sudden virulent anti-Freudianism" and later spoke of my "silence" on this question, she was using the words "answer" and "silence" to imply that I had secret motivations I was trying to conceal. But, in fact, I did answer at great length—what is my book, but an extended answer to this important question? What Malcolm meant, she explained to Romano, was that I did not give her a *satisfactory* answer. But she omitted to warn her readers that she was using the verb "to answer" in this unusually restricted sense. Romano concluded that "a comparison of the articles with the book supports Masson's allegations that Malcolm reconstructs conversations—an unacceptable journalistic technique." Romano's piece caught the attention of Geoffrey Stokes of the *Village Voice,* who wrote about it in his *Press Clips* (June 28, 1984). For the next month, there was a series of letters and responses published in the *Voice*. Stokes (July 17, 1984) summed up his belief that Malcolm had engaged in dishonest journalism:

> This sort of selective (mis)quotation calls Malcolm's good faith into question, and it is only on an almost preternatural amount of good faith that readers can rely when reporters start creating composite quotations. The net effect of what Malcolm has done—because it is

central to her portrait of Masson, which was in turn central to her articles and book—seems to me far worse than the comparatively minor atmospheric details invented by Alastair Reid. [In the spring of 1984 Reid, a *New Yorker* writer, confessed to creating composite characters in pieces he presented as factual reporting.]

Sanskrit scholar Robert Goldman, who had also been misquoted in the Malcolm pieces, pointed to what he saw as the damage these pieces had done in an article he wrote for *California Monthly* (July 1984):

Malcolm's articles appeared in advance of the publication of Masson's *The Assault on Truth* and set the intellectual tone for the reviews Masson would receive. Her articles provided Masson's critics both with the precedent for ignoring his discoveries (while focusing on his personality) and with the ammunition for attacking him—his credentials, his competence, and his motives—without the need to conduct any independent inquiry of their own. To be blunt: Malcolm's account of Jeffrey Masson is a tendentious, dishonest, and malicious piece of character assassination, all the more pernicious because of its studied tone of mildly amused detachment. Had her articles (and now book) never appeared, the arguments of Masson's book surely would have been given a fairer and more dispassionate hearing than is now seemingly possible.

I believe that Goldman is correct, and his points are interesting because they raise issues that are far more important than whether the portrait of me is an accurate one. What is at issue is how one responds to the new information recently becoming available on the abuse of women and children. Many reviewers (almost all men, interestingly) have followed Janet Malcolm's lead in focusing their attention on my personality and motivation, thereby avoiding the substantive issues raised by my discoveries. Nor do I believe that the driving force of this hostile response lies in any personal animus against me. One cannot escape the feeling that most men (and some women) have terrible difficulty when it comes to even hearing about the miseries of childhood, and about the suffering many girls undergo in their early years, first at the hands of a trusted adult (generally a close male relative) and later at the hands of a therapist (generally male) who does not believe their memories and will not take seriously what has really happened to them in childhood, ascribing it, more often than not, to a perverted imagination or to an allegedly normal childhood fantasy—a desire to be raped by the father.

Many women, sympathetic to the research I have done in this book, have been puzzled by my lack of explicit recognition of the work done by feminist authors in the field of the sexual abuse of children. Since I am not an expert in the issues involved in child abuse as it exists today, and felt that I was addressing an explicitly historical issue (and one confined to psychoanalysis and the role it played in ignoring the extent of child abuse), I did not feel competent to comment on the modern literature. But I believe, in retrospect, that this was a mistake. For one thing, it cannot be taken for granted that all or even most of my readers will be aware of the dimensions of the problem; and for another, it now strikes me as wrong not to acknowledge my predecessors in this field and the important contribution they made. There are three books in particular that deeply impressed me and taught me a great deal about the subject of the sexual abuse of children, which I highly recommend to readers: David Finkelhor's *Sexually Victimized Children* (The Free Press, 1979); Florence Rush's *The Best Kept Secret: Sexual Abuse of Children* (Prentice Hall, 1980); and Judith Herman's *Father/Daughter Incest* (Harvard, 1981). All three authors, writing in the wider context of a feminist perspective, one I lacked when I wrote my book, reached very similar conclusions to mine with respect to Freud. From these authors I learned that the problem was far greater than I had realized. This became clearer still after reading the authoritative article by Diana E. H. Russell, "The Incidence and Prevalence of Intrafamilial and Extrafamilial Sexual Abuse of Female Children"

(*Child Abuse & Neglect*, 7: 133–146, 1983). Russell concludes that "over one-quarter of the population of female children have experienced sexual abuse before the age of 14, and well over one-third have had such an experience by the age of 18 years." Her article was based on interviews with a random sample of 930 adult female residents of San Francisco. It was the first time that such a survey was undertaken, and the results are staggering. We can assume, I think, that if such abuse is so prevalent in this segment of the general population, then among people who seek psychotherapy, it is likely to be even higher. This assumption is supported by the findings of Elaine Carmen, Patricia Rieker, and Trudy Mills in "Victims of Violence and Psychiatric Illness" in the *American Journal of Psychiatry* (141: 378–383, 1984): "Almost half of the patients had histories of physical and/or sexual abuse." These authors then admit candidly: "Our research underscores the discrepancy between the alarming number of people who are physically and sexually abused and the relative lack of attention that is given to these topics in taking routine psychiatric histories."

In the end, it is the reality and the extent of the abuse that matters, and, equally important, the fact that both are routinely denied or in some other fashion neglected by psychoanalysts and psychiatrists. It is irrelevant where this neglect originates. I believe that Freud is largely responsible for this neglect by having given intellectual sophistication to a wrong view (that women invent rape) for the perpetuation of a view that is comforting to male society; but I do not believe that this is the reason we persist in ignoring the reality of this abuse. To understand this, one must take into account the wider issues raised by Florence Rush and Judith Herman and other feminist authors. There is no doubt in my mind that it was the feminist literature of the 1970s that finally broke the silence about the incidence and prevalence of incest. It was only the feminists who were able to place what had happened in the past in a perspective that made sense, and who pointed at the same time to the urgency and depth of the problem.

Not only is the best literature on this topic written by feminists, but the courageous books that talked about personal incest experiences, the first autobiographical accounts, were all by women: Maya Angelou's *I Know Why the Caged Bird Sings* (Random House, 1970); Sandra Bulter's *Conspiracy of Silence: The Trauma of Incest* (New Glide Publications, 1978); Louise Armstrong's *Kiss Daddy Goodnight: A Speak-Out on Incest* (Hawthorn Books, 1978); Susan Forward's *Betrayal of Innocence: Incest and Its Devastation* (Penguin, 1979); Katherine Brady's *Father's Days* (Seaview, 1979); and Charlotte Vale Allen's *Daddy's Girl: A Memoir* (Simon and Schuster, 1980). How different this literature is from the standard psychiatric literature, not just in its power to move us emotionally, but also in the courage to tell the truth, and to tell it in the words that belong to the real events. This is perhaps nowhere better evidenced than in the moving novel about incest by Michelle Morris, *If I Should Die Before I Wake* (J. P. Tarcher, 1982), and three books by Alice Miller, the noted Swiss psychoanalyst: *Prisoners of Childhood* (Basic Books, 1981); *For Your Own Good: Hidden Cruelty in Childrearing and the Roots of Violence.* (Farrar, Straus and Giroux, 1983); and *Thou Shall Not Be Aware: Psychonalysis and Society's Betrayal of Children* (Farrar, Straus and Giroux, 1984).

Now that the storm raised by the appearance of my book has calmed down somewhat, it may be possible to evaluate the documents and their significance in a more objective manner. No doubt my speculations about Freud's motivations, being merely an interpretation, are not conclusive or definitive. I can only look forward to a time when the whole matter can be discussed in a more scholarly fashion, when objections to my position will be based on a different understanding of the documents, rather than a dislike for the subject matter or the imagined personality of the author.

PREFACE TO THE HARPERPERENNIAL EDITION

S INCE I first began writing this book ten years ago, a great deal has happened relating to the sexual abuse of children. Nobody, now, denies that it happens. Few, now, deny that it happens frequently. Almost everybody recognizes that it happens across all lines of class, income, and education. Ten years ago this was not the case. Then there was a lonely contingent of courageous feminist researchers—among them Louise Armstrong, Florence Rush, Judith Herman, and Diana Russell—whose works were ignored, by and large, by the mainstream media and especially by psychiatry, the very profession women who were abused as children often turned to in their tragically mistaken belief that they would find help. Psychiatry was largely responsible for the climate of disbelief that surrounded those women who braved the scorn of male professionals and spoke up about their own experience of abuse.

What has happened over these ten years to make this change possible? A growing body of scholarly writing (by people such as David Finkelhor, Roland Summit, Ann Burgess, Kee MacFarlane, Sandra Butler, and especially, again, Diana Russell and Judith Herman); the justly popular books by Alice Miller that speak passionately and eloquently on the reality of child sexual abuse; many firsthand reports from women who had experienced incest and were able to publish their stories (Katherine Brady, Charlotte Vale Allen, Eleanore Hill, Sylvia Fraser, Trudi Chase); and finally, accounts in all major media of two sexual abuse scandals that mesmerized the nation, one in Jordan, Minnesota, and one at the McMartin Preschool in

Manhattan Beach, California. All of these factors shattered society's apathy and disbelief, and many reports flooded in.

How has psychiatry reacted? As if all along these professionals were the ones fighting to have an unwanted truth recognized. And now they were prepared to accept their reward in the form of being called upon as experts. From having denied the existence of child sexual abuse, or at least its importance, they were now offering workshops in its treatment methodology. The change was caused by the profession's realization that there was a profit to be made either through a new patient population or through "educating" the public.

The picture, however, is not monochromatic. Society as a whole has been willing to recognize the reality of child sexual abuse. Witness the cover story in the October 7, 1991 issue of *People* magazine about Roseanne Barr, which was an excellent article. But the price to be paid was in the backlash. This backlash is really a reflection on a societal level of the vehement rejection of an accusation at the individual level. That is, most men, when accused of child sexual abuse, become outraged at the very idea, and flat out deny that they did any such thing. Pressed to explain a two- or three- or ten-year-old child's possible motivation for lying about such an event, especially when that same child manifests every sign of great affection, warmth, and even love for the man, the abuser will say: "She is fantasizing." In the past psychiatrists had often helped men evade their responsibility by invoking Freud's explanation for the pervasiveness of child sexual abuse. It was too improbable, said Freud, forgetting his teacher Charcot's ringing words, which he had so often evoked: *La théorie c'est bon, mais ça n'empeche pas d'exister* ["Theory is fine, but it does not prevent facts from existing"].

But Freud was rapidly losing credibility when it came to child sexual abuse. Florence Rush, Alice Miller, Judith Herman, and I all in our own ways, and separately, have pointed out the inconsistencies and historical inaccuracies on which the psychoanalytic approach to the issue was based. The publication of the complete letters of Sigmund Freud to Wilhelm Fliess by Harvard University Press in 1985, which I edited and translated, provided for the first time the real historical account of Freud's views on sexual abuse, which were more complicated than we had been led to believe by the standard psychoanalytic histories. The hard data Diana Russell provided in a landmark essay in 1983 stated that "over one-quarter of the population of female children have experienced sexual abuse before the age of fourteen, and well over one-third have had such an experience by the age of eighteen years," was universally accepted by other researchers and showed Freud's error revealed for what it was; he was simply wrong in claiming that most women who complain are fantasizing, as opposed to remembering sexual abuse. (The implication for psychoanalysis, psychiatry, and psychology in general is another story, and one that I have tried to address in three subsequent books: *A Dark Science; Against Therapy;* and *Final Analysis*).

I would like to take this opportunity to clarify a misunderstanding about my attitude toward Freud. I found a large number of previously unpublished documents that clarified the question of Freud's abandonment of the seduction hypothesis. But these documents, while permitting a much fuller explanation of the historical circumstances surrounding this crucial event in Freud's intellectual life, do not permit anybody to claim with certainty that he or she now understands Freud's motivation. I certainly speculate in this book what that motivation might be: a fear of losing his friendship with Fliess; a fear of standing up for the least advantaged in society; a desire to distance himself from any responsibility in the failed operation on a favorite patient; a fear of the wrath of the more powerful men—men of the middle class elite whom Freud's patients were accusing of sexual abuse, and a desire to remain in the good graces of these men so that he could continue to practice his profession. However, I must emphasize that these are mere speculations. I do not know for certain what Freud's motivation was, and I cannot imagine that any document as yet undiscovered will eventually disclose it. I may disapprove of what I call Freud's loss of moral courage, but I cannot claim that I understand it.

Nevertheless, new documents may well shed some light on Freud's reversal. Since the first edition of this book, I have come across one document that I did not know of when I published *Assault*. In 1899 Leopold Löwenfeld, in his book *Sexualleben und Nervenleiden*, wrote that "one of the cases in which Freud used his analytic method [to uncover a sexual event in early childhood] came under my observation by chance. The patient in question told me with absolute certainty that the infantile sexual scene which Freud's analysis had apparently uncovered was pure fantasy and was never experienced by him in reality." This account no doubt distressed Freud. Here was a well-known German psychiatrist saying that Freud's patients were merely engaged in fantasies, that they were not remembering, and for proof he had a retraction from one of these very patients whom Freud had relied on to devise his original seduction theory. I think we must add this piece of evidence to the ones I cited earlier. It strengthens my belief that Freud was extremely upset by the response his initial theory evoked among his male colleagues.

Even in light of the recent evidence described above, Freud's subsequent seduction theory remained so entrenched in the psychological literature, and so enormously beneficial to those with power that it wouldn't totally disappear without a last ditch struggle. That struggle has come to be known as the backlash against accusations of child sexual abuse. That is, at first people were not prepared to believe the phenomenon existed at all. Then they did. And now, claim the revisionists, we have gone too far in the other direction, and believe all accounts, no matter how wild or improbable or devoid of evidence. This backlash is not dependent on psychiatry; it has its own organization, VOCAL (Victims of Child Abuse Legislation), whose members are primarily, though not exclusively, men accused of child sexual abuse. It has one or two prominent speakers, such as Lee Coleman, who happens to be a psychiatrist but has a rather enlightened view of the profession's uselessness in these and other matters. VOCAL has produced a body of literature that is in no way comparable to the serious literature on the other side (best summed up in Diana Russell's superb book, *The Secret Trauma*), but mostly centers around the "improbable" and "impossible" stories from day-care centers, with Jordan and McMartin as the showpieces.

Fantasy—the notion from Freud that women invent allegations of sexual abuse because they desire sex—continues to play a role in undermining the credibility of victims of sexual abuse. This was recently showcased in the Senate hearings on the confirmation of Judge Clarence Thomas, in which his accuser was alternately portrayed as an "erotomaniac," a woman who fantasizes that powerful men want to have sex with her, and a vengeful spurned woman. The vengeful woman also makes an appearance as the mother who fabricates sexual abuse of her children by their father to win custody. As Louise Armstrong and others, particularly Phyllis Chesler in her strong book *Mothers on Trial*, have documented, women who accuse their husbands of sexual abuse of their children as part of divorce proceedings often lose custody precisely because they made the accusation.

There is a growing body of writing about false accusations of child sexual abuse, but much of it is partisan, and some of it is extremely unreliable. Of course, one cannot say that false accusations never happen, and that children, for one reason or another, never recant. But such cases are rare. However, some authors take the position that abuse never occurs. For example, Paul and Shirley Eberle's book *The Politics of Child Abuse*, a so-called exposé of the McMartin case, attempts to exonerate all the accused. But as *Ms.* magazine pointed out (December 1988), these same authors also edit a soft-core pornography magazine, and were formerly responsible for publishing a hard-core pornography magazine, *Finger*, which contained such edifying articles as "Sexpot at Five" and "My First Rape."

Two excellent, balanced, and informative books have been written about the backlash, especially the Jordan, Minnesota, and McMartin cases. One is by John Crewdson, *By Silence Betrayed: Sexual Abuse of Children in America* (1988), and the other is David Hechler's *The Battle and the Backlash: The Child Sexual Abuse War* (1988). Both authors tackle the thorny question of the statistics on false charges of sexual abuse. The key article is by Douglas Besharov, who was the first director of the National Center on Child Abuse and Neglect, entitled "Doing Something About Child Abuse" and published in the *Harvard Journal of Law and Public Policy* in 1985. In that article Besharov writes: "More than sixty-five percent of all reports of suspected child maltreatment—involving over 750,000 children per year—turn out to be 'unfounded.'" (Note that Besharov is speaking not just about sexual abuse cases, but also about physical abuse and neglect, a fact that many writers ignore when attempting to imply that most sexual abuse cases are later proven false). Moreover, "unfounded" and false are not the same, as both Hechler and Crewdson point out. Sometimes an "unsubstantiated" case merely means that no investigation was possible because the family moved away, because a case worker has no time to investigate it, or because the child cannot or will not speak to an investigator. If a child is pre-verbal, and cannot name her accuser, some reporting systems then legally require that the case be called "unfounded." In California, the Department of Social Services admits that it investigates fewer than half of the fifty thousand child abuse reports it receives each year. "If they cannot determine within a week or ten days whether an accusation of abuse is true, the report in question is either labeled "unfounded" or purged from the state's central registry altogether. "During an average month in 1985, nearly five thousand Los Angeles children who were suspected of being physically or sexually abused were never visited by a child protection worker at all" writes Crewdson (*By Silence Betrayed*, p. 23).

We are only slowly beginning to recognize that child sexual abuse is not confined to the United States, but is a worldwide problem. In other countries, while material has been gathered about child abuse in general, the tendency has been to overlook sexual abuse. But that is changing, and there has been a number of publications about the topic in Germany, especially, but also in Switzerland, Holland, England, and Italy.

This popular and scholarly activity around the world, especially in the United States, demonstrates that society has, even if reluctantly and belatedly, come to recognize that the sexual abuse of children is real, widespread, serious, and long-silenced. I am glad that this book has played a role in ending that silence.

INTRODUCTION

I N 1970, I became interested in the origins of psychoanalysis and in Freud's relationship with Wilhelm Fliess,
the ear, nose, and throat physician who was his closest friend
during the years Freud was formulating his new theories.

For some time I had been corresponding with Anna Freud
about the possibility of preparing a complete edition of
Freud's letters to Fliess, an abridged version of which had
been published in 1950 in German and in 1954 in English
as *The Origins of Psychoanalysis* (New York: Basic Books).
This edition had been edited by Anna Freud, Ernst Kris, and
Marie Bonaparte. In 1980, I met with Dr. K. R. Eissler, the
head of the Freud Archives and Anna Freud's trusted adviser
and friend, and with Anna Freud in London, and Miss Freud
agreed to a new edition of the Freud/Fliess letters. As a
result, I was given access to this sealed correspondence (the
originals are in the Library of Congress), which constitutes
our most important source of information concerning the
beginnings of psychoanalysis.

In addition to including all the letters and passages which
previously had been omitted (which amounted to more than
half the text), I thought it necessary to annotate the book
fully. I would thus need access to other relevant material.
Anna Freud offered her complete cooperation, and I was
given the freedom of Maresfield Gardens, where Freud spent
the last year of his life.

Freud's magnificent personal library was there, and many

of the volumes, especially from the early years, were annotated by Freud. In Freud's desk I discovered a notebook kept by Marie Bonaparte after she purchased Freud's letters to Fliess in 1936, in which she comments on Freud's reactions to these letters, which he had written years before. I also found a series of letters concerned with Sándor Ferenczi, who was in later years Freud's closest analytic friend and colleague, and with the last paper Ferenczi delivered to the 12th International Psycho-Analytic Congress in Wiesbaden. This paper dealt with the sexual seduction of children, a topic that had engrossed Freud during the years of his friendship with Fliess.

In a large black cupboard outside Anna Freud's bedroom, I found many original letters to and from Freud written during this same period, letters that were previously unknown— a letter from Fliess to Freud, letters from Charcot to Freud, letters from Freud to Josef Breuer, to his sister-in-law Minna Bernays, to his wife Martha, and to former patients.

A short time later, Dr. Eissler asked me if I would be willing to succeed him as director of the Freud Archives. I agreed and was appointed provisional Projects Director. The Archives had purchased Freud's house in Maresfield Gardens, and I was to convert the house into a museum and research center. Anna Freud gave me access to the restricted material she had already donated to the Library of Congress, to enable me to prepare a catalogue of all the Freud material at the Library (most of it from the Archives), which came to nearly 75,000 documents. The Library agreed to supply copies of these documents to the projected museum. I also became one of the four directors of Sigmund Freud Copyrights, which allowed me to negotiate with Harvard University Press for the publication of Freud's letters in scholarly, annotated, complete editions.

As I was reading through the correspondence and preparing the annotations for the first volume of the series, the Freud/Fliess letters, I began to notice what appeared to be a pattern in the omissions made by Anna Freud in the original, abridged edition. In the letters written after September 1897 (when Freud was supposed to have given up his "seduction" theory), all the case histories dealing with sexual seduction of children were excised. Moreover, every mention of Emma Eckstein, an early patient of Freud and Fliess who seemed connected in some way with the seduction theory, was deleted. I was particularly struck by a section of a letter written in December 1897 that brought to light two previously unknown facts: Emma Eckstein was herself seeing patients in analysis (presumably under Freud's supervision); and Freud was inclined to lend credence, once again, to the seduction theory.

I asked Anna Freud why she had deleted this section from the December 1897 letter. She said she no longer knew why. When I showed her an unpublished letter from Freud to Emma Eckstein, she said that she could well understand my interest in the subject, as Emma Eckstein had indeed been an important part of the early history of psychoanalysis, but the letter should nevertheless not be published. In subsequent conversations, Miss Freud indicated that, since her father eventually abandoned the seduction theory, she felt it would only prove confusing to readers to be exposed to his early hesitations and doubts. I, on the other hand, felt that these passages not only were of great historical importance, they might well represent the truth. Nobody, it seemed to me, had the right to decide for others, by altering the record, what was truth and what was error. Moreover, whatever Freud's ultimate decision, it was evident that he was haunted by this theory all his life.

I showed Miss Freud the 1932 correspondence I found in Freud's desk concerning his close friend Sándor Ferenczi's last paper, which dealt with this very topic. Clearly, I thought, it was her father's continued preoccupation with the seduction theory that explained his otherwise mysterious turning away from Ferenczi. Miss Freud, who was very fond of Ferenczi, found these letters painful reading and asked me not to publish them. But the theory, I insisted, was not one that Freud had dismissed lightly as an early and insignificant error, as we had been led to believe.

Anna Freud urged me to direct my interests elsewhere. In conversations with other analysts close to the Freud family, I was given to understand that I had stumbled upon something that was better left alone. Perhaps, if the seduction theory had really been only a detour along the road to truth, as so many psychoanalysts believe, it would have been possible for me to turn my attention to other matters. But the seduction hypothesis, in my opinion, was the very cornerstone of psychoanalysis. In 1895 and 1896 Freud, in listening to his women patients, learned that something dreadful and violent lay in their past. The psychiatrists who had heard these stories before Freud had accused their patients of being hysterical liars and had dismissed their memories as fantasy. Freud was the first psychiatrist who believed his patients were telling the truth. These women were sick, not because they came from "tainted" families, but because something terrible and secret had been done to them as children.

Freud announced his discovery in a paper which he gave in April 1896 to the Society for Psychiatry and Neurology in Vienna, his first major public address to his peers. The paper—Freud's most brilliant, in my opinion—met with total silence. Afterwards, he was urged never to publish it, lest his reputation be damaged beyond repair. The silence around him deepened, as did his loneliness. But he defied his colleagues and published "The Aetiology of Hysteria," an act of great courage. Eventually, however, for reasons which I will attempt to elucidate in this book, Freud decided that he had made a mistake in believing his women patients. This, Freud later claimed, marked the beginning of psychoanalysis as a science, a therapy, and a profession.

It had never seemed right to me, even as a student, that Freud would not believe his patients. I did not agree that the seduction scenes represented as memories were only fantasies, or memories of fantasies. But I had not thought to doubt Freud's historical account (often repeated in his writings) of his motives for changing his mind. Yet, when I read the Fliess letters without the omissions (of which Freud, by the way, would undoubtedly have approved), they told a very different, agonizing story. Moreover, wherever I turned, even in Freud's later writing, I encountered cases in which seduction or abuse of children played a role.

Muriel Gardiner, a psychoanalyst and a friend of both Anna Freud and Kurt Eissler, supported my work both financially and by giving me every possible encouragement. She asked me to go through the unpublished material she had in her home concerning the Wolf-Man, one of Freud's most famous later patients, who had been financially supported by Dr. Gardiner and Dr. Eissler. There I found some notes by Ruth Mack Brunswick for a paper she never published. At Freud's request, she had re-analyzed the Wolf-Man and was astonished to learn that as a child he had been anally seduced by a member of his family—and that Freud did not know this. She never told him. Why? Did Freud not know because he did not want to know? And did Ruth Mack Brunswick not tell him because she sensed this?

In my search for further data, I tried to learn more about Freud's trip to Paris in 1885–1886. I visited the library of his early teacher, Charcot, in the Salpêtrière, and that led me to the Paris morgue, for I knew that Freud had attended autopsies performed there by a friend and collaborator of Charcot's, Paul Brouardel. Hints dropped by Freud indicated that he had seen something at the morgue "of which medical science preferred to take no notice." At the morgue, I learned that a whole literature of legal medicine existed in French devoted to the topic of child abuse (especially rape), and Freud had this material in his personal library, though he did not refer to it in his writings. I discovered, moreover, that some of the autopsies attended by Freud may have been autopsies done on children who had been raped and murdered.

I found myself in a strange position. When I became a psychoanalyst, I believed that Freud had fearlessly pursued truth, that he wanted to help his patients face their personal histories, and the wrongs inflicted on them, no matter how unpleasant. My analytic training taught me early on that these ideals were not shared by the profession at large. But I did not think they had altogether vanished from the science; surely there were still people who uncompromisingly sought out truth. That is why, I argued to myself, I had been encouraged in my research; no restrictions had been placed on it.

The information I was uncovering, I felt, was vital to an understanding of how psychoanalysis had developed, and I reported the results of my research to those responsible for it in the first place, Anna Freud, Dr. Eissler, and Dr. Gardiner. I thought that although they might not agree with my interpretations, they would not discount the significance of my discoveries.

My disappointment with psychoanalysis as I knew it was well known, and in fact it was shared by many of my colleagues. In this connection, one meeting with Anna Freud seems to me important enough to merit recounting. Generally, my relations with Miss Freud were formal, confined to discussions of research matters. One afternoon, however, we both began to talk more personally. I told her how disillusioned I was with my training in Toronto, and said that I had not found much improvement in San Francisco and I doubted it would be different anywhere else. I asked her whether, if her father were alive today, he would want to be part of the psychoanalytic movement, or even would want to be an analyst. "No," she replied, "he would not." Anna Freud, then, understood my criticism of psychoanalysis as it is practiced today, and seemed to support me in this criticism. However, when my research carried me further back, to Freud himself, this support ceased.

Indeed, what I was finding pointed back to Freud's early period, 1897–1903, as the time when fundamental changes set in that would, in my opinion, undermine psychoanalysis. With the greatest reluctance, I gradually came to see Freud's abandonment of the seduction hypothesis as a failure of courage. If I was wrong in my view, surely I would meet with intelligent rebuttal and serious criticisms of my interpretation of the documents. Wherever it lay, the truth had to be faced, and the documents I found had to be brought out into the open.

At the invitation of Anna Freud, I presented a preliminary account of my findings to a meeting of psychoanalysts at the Hampstead Clinic in London in 1981. The participants had been invited by Anna Freud to a conference on "Insight in Psychoanalysis," and many of the leading analysts from around the world were present. The negative response to my paper alerted me to the political overtones of my research, to the possibility that it would have an adverse effect on the profession. But I dismissed such considerations as not worthy of attention by a serious researcher.

In June 1981 I was asked to make a more detailed presentation of the documents and their implications before a closed meeting of the Western New England Psychoanalytic Society in New Haven. The paper I gave was entitled "The Seduction Hypothesis in the Light of New Documents." The anger aroused by this paper, most of it directed at me rather than focused on the documents I had uncovered, brought home the realization that my views would not be treated simply as one man's attempt to come closer to the historical truth behind Freud's abandonment of the seduction theory. The truth or falsity of my research was not questioned, only the wisdom of making the material available to the public. My interpretations, the critics seemed to feel, put in jeopardy the very heart of psychoanalysis.

It was my conviction that what Freud had uncovered in 1896—that, in many instances, children are the victims of sexual violence and abuse within their own families—became such a liability that he literally had to banish it from his consciousness. The psychoanalytic movement that grew out of Freud's accommodation to the views of his peers holds to the present day that Freud's earlier position was simply an aberration. Freud, so the accepted view goes, had to abandon his erroneous beliefs about seduction before he could discover the more basic truth of the power of internal fantasy and of spontaneous childhood sexuality. Every first-year resident in psychiatry knew that simple fact, yet I seemed incapable of understanding it. And I now claimed that this accepted view actually represented a travesty of the truth. The prevalent opinion in psychotherapy was that the victim fashioned his or her own torture. In particular, violent sexual crimes could be attributed to the victim's imagination, a position held by Freud's pupil Karl Abraham and enthusiastically accepted by Freud himself. It was a comforting view for society, for Freud's interpretation—that the sexual violence that so affected the lives of his women patients was nothing but fantasy—posed no threat to the existing social order. Therapists could thus remain on the side of the successful and the powerful, rather than of the miserable victims of family violence. To question the basis of that accommodation was seen as something more than a historical investigation; it threatened to call into question the very fabric of psychotherapy.

When a series of articles in *The New York Times* in August 1981 reported on my findings, the resulting wave of protest culminated in a demand for my removal from the Archives. I was dismissed, to the evident relief of the analytic community; the reason offered was that I had shown "poor judgment" in expressing opinions before a non-professional audience.

Here, then, is the story of Freud's abandonment of the seduction theory, including the documents and my interpretations. My pessimistic conclusions may possibly be wrong. The documents may in fact allow a very different reading. However they are evaluated, I believe that anybody who reads them will come away with a new understanding of psychoanalysis.

It might be helpful if the reader, before proceeding, would at this point turn to Freud's 1896 essay "The Aetiology of Hysteria," which will be discussed often in the pages that follow. It is reproduced in Appendix B.

The Assault
on Truth

1 *"The Aetiology of Hysteria"*

*I had shown them the solution
to a more than thousand-year-
old problem—a* caput Nili.
— SIGMUND FREUD, 1896

O N the evening of April 21, 1896, Sigmund Freud gave
a paper before his colleagues at the Society for Psychiatry and Neurology in Vienna, entitled "The Aetiology
of Hysteria."[1] (The paper has been included below as Appendix B.) Freud realized that in giving this paper he would
become "one of those who had disturbed the sleep of the
world."[2] The address presented a revolutionary theory of
mental illness. Its title refers to Freud's new theory that the
origin of neurosis lay in early sexual traumas which Freud
calls "infantile sexual scenes" or "sexual intercourse in childhood." This is what later came to be called the "seduction
theory"—namely, the belief that these early experiences were
real, not fantasies, and had a damaging and lasting effect on
the later lives of the children who suffered them.

Freud uses various words to describe these "infantile sexual
scenes": *Vergewaltigung* (rape), *Missbrauch* (abuse), *Verführung* (seduction), *Angriff* (attack), *Attentat* (the French
term, meaning an assault), *Aggression* (aggression), and
Traumen (traumas). All of these words explicitly state something about the violence being directed against the child
expressed in the sexuality of the adult, with the exception
of the word "seduction," which was an unfortunate choice,

3

Freud, ca. 1896

since it implies some form of participation by the child. These terms, used by Freud in his early papers, are replaced in his later writings, in the overwhelming majority of cases, by the word "seduction." In Freud's later theories and in psychoanalytic theory after Freud, this ambiguity inherent in the word is exploited. The implication is that the "seduced" child is also the seducer and has brought on the sexual act by his or her behavior. However, in this early paper, there is no doubt as to what Freud meant by a sexual seduction: a real sexual act forced on a young child who in no way desires it or encourages it. A seduction, in this context, is an act of cruelty and violence which wounds the child in every aspect of her (or his, though Freud makes it clear that usually it is a young girl who is the victim) being. Her body is not ready for the adult act of intercourse (which is often an actual rape with life-threatening consequences), nor are the child's emotions prepared either for the immediate impact of the sexual passion of the adult or for the later inevitable feelings of guilt, anxiety, and fear. The adult is venting his own sexual and emotional unhappiness on a child too frightened to protest, too weak to defend herself, and too dependent on the continuing care of the adult for her very survival to seek any form of redress. The imbalance in the relationship and the sadistic willingness of the adult to exploit his power over the child are made explicit by Freud in these searing words, which have lost none of their truth today:

> All the strange conditions under which the incongruous pair continue their love relations—on the one hand the adult, who cannot escape his share in the mutual dependence necessarily entailed by a sexual relationship, and who is at the same time armed with complete authority and the right to punish, and can exchange the one role for the other to the uninhibited satisfaction of his whims, and on the other hand the child,

who in his helplessness is at the mercy of this arbitrary use of power, who is prematurely aroused to every kind of sensibility and exposed to every sort of disappointment, and whose exercise of the sexual performances assigned to him is often interrupted by his imperfect control of his natural needs—all these grotesque and yet tragic disparities distinctly mark the later development of the individual and of his neurosis, with countless permanent effects which deserve to be traced in the greatest detail.[8]

One wonders how the medical journals reported Freud's lecture, and whether they were in any way aware of the theoretical impact of the address. Since I had found no reference in the psychoanalytic literature to any mention of the paper by the medical community, when I was in Vienna I went through the medical journals in an attempt to find out what the response had been. I was startled to discover something that had gone unnoticed: in the *Wiener klinische Wochenschrift*, published weekly in Vienna, on May 14, 1896, three papers were reported from the April 21 meeting (p. 420). Two of the papers were reported in the usual manner. (Generally—in fact, invariably—the practice was to give the title of a paper, a brief summary of its contents, and an account of the ensuing discussion.) But in the citation of the last paper, there was a break with tradition. The report read as follows:

Docent Sigm. Freud: Über die Aetiologie der Hysterie. (Sigmund Freud, lecturer: On the Aetiology of Hysteria.)

There was, I found, no summary and no discussion.

Nor did any member of the audience leave for posterity an account of what was heard that night. But five days later, on April 26, Freud wrote a letter to his closest friend which speaks of the events of that evening. This letter, to the Berlin ear, nose, and throat specialist Wilhelm Fliess (1858–1928),

Wiener klinische Wochenschrift

unter ständiger Mitwirkung der Herren Professoren Drs.

E. Albert, G. Braun, V. R. v. Ebner, S. Exner, M. Gruber, E. R. v. Hofmann,
R. Freih. v. Krafft-Ebing, C. Toldt, A. Vogl, H. Widerhofer, E. Zuckerkandl

begründet von weil. Hofrath Prof. **H. v. Bamberger**

herausgegeben von

**Rudolf Chrobak, Ernst Fuchs, Karl Gussenbauer, Ernst Ludwig,
Edmund Neusser, L. R. v. Schrötter** und **Anton Weichselbaum.**

Organ der k. k. Gesellschaft der Aerzte in Wien.

Redigirt von Dr. Alexander Fraenkel. (Telephon Nr. 3373.)

Verlag von Wilhelm Braumüller, k. u. k. Hof- und Universitäts-Buchhändler, I. Graben 21. (Telephon Nr. 6834.)

IX. Jahrgang. | **Wien, 14. Mai 1896.** | **Nr. 20.**

Verein für Psychiatrie und Neurologie in Wien.

Officielles Protokoll der Sitzung vom 21. April 1896.

Vorsitzender: Hofrath **v. Krafft-Ebing.**

Schriftführer: Dr. **Starlinger.**

Discussion: Docent Sigm. Freud erwähnt einen ähnlichen Fall aus seiner Praxis, wo er bei einer Bäuerin durch mehrere Jahre Cyanose der Hände und Füsse mit Sklerodermie beobachten konnte.

Docent H. Schlesinger verweist auf einen Fall der Klinik Schrötter, der von Dr. Kalmann im nächsten Hefte der psychiatrischen Jahrbücher eine ausführlichere Darstellung findet, bei dem die Sklerodermie durch die Raynaud'sche Krankheit bedingt erscheint.

3. Docent Sigm. Freud: Ueber die Aetiologie der Hysterie.

Page from the Wiener klinische Wochenschrift *announcing Freud's 1896 paper* "The Aetiology of Hysteria"

Krafft-Ebing

was omitted from the published edition of Freud's letters to Fliess. Max Schur, however, included it in his book *Freud: Living and Dying*. From this letter we learn that Baron Richard von Krafft-Ebing (1840–1902), the distinguished professor and head of the Department of Psychiatry at the University of Vienna, was in the chair that evening. Freud reports:

> A lecture on the aetiology of hysteria at the Psychiatric Society met with an icy reception from the asses, and from Krafft-Ebing the strange comment: It sounds like a scientific fairy tale. [*Es klingt wie ein wissenschaftliches Märchen.*] And this after one has demonstrated to them a solution to a more than thousand-year-old problem, a "source of the Nile"!⁴

But Schur did not include Freud's final sentence, in which he expresses open contempt for his colleagues: "They can all go to hell." (*Sie können mich alle gern haben.*) Freud evidently felt that his discoveries were important enough for him to risk the displeasure of his colleagues. The prospect of being ostracized by medical society was negligible in the face of his knowledge that he had discovered an important truth.

Freud's female patients had the courage to face what had happened to them in childhood—often this included violent scenes of rape by a father—and to communicate their traumas to Freud, no doubt hesitating to believe their own memories and reluctant to remember the deep shame and hurt they had felt. Freud listened and understood and gave them permission to remember and speak of these terrible events. Freud did not think they were fantasies:

> Doubts about the genuineness of the infantile sexual scenes can, however, be deprived of their force here and now by more than one argument. In the first place, the behavior of patients while they are reproducing these infantile experiences is in every respect incompatible with the assumption

that the scenes are anything else than a reality which is being felt with distress and reproduced with the greatest reluctance.[5]

Nor are these memories mere intellectual insights, the product of quiet reflection. Freud's patients recalled their traumas "with all the feelings that belonged to the original experiences," that is, the permission to remember seemed also a permission to feel, and the feelings apparently absent from the original assault were now experienced; the anger, the disgust, the sense of helplessness and betrayal, all these powerful emotions surfaced. Freud must have felt like an explorer who has chanced upon a long-submerged world.

Freud knew how reluctant his colleagues were to think about truths of this nature, having encountered a similar reluctance in himself and his teachers:

> . . . the singling out of the sexual factor in the aetiology of hysteria springs at least from no preconceived opinion on my part. The two investigators as whose pupil I began my studies of hysteria, Charcot and Breuer, were far from having any such presupposition; in fact they had a personal disinclination to it . . .[6]

Freud was admitting here that he too had to overcome resistances before accepting the unpalatable truth. So he was not unprepared for the reaction of his colleagues. However, we did not know the full extent of Freud's isolation, because Freud's words to Fliess of May 4, less than two weeks after he gave the paper, were omitted from the published edition of the Freud/Fliess letters:

> I am as isolated as you could wish me to be: the word has been given out to abandon me, and a void is forming around me.

It must have come as no great surprise to Freud, then, when ten days later he opened the *Wiener klinische Wochen-*

schrift—a journal he suspected of anti-Semitic leanings[7]—to see that his paper was listed by title alone, without summary or discussion, without even the remark that it would be published. On May 30, Freud wrote to Fliess: "In defiance of my colleagues I have written down in full my lecture on the aetiology of hysteria."

He published it a few weeks later.[8] We are fortunate that he did, for in a few years Freud would wish he had not been so hasty. The early traumas his patients had had the courage to face and report to him he was to later dismiss as the fantasies of hysterical women who invented stories and told lies. He was to view his own courage in reporting these findings as rash:

> I believed these stories, and consequently supposed that I had discovered the roots of the subsequent neurosis in these experiences of sexual seduction in childhood. . . . If the reader feels inclined to shake his head at my credulity, I cannot altogether blame him.[9]

Freud was to retract his views on the etiology of hysteria, the belief that external, real sexual traumas lay at the very heart of neurosis. His patients, he now felt, had been lying to themselves and to him:

> . . . I was at last obliged to recognize that these scenes of seduction had never taken place, and that they were only fantasies which my patients had made up.[10]

These patients, primarily women, were laboring under a common fantasy, one that, moreover, dominated their entire lives:

> Since childhood masturbation is such a general occurrence and is at the same time so poorly remembered, it must have an equivalent in psychic life. And, in fact, it is found in the fantasy encountered in most female patients—namely, that

the father seduced her in childhood. This is the later rework-
ing which is designed to cover up the recollection of infantile
sexual activity and represents an excuse and an extenuation
thereof. The grain of truth contained in this fantasy lies in
the fact that the father, by way of his innocent caresses in
earliest childhood, has actually awakened the little girl's sexuality (the same thing applies to the little boy and his mother).
It is these same affectionate fathers that are the ones who then
endeavor to break the child of the habit of masturbation, of
which they themselves had by that time become the unwitting
cause. And thus the motifs mingle in the most successful
fashion to form this fantasy, which often dominates a woman's
entire life (seduction fantasy): one part truth, one part gratification of love, and one part revenge.[11]

Giving up his "erroneous" view allowed Freud to participate
again in a medical society that had earlier ostracized him.
In 1905 Freud publicly retracted the seduction theory. By
1908, respected physicians had joined Freud: Paul Federn,
Isidor Sadger, Sándor Ferenczi, Max Eitingon, Karl Jung,
Ludwig Binswanger, Karl Abraham, Abraham Brill, and
Ernest Jones. The psychoanalytic movement was born but
an important truth had been left behind.
    What had happened? Why did Freud abandon the "seduc-
tion theory"? What caused this momentous about-face that
would affect the lives of countless patients in psychotherapy
from 1900 to the present? Psychoanalysts have not been
overly curious about the reasons for Freud's change of heart,
even though they, along with Freud, are convinced that,
without the abandonment of this theory, the development
of psychoanalysis would not have been possible. The
standard explanation that clinical experiences taught Freud
that he had made a mistake is not a very satisfying one. The
purpose of this book is to make public evidence hitherto
unknown, ignored, or discounted that would point to a more

illuminating explanation for the single most important step Freud took, one that helped shape the world we live in.

It seemed to me that one reason we could not satisfactorily explain the abandonment of the seduction theory was that we had no explanation either from Freud himself or from later historians of how Freud came to develop the theory in the first place. We did not know what experiences played the key role. Until we understood these questions, we had an *account* of the origins of psychoanalysis, but no real history. To find the real history, it seemed to me necessary first of all to reexamine Freud's stay in Paris, for he had hinted, in later years,[12] that the time he spent in Paris was critical to the development of psychoanalysis.

2 *Freud at the Paris Morgue*

AMBROISE TARDIEU AND THE

LITERATURE ON RAPE AND OTHER

VIOLENT ACTS AGAINST CHILDREN

I N 1885, when Freud was twenty-nine years old and just finishing his medical studies, he made a study trip to Paris, to work under the great Jean Martin Charcot (1825–1893), France's most illustrious neurologist, defender of hypnosis, and physician of hysteria, at the celebrated Salpêtrière hospital. Ernest Jones, in his authorized three-volume biography of Freud (1, p. 227), writes of this period:

> Charcot was then at the zenith of his fame. No one, before or since, has so dominated the world of neurology, and to have been a pupil of his was a permanent passport to distinction.

It is well known that Freud admired Charcot—Freud's obituary of him speaks of the magic that seemed to radiate from his person.[1]

It is not surprising, then, that a number of studies have been devoted to Freud's relationship with Charcot, and to the influence Charcot may have had on Freud's later thinking. Little that is new has come from these studies. There is not much in Charcot's writings that could illuminate the origins of psychoanalysis. Freud, however, hints that the

14

seeds of his new science were sown in Paris, though so far the evidence for this has remained elusive.

I believe that I was able to fill in the lacunae of these years with two startling discoveries: Freud was exposed to a literature attesting to the reality and indeed the frequency of sexual abuse in early childhood (often occurring within the family); furthermore, in all probability, he witnessed autopsies at the Paris morgue performed on the young victims of such abuse. This was unsuspected by historians of psychoanalysis and consequently any new evaluation of Freud's stay in Paris must take into account an entirely new body of literature, the importance of which has not been previously recognized.

This literature deals with both physical and sexual abuse of children. The French authors were the first to write on these subjects, and though they were unable to draw any psychological conclusions from the material at their disposal, they did not hesitate to recognize its reality.

In 1860, an article was published in the distinguished *Annales d'hygiène publique et de médecine légale* which catalogued in horrifying detail the brutal abuses suffered by children at the hands of their caretakers, often their own parents. The title of the article was "Etude médico-légale sur les sévices et mauvais traitements exercés sur des enfants" (A Medico-legal Study of Cruelty and Brutal Treatment Inflicted on Children).[2] The author, Ambroise Auguste Tardieu (1818–1879), was professor of legal medicine at the University of Paris, dean of the Faculty of Medicine, and president of the Academy of Medicine in Paris, "the most eminent representative of French legal medicine."[3] What Tardieu discovered, and what he had the courage to describe for the first time, in the precise terms of the legal physician working under the directions of a court of law, was the full range of abuses that adults, most often parents, inflict on young and helpless children. The article deals with thirty-two cases that

MÉDECINE LÉGALE.

ÉTUDE MÉDICO-LÉGALE

SUR LES

SÉVICES ET MAUVAIS TRAITEMENTS

EXERCÉS SUR DES ENFANTS,

Par le Dr Ambroise TARDIEU,

Professeur agrégé de médecine légale à la Faculté de médecine.

Parmi les faits si nombreux et de nature si diverse dont se compose l'histoire médico-légale des coups et blessures, il en est qui forment un groupe tout à fait à part, et qui, laissés jusqu'ici dans l'ombre la plus complète, méritent à plus d'un titre d'être mis en lumière. Je veux parler de ces faits qualifiés sévices et mauvais traitements, et dont les enfants sont plus particulièrement victimes de la part de leurs parents, de leurs maîtres, de ceux en un mot qui exercent sur eux une autorité plus ou moins directe.

S'ils nous offrent un sujet d'étude intéressant et neuf au point de vue de la médecine légale, en raison de l'âge et de la constitution des blessés, de la diversité des agents vulnérants, de la nature très variable des lésions, et de leurs conséquences toujours graves, souvent terribles, nous sommes assuré que les exemples nombreux recueillis par nous et cités dans ce travail, éveilleront en même temps de tristes et profondes réflexions sur les causes morales de pareils crimes. La sévérité inflexible d'un maître, la dureté d'un patron avide, l'aversion d'une marâtre, peuvent expliquer des châtiments corporels même excessifs infligés à de jeunes enfants ; mais que dès l'âge le plus tendre de pauvres êtres sans défense soient voués chaque jour et presque à

*First page of Ambroise Tardieu's article
on violence against children*

Ambroise Tardieu

Tardieu was commissioned by the court to examine from a medico-legal point of view.

The cases reveal some important facts that had not been previously acknowledged:[4] the perpetrators of these crimes are, more often than not (in twenty-one cases), the parents of the child; the children are often very young; the cruelty inflicted on them can result in death. What Tardieu does not tell us, but what a careful reading of the article allows us to infer, is that he was often charged with performing autopsies at the Paris morgue on children who had died as a result of "accidents," and that only his astute observations permitted a correct diagnosis of the cause of death. Tardieu begins his article fully aware of the importance of what he is bringing to light:

> Among the numerous and very diverse facts which make up the medico-legal history of blows and wounds, there is one that forms a group completely separate from the rest. These· facts, which until now have remained in total obscurity, deserve, for more than one reason, to be brought to the light of day. I am speaking of the facts of cruelty and brutal treatment of which children are particularly the victims and which derive from their parents, their teachers, from those, in a word, who exercise more or less direct authority over them.

Tardieu says that he can understand the inflexibility of a teacher, or the hardness of a greedy employer, or even the aversion of a cruel stepmother,

> but that, from the most tender age, those defenseless unfortunate children should have to experience, every day and even every hour, the most severe cruelty, be subjected to the most dire privations, that their lives, hardly begun, should be nothing but a long agony, that severe corporal punishments, tortures before which even our imagination recoils in horror, should consume their bodies and extinguish the first rays of reason, shorten their lives, and, finally, the most unbelievable

thing of all, that the executioners of these children should more often than not be the very people who gave them life—this is one of the most terrifying problems that can trouble the heart of man (pp. 361–362).

Tardieu was aware that society at large, and medical practitioners in particular, preferred to deny the reality of what he observed. Participating in this denial, strangely enough, was the victim. But the denial was not total—somewhere these children kept their knowledge of the horrible crimes that had been committed on their bodies sealed off from the world. Tardieu noticed that this recognition of what had been done to them was sometimes apparent in the eyes of these children:

> Their features reveal the deepest sadness; they are timid and apprehensive, often they look dazed and the expression in their eyes is lifeless. But sometimes, often in fact, it is very different: they have a precocious intelligence which only reveals itself in a dark fire in their eyes (p. 365).

Tardieu goes on to say that these same children will alter their expression when they perceive acts of kindness and tenderness to which they have become unaccustomed (p. 365). He notes (p. 370) that the vicious parents who torture their children in this way do not hesitate to claim that in so doing they are merely exercising their parental rights, that the child deserves such treatment because of his "bad disposition," and they are only teaching the child to behave. Tardieu recognized the absurdity of such statements.

A summary of one of Tardieu's cases will provide the reader with a more concrete idea of the material. It is the most elaborate case in the article, with thirteen pages devoted to it (pp. 377–389), and the only one involving sexual abuse. For Tardieu, physical abuse is the larger category; he regards sexual abuse as a kind of physical abuse, as is evident from his inclusion of this case history in the article.

The criminal court at Reims, on December 3, 1859, heard the case of Adelina Defert, seventeen years old. Dr. Nidart, a physician in Sainte-Ménehould, was commissioned by the court to examine this girl. She lived in the house of her maternal grandfather until she was eight. Upon her return to the home of her mother and father a life of torture began. What Dr. Nidart discovered, to his evident puzzlement, was that Adelina would "invent stories" of what had happened to her, in order to cover up the crimes of her parents against her own person, "imagining" falls and accidents, rather than allow others to know the horrible truth of what had been done to her. As we shall see, her parents had kept her literally hermetically sealed off from the real world outside, and in a pathetic, heartbreaking gesture of tenderness toward her own tormentors, she wished to protect them, too, from the world. Dr. Nidart, none too eager himself to uncover the truth, was nevertheless forced by the court to pay a visit to the Deferts' home. There he found the world of Adelina: a small wooden chest. Dr. Nidart provides exact measurements: it was 1 meter 86 centimeters long, 48 centimeters high, and 70 centimeters wide. It was fastened shut by a heavy chain and lock. There was a small hole in the chest barely large enough to let in sufficient air to sustain life. The box was lined with straw mixed with thistles and nettles. The straw had never been changed and was teeming with insects. Rags, soaked with pus, served as blankets. An indentation in the straw betrayed the contours of an undersized human body. It gradually dawned on the good doctor that a human being had been sleeping in this coffin. Only later did he learn that most of her day was spent in the coffin as well.

Dr. Nidart wrote the first of two reports on July 22, 1859. He discovered that Adelina Defert had been tied to a wooden bench, that after beating her with a strap, her father took red-hot charcoals and rolled them along her back and legs, rekindling them in a fire of live coals as they cooled. Her neck had already been burned in this way. She was then put to bed in her coffin. The next evening she was taken out, again tied to the bench, and again whipped with a strap. Her mother came into the room with a sponge dipped in nitric acid tied to the end of a stick, and washed the wounds of the night before with this hellish medicine. The neighbors could hear the girl screaming for hours. She "admitted" that her father then made "cynical advances" of a "vulgar" kind, and had tried to engage her in conversations that referred to "knowledge of a whole order of ideas that should have been kept carefully secret from her." He had even tried to touch her—but here her confessions ceased, and she could not be persuaded to say anything further (p. 379). One evening her parents had her lie on a table and tied one leg to the table and the other to a door handle, thus lifting her legs and spreading them apart. Her father, aided by her mother, then forcibly inserted a block of wood from an elder tree into her body. The piece of wood was found and "the physician was able to observe the strange disorders to which this barbarous act had led." Nidart is a physician of his time: he inserts his finger into her vagina, and reports: "Medically, Adelina has been deflowered, but it is possible that this tearing of the hymen is the result of manual and personal masturbation" (p. 383).

In his second report, on July 29, Dr. Nidart gives a detailed account of the scars and wounds on Adelina:

> Her lower back, buttocks, and thighs presented one immense wound, secreting daily at least one liter of pus; for one must not forget the dimensions of this frightening wound: 44 centimeters by 24 centimeters. During this time Adelina lay on her stomach, not able to make the slightest movement . . . without experiencing the most agonizing pain. She was not

able to urinate or defecate without experiencing indescribable torture. . . . A similar wound in the hands of an experienced surgeon would require a minimum of 40 days of treatment in bed with absolute immobility. . . . The pain suffered by this unfortunate child surpasses the most atrocious punishment the mind is capable of imagining (p. 388).

This article was not referred to in the later literature, but Tardieu decided to reproduce it in his book on wounds published nineteen years later, in 1879, the year of his death. The chapter is identical with the article except for one passage. Tardieu laments the fact that in the intervening years his article had not awakened the indignation and interest he had expected:

This study, undertaken eighteen years ago, is the first to have been attempted on this subject, about which writers in the field of legal medicine have subsequently remained completely silent (p. 70).

The singular importance of this work has been ignored[5] for more than 120 years. No trace of any influence it may have had has survived in any direct form (it was never quoted in the subsequent literature on infanticide,[6] for example, which became a popular theme in European medico-legal literature of the late nineteenth century). The work which brought Tardieu temporary fame, his *Etude médico-légale sur les attentats aux moeurs*[7] (A Medico-legal Study of Assaults on Decency), first published in 1857,[8] has never been quoted in the psychoanalytic or psychiatric literature. It was the first such book written in Europe.

In this book, and in its six later editions (the last appeared in 1878), Tardieu drew attention to the frequency of sexual assaults on children, especially young girls. The statistics he provides are chilling: on p. 62 of the last edition, Tardieu gives the figures for 1858–1869 in France. In all, there were

11,576 cases of people accused of rape or attempted rape
during this time. Of these, 9,125 were accused of rape or
attempted rape of children. Tardieu points out that almost all
the victims are girls. By children he means those under the
age of sixteen, though in the vast majority of cases he describes, the victims are between the ages of four and twelve.
The book, in effect, is about sexual abuse of children.

On p. 8 of the fifth edition (1867), Tardieu explains that
the histories that follow are based on the analysis of 616
cases which he personally examined as medical expert. Later
(p. 14), he states that of these 616 cases, 339 were of rape
or attempted rape of children under the age of eleven. On pp.
158 and 159, Tardieu presents cases of rape committed by
fathers on their daughters, and on p. 170, a case of rape of
a seven-year-old girl which resulted in her death. Whether
Tardieu himself recognized a link between his earlier work
on the physical abuse of children and this later work on the
sexual abuse of children is not known. But it was evident to
Tardieu that a sexual assault on a young child, like a physical
assault, was a violent act which *could* and *did* result in death.

In his preface, Tardieu explains that he is breaking with
tradition in not reverting to the obscuring blanket of Latin.
He says plainly (in the 1878 edition, p. 62) that fathers often
abused their daughters:

> What is even sadder is to see that ties of blood, far from con-
> stituting a barrier to these impardonable allurements, serve
> only too frequently to favor them. Fathers abuse their daugh-
> ters, brothers abuse their sisters. These facts have been coming
> to my attention in increasing numbers. I can count twelve
> more cases since the last but one edition of this book.

By and large, Tardieu is convinced that those accused—
the number of accused is always smaller than the actual
number of those guilty of such crimes—actually did what

their accusers said they did. He has a chapter entitled "Simulation" (pp. 131 ff.), for many authorities were convinced that children pretended to have been abused or harmed. (It is of interest that nobody thought that these tales of rape and seduction were fantasies, but rather conscious attempts to extort money or gain some material advantage from the accused.) Tardieu believed that the vast majority of the cases he investigated could not have been simulated. He gives simple reasons: There were anatomical changes that could not be imagined—anal fissures and other physical evidence of violent attacks on the sexual parts of young girls. He points out that the children who accused their fathers did so very reluctantly, and with great fear. They provided details which were decisive, and furthermore, in almost every case they suffered the physiological effects of the act, often with fatal results. Some of the case histories he gives (in particular, on pp. 144–145; 148–149, and 150–151 of the last edition) are of girls as young as four and five who were both anally and vaginally raped. In one case (p. 145) he notes the following:

> From the information provided by the child in the midst of hesitations and tears, it turns out that the accused engaged in violent attempts on her, that, notably, on the tenth of January he lured her into his room, and after throwing her on his bed, he lay on top of her. He then introduced a piece of very hard wood between her buttocks, and remained in this position for about a quarter of an hour. Finally she felt something wet on her sexual parts. She added that she suffered and the pain caused her to scream.

What the book does *not* do, nor does any other book in this tradition or of this time, is mention the psychological effects on the children.[9]

On the basis of Tardieu's book (which, unlike the more

passionately written article, was not ignored), an entire literature sprang up and a tradition was established, quite consciously based on this pioneering work. Alexandre Lacassagne
(1834–1924), who held the chair of legal medicine at the
University of Lyon, founded the *Archives d'anthropologie
criminelle et des sciences pénales* and encouraged his students
to write on the topic of sexual assaults on children. His valuable collection of 12,000 works, which was given to the
Bibliothèque de la Ville de Lyon, contains many works in
this area.[10] In the very first issue of his journal, in 1886, he
published an article, "Attentats à la pudeur sur les petites
filles" (Sexual Assaults on Young Girls),[11] in which he noted
that in the criminal courts often one third of the cases involved this crime (p. 59) and that "more than two thirds of
the cases related to assaults on virtue have to do with sexual
assaults on young girls" (p. 60). He stresses the fact, which
the courts ignored, that "sexual assaults, even when repeated
over a long period of time, and frequently engaged in, are
capable of leaving absolutely no trace" (p. 67)—in other
words, that the fact that a child shows no physical sign of
having been sexually abused does not mean that the child was
not so abused in actuality.

The same issue contains an article by R. Garraud, who
was professor of criminal law at the Faculty of Law in Lyon,
and Paul Bernard: "Des Attentats à la pudeur et des viols
sur les enfants. Législation-statistique" (Sexual Assault and
Rape Committed on Children: Legislation and Statistics).[12]
In the same year, 1886, Paul Bernard (1828–1886) published *Des Attentats à la pudeur sur les petites filles* (Sexual
Assaults on Young Girls).[13] According to the tables published at the end of this book, between 1827 and 1870 in
France there were 36,176 *reported* cases of "rape and assaults on the morality" of children fifteen years and under
(the corresponding number reported for adults is much lower:

9,653). Some of Bernard's observations are worthy of note: on p. 49 he remarks that children are vulnerable to these sexual attacks as early as the age of four. When they occur, "parents would rather remain silent."

One might have thought that rape was exclusively the province of single men. But Bernard is surprised to discover that

> the influence of the family does not make itself felt to any significant degree, and it would seem that, on the contrary, children living at home constitute rather a stimulus to evil acts. In our observations, we have been struck by the large number of cases of incest that figure in them (p. 65).

What Bernard finds "most astonishing" is that

> the number of individuals with a higher education who have been charged with sexual assaults on children has been increasing regularly up to 1880, when it reaches its maximum (p. 68).

The most important aspect of the book, for our purposes, is the faith its author places in the truthfulness of the children, no doubt following the example of his teacher Lacassagne. For he quotes Lacassagne (p. 108) as saying: "The experiences we have undergone confirm this manner of seeing things and prove the truth of the assertions of the child." An example of a case where one might have disbelieved the child is given on p. 114. A man was accused, in 1884, of having attempted rape on two girls. One of the girls was nine, the other eleven. Both of them claimed that he had something colored (one said it was bright blue, the other bright red) on his penis. Lacassagne was instructed by the court to examine the accused. Sure enough, the thirty-three-year-old man had "a tattoo drawn on the back of his penis representing a horned devil whose cheeks and lips were colored red"

(p. 113). Lacassagne restricts himself to recounting only the physiological facts, and concludes: "If there was an assault on the children such as they tell it, it has left no trace" (p. 116).

But Bernard (p. 138) is less cautious and more logical when he points out that the fact that the children remembered the peculiar nature of his penis was enough to establish the identity of the guilty party who had lured the girls to him by saying that he intended to show them the devil. And then Bernard, departing somewhat from his teacher, quotes Tardieu and says:

> The medical examiner should never forget the sound advice of Tardieu. In cases where the examination is inconclusive, the physician should not be satisfied with pointing out negative signs when it is possible that the act took place without leaving traces; to be completely truthful it is necessary to indicate at least the possibility of the act [having taken place] even in the absence of positive signs (p. 139).[14]

Bernard reaches the following conclusions:

> Sexual acts committed against children are very frequent, especially in highly populated areas and industrial centers.
> Those charged with this sort of crime are most often men of mature age or elderly men, and one can say that the age of the aggressor is almost always in inverse proportion to that of his victim.
> Education does not seem to be an inhibiting factor in the commission of this criminal act (p. 141).

FREUD, CHARCOT, AND PAUL BROUARDEL

FREUD was in Paris from October 3, 1885, until February 28, 1886. He had gone there to study under Charcot, but seemed unaware that Charcot had written directly about sexuality. Alerted by E. Gley's article[15] cited by Freud in *Three Essays on the Theory of Sexuality*,[16] I found that, in collaboration with Valentin Magnan (1835–1916), a well-known French psychiatrist, Charcot had written an article in 1882 entitled "Inversion du sens génital et autres perversions sexuelles" (The Inversion of the Genital Sense and Other Sexual Perversions).[17] In the second part of that article (p. 300), the authors make a plea for taking into account madness as a factor in sexual assaults:

> Physicians interested in legal problems who have had to occupy themselves with sexual assaults, and before whose eyes essentially vicious individuals have appeared, have seemed, until now, little disposed to attribute to mental illness the share it deserves in these matters.

They then cite Tardieu's book on *attentats aux moeurs*, which, they say, "barely touches on the question of madness." The people accused of sexual assaults are usually what they call *fous lucides* (lucid lunatics), whose "appetites and instincts dominate their will and push them to the irresistible satisfaction of their morbid needs" (p. 301). Charcot and Magnan wished to establish that people with perverted sexual appetites are capable of intellectual achievements but are what Magnan calls elsewhere *dégénérés supérieurs*. The cases they presented are of psychological interest (e.g., pp. 307–314), though they are not given for that reason.

One case reported in the article (p. 321) is that of a twenty-nine-year-old woman who lives under a continual irresistible urge to sleep with her nephew, who is three years old. She has constant fantasies of seeing him naked in front of her, and of his lying on top of her, his small penis on her vagina. These fantasies are so intense that they often reach the point of an actual hallucination, and she must then anxiously ask her neighbors whether they saw her so engaged. When the family meets for dinner, she sees to it that the boy is seated as far from her as possible, but nonetheless the very sight of him is enough to produce *"spasmes et sécrétions vaginales."* This same case was reported by Magnan in a number of his other publications as well.[18] Thus, for Charcot and Magnan (no doubt under the influence of Tardieu), sexual impulses (which often led to sexual acts) on the part of adults toward children were *real.*

On January 13, 1885, Magnan gave a widely reported lecture at the Académie de Médecine,[19] entitled "Des Anomalies, des aberrations et des perversions sexuelles" (On Sexual Anomalies, Aberrations, and Perversions). In this article (p. 65) Magnan mentions that Charcot and he visited a patient together, and it is therefore clear that Charcot was aware of cases involving sexual perversions, although he does not betray any interest in the etiological significance of sexuality in his better-known articles on hysteria. It is possible that Freud heard Charcot lecture on some of these cases.

Magnan seems to be unique in having reported a case of reverse child molestation. In an 1893 publication entitled *Leçons cliniques sur les maladies mentales* (2nd ed.; Paris: Bureaux du Progrès Médical, p. 187), he gives the case of the twelve-year-old Georgette, who would not, at first glance, appear to be *dégénérée* but whose *mauvais instincts* reached an extent that Magnan had not previously observed. She began masturbating at the age of five, after "a young man apparently abused her, and she affirms that since that time she has been experiencing an irresistible need to feel the same sensations again." At eleven

her moral perversity reached its heights: she drank urine, and masturbated with cutlets, which she then ate. Finally she turned her lewdness toward her own mother. She often asked her to sleep with her, with the sole purpose of touching her genitals. One day, taking advantage of the fact that her mother did not feel well and was lying down, she touched her genitals, masturbating at the same time. She had chosen a moment when her mother was in a semi-faint. She proposed, one day, to run her tongue along her mother's genitals.

To Magnan's evident satisfaction, she was placed in an asylum for the mentally insane.

Freud probably knew of these cases, for Möbius, whom Freud much admired, had translated Magnan's works into German, fascinated as he was with Magnan's concept of degeneracy. Freud had the six volumes of this translation in his personal library.[20] The article in collaboration with Charcot is included (2, pp. 33 ff.). Furthermore, this work contains other cases of a similar nature in an article, again in collaboration with Charcot, entitled "Onomatomanie"—the urge to say obscene words (4, pp. 3–32)

Whether or not Freud knew this work from his Paris days is impossible to say, but it is worth observing that Charcot was a man of greater experience than had been realized in matters that were to absorb the interest of Freud in later years.

One of Charcot's assistants at the Salpêtrière was Georges Gilles de la Tourette, three of whose books Freud had in his personal library.[21] In an address entitled "Le Viol dans l'hypnotisme et les états analogues" (Rape during Hypnotism and Similar States),[22] given in Paris on August 2, 1886, he reports (p. 392) on a "remarkable account, as yet unpublished, by Brouardel," a case of rape that could not fail to arouse Freud's interest since it took place during a hypnotic trance, often the subject of Charcot's lectures at the Salpêtrière.

Paul Camille Hippolyte Brouardel[23] (1837–1906), known as the "Pontifex Maximus"[24] of French medicine, was Ambroise Tardieu's successor to the chair of legal medicine in

Paul Brouardel

Paris. In 1876–1877, he was Tardieu's assistant. With Tardieu's death in 1879, he occupied the chair and immediately instituted a change in policy: medical students were allowed to come to the Paris morgue three times a week; thus, the autopsies became public. "All the bodies of victims of crimes are brought to the morgue . . . every year the morgue receives about one thousand corpses. Three hundred of these are subjected to autopsy by judicial decree."[25]

Freud knew Brouardel and attended these autopsies. In his "Report on My Studies in Paris and Berlin Carried Out with the Assistance of a Travelling Bursary Granted from the University Jubilee Fund, October, 1885—End of March, 1886"[26] (1886), Freud writes:

> I abandoned my occasional attempts at attending other lectures after I had become convinced that all they had to offer were for the most part well-constructed rhetorical performances. The only exceptions were Professor Brouardel's forensic autopsies and lectures at the morgue, which I rarely missed.

In a published letter from Freud to his wife, Martha, written on January 20, 1886, Freud tells of meeting Brouardel in Charcot's home:

> I also received permission to attend Professor Brouardel's course in the morgue, where I have been today. The lecture was fascinating, the subject matter not very suitable for delicate nerves. It is described as the latest murder in every Paris newspaper.[27]

After reading Freud's preface[28] to Captain John Gregory Bourke's *Scatologic Rites of All Nations*, it became clear to me that Freud witnessed something more important than an ordinary murder in his subsequent visits to the morgue. Freud begins his preface with these curious words:

> While I was living in Paris in 1885 as a pupil of Charcot, what chiefly attracted me, apart from the great man's own

lectures, were the demonstrations and addresses given by Brouardel. He used to show us from post-mortem material at the morgue how much there was which deserved to be known by doctors *but of which science preferred to take no notice* [emphasis added].

This is a puzzling passage. What was it that Brouardel was able to show his audience but "of which science preferred to take no notice"?

A well-known anecdote which appears in Freud's 1914 essay "On the History of the Psycho-Analytic Movement" links Brouardel, Charcot, and the role of sexuality in mental illness.[29] It is this topic, no doubt, that Freud is referring to. In fact, Brouardel wrote a book on the rape of children. The book was published posthumously (but included lectures given before and possibly during the time Freud was in Paris) with the by now familiar title *Les Attentats aux moeurs*, the last of his series *Cours de médecine légale de la Faculté de Médecine de Paris*.[30] What emerges is the unsuspected close collaboration between Charcot and Brouardel on the study of the rape of small children by adults. Brouardel writes (p. 1):

> May I be permitted, in this respect, to remind [my audience] that Charcot and I have attempted, many times, not to remain satisfied with this somewhat unilateral examination, and to extend our investigations to include not only the victim but the accused as well.

(The exact nature of their collaboration is not known, nor, as far as I am aware, did Charcot indicate in his writings that he was interested in the topic of sexual abuse of children, beyond the quotations cited above from the articles he wrote with Magnan.[31])

Brouardel is most concerned, not with the victim, but with the rapist, as he confesses several times in this book. He says of convicted rapists that they are often *"excellents pères de famille"* (excellent family men) (p. 3). Yet, like Tardieu and Toulmouche, in whose tradition he follows, he describes what he saw. Thus, he writes: "Sexual assaults are crimes of the home" (p. 8). In spite of his reluctance to acknowledge a father's guilt in such a crime, he writes that, within his personal practice, out of 232 cases, the father was guilty in 19, the father-in-law in 4, and the uncle in 6. Brouardel's definition of *attentat à la pudeur* (assault on virtue) is quite simple: "rape without penetration" (p. 22). He recognizes that it is a crime directed against females in particular and cites with approval the words of his student Thoinot:[32] "The characteristic sexual assault is the sexual assault on a young girl" (p. 26).

Most of the case histories in Brouardel's book date from 1880–1885. Some of the cases involved father/daughter incest. For example, on p. 183 Brouardel mentions a case of rape by a father of his twelve-year-old daughter whom he examined in 1882. Many of the children were very young. On p. 171 he mentions having examined a seven-year-old rape victim in 1885, the year that Freud was in Paris. Moreover, it was clear to Brouardel that many of the cases involved violence and sadism. He writes, for example (p. 90): "I know three or four cases where the nipples were bitten off"; and mentions as well that "wounding of the genitals is not a rare occurrence" (p. 129). Finally, he cites (p. 93) murder victims who had been raped. But is there any reason to believe that Brouardel may have had occasion, during a class that Freud might have attended, to perform an autopsy on a sexually brutalized child?

Unfortunately, at the present morgue in Paris, near the Gare d'Austerlitz, records of autopsies from the nineteenth century have not been kept. However, the library there contains an obscure thesis (which is printed, but not listed in the *National Union Catalogue*) by Antonin Delcasse entitled *Etude médico-légale sur les sévices de l'enfance* (A Medico-legal Study of Cruelty toward Children) (Paris: Librairie Ollier-Henry, 1885).[38] In the introduction to that work appears the following passage:

> In the remarkable conferences he gives each week at the morgue, Professor Brouardel, who has been able in a few years to acquire, as a physician interested in legal matters, an authority and a celebrity which are as great as those of his predecessor, Professor Ambroise Tardieu, has often called our attention to the fact of cruelty and brutal treatment, of which children in particular are the victims of their parents, their teachers, in short, of those who exercise over them a more or less direct authority.

Thus, in 1885, just before Freud arrived in Paris, Brouardel was "often" drawing the attention of his audience at the autopsies to the abuse of children by their parents and teachers.

Delcasse provides many examples drawn from Brouardel's presentations at the morgue. Brouardel once presented the case of a four-and-a-half-year-old girl evidently beaten to death (p. 46). He pointed out that "most of the blows were administered by a relentless hand, hitting blindly, without aim. Two contusions give witness to even greater violence." Delcasse also cites Brouardel on a seven-year-old girl burned and tortured by her mother (p. 41).

Thus, at the Paris morgue Brouardel presented cases of young children murdered by a parent. Since, as we know from Brouardel's writings, he was interested in sexual assaults (*attentats aux moeurs*—by now a traditional interest of occupants of the chair of legal medicine, as evidenced by the writings of his predecessor, Ambroise Tardieu, on the same topic)—and since it is now common knowledge that sexual violence (rape) often ends in physical violence (murder), it is likely that among the cases Brouardel demonstrated at the morgue were rape/murders of small children by a parent or close relative. In any event, the two topics, violent physical acts against children by a parent and violent sexual acts against children by a parent, were subjects that both Brouardel and Tardieu wrote about. We know that Freud attended Brouardel's classes at the Paris morgue and saw things "of which science preferred to take no notice." If Brouardel was presenting a case of a brutally murdered child, it would be only natural for him to link that case with cases of brutal sexual assaults on children, which he had also investigated. Freud, then, in all likelihood, heard Brouardel speak about cases of violent sexual assaults on children and may have witnessed the evidence of such assaults directly. Even if Brouardel saw no similarity between the two types of crimes, when Freud came to evaluate the psychological significance of such acts in 1895 and 1896, it is inevitable that he would think back to the experiences of his Paris days, both his reading and what he witnessed at the morgue. The very word that Freud uses in his 1896 paper on the etiology of hysteria, *Vergewaltigung* (rape), speaks for the violence (*Gewalt*) that is part of the act. And when Freud speaks, in that same paper, of the punishment that a seducer often metes out to the child he seduces, he makes it clear that he is aware of the physical abuse that often accompanies sexual abuse of a child.

FREUD'S LIBRARY—*Attentats aux moeurs:*
TARDIEU, BERNARD, BROUARDEL

TARDIEU, Bernard, and Brouardel were the authors of the major works in this field, but there is another reason why they have been the main focus of this chapter.

In 1938, before leaving for England, Freud went through his library with the help of his daughter Anna, and selected those books which he did not wish to take with him.[34] Freud gave these books to Paul Sonnenfeld, who had a bookstore near Freud's home. Sonnenfeld sold the books to Heinrich Hinterberger (1892–1970), who owned a large secondhand bookstore. Hinterberger made a catalogue of the books, "Books and Pamphlets on Neurology, Psychiatry, and Allied Branches of Science," and offered them for sale in 1938. This 26-page catalogue contains a list of 814 books, 54 of which had Freud's name written in them; others had his stamp. The collection was sold to the New York State Psychiatric Institute in 1939, and is now housed in the Augustus Long Rare Books Library of Columbia University College of Physicians and Surgeons.[35] K. R. Eissler, who was in contact with Hinterberger, drew up a list of those books (some 65 volumes) which possibly did not belong to Freud. We can be reasonably certain that the remaining volumes had been his. Among those volumes are the following three titles, which are reproduced here from the catalogue; they appear under the heading "Sexual Life, normal and abnormal, Sexual Pathology, etc."

648 Brouardel, P., *Les Attentats aux Moeurs*. Préf. de Thoinot. Paris 1909. In.-8. VII, 231 pp. Br.   2.-(Marks)

646 Bernard, Paul. *Des Attentats à la Pudeur sur les petites Filles*. Paris 1886. In.-8. 145 (1) pp., 2 planches. Br.   2.-

702 Tardieu, Ambroise. *Etude médico-légale sur les Attentats aux Moeurs*. 7. éd. Accomp. de 3 planches gravées. Paris 1878. In.-8 VI. 296 pp. Br.   2.-

In other words, Freud had had all three books, the major French works dealing with sexual violence against children, in his personal library. When he departed for England, he left them behind, and it would seem that he had eradicated all traces of their content from his mind as well.

None of the three volumes is annotated by Freud. But given the central importance in Freud's thinking of the themes dealt with in all three books, it is unlikely that Freud left them unread. Many of the volumes I saw in Freud's library in Maresfield Gardens, even those which he cites frequently in his papers, are not marked. It is possible that Freud read the Bernard and the Tardieu in a library while he was in Paris and only purchased them later. All three volumes have been rebound, so it is difficult to judge from their appearance whether they were extensively used. Freud does not cite any of these books anywhere in his writings. Why he would not have referred to Bernard and Tardieu in his publications of 1896, when these authors could have offered support for his new and unpopular theories, is a puzzle upon which we can only speculate. Possibly Freud did not wish to concede priority to the French authors, knowing that he was the first to discover the psychological relevance of the material so carefully collected and presented by them. (Brouardel's book, though published in 1909, represents his thinking at the time Freud was in Paris— 1885–1886—as an examination of Brouardel's articles from this period makes clear. Freud purchased the book in 1909 or later, no doubt because of his regard for Brouardel and

Title pages of Freud's personal copies of Paul Brouardel's *Les Attentats aux moeurs; Paul Bernard's Des Attentats à la pudeur sur les petites filles;* and *Ambroise Tardieu's Etude médico-légale sur les attentats aux moeurs*

possibly as a reminder of the lectures by Brouardel that he had attended.)

In any case, this new information indicates that Freud's visit to Paris may have been of greater historical significance than he himself either realized or chose to reveal. We can reach the unexpected conclusion that, in all likelihood, Paris provided Freud with experiences and evidence on which he built his thesis, in 1896, that real sexual traumas in childhood lay at the very heart of neurotic illness.

There is another body of literature originating in France, however, whose importance has been overlooked, which may have exercised considerable influence on Freud's later decision to abandon this thesis—though, again, Freud does not refer to this literature in his writings.

CHILDREN WHO LIE: FOURNIER
AND THE FANTASY OF VIOLENCE

THE French authors who wrote about childhood rape were medical specialists called in by the courts to determine the nature of the criminal acts being prosecuted. For them, these acts were all too real. But early on there developed a current within the literature which, in the long run, exercised an enduring influence, and in my opinion a sinister one. This is the literature that concerns itself with simulations and the supposed lies of children. There existed a whole series of authors interested in the *pseudologica phantastica* of children. Toulmouche and Tardieu, the original writers on *attentats*, at first devoted brief chapters in their works to this topic. They warn that, in the very nature of things, there are bound to be a small number of simulations arising out of greed or motives of revenge. Neither author attributed any particular significance to this, and certainly did not accord the topic any undue theoretical importance. But some thirty years later, matters had changed, and two articles within this tradition were to take root in all later thinking.

The first is by Alfred Fournier (1832–1914), given as an address to a well-attended meeting of the Academy of Medicine in 1880, elegantly delivered and often cited (for example, Bernard's book on *attentats* begins with the opening words of this address),[36] entitled "Simulation d'attentats vénériens sur de jeunes enfants" (Simulation of Sexual Attacks on Young Children). Fournier, a senior medical figure in Paris academic life, is out to unmask the pretenses of the child.

A child of eight came to Fournier's office "literally bathed in yellow pus oozing from her vagina." Something in her account of how she was molested by a man awakened Fournier's suspicions and he decided to win her confidence by means of money, candy, sweet words, and finally "a doll whose eyes moved" which "decided my triumph." She told Fournier, with great difficulty, and with much fear and hesitation, that "it was not a man who touched her, but that her mother, three times, brushed her sexual parts with a waxing brush, forbidding her to tell anyone about it, and threatening to do it more if she told" (p. 502).

Fournier was pleased that the case against the man was dropped; "simulation" had been demonstrated. As far as Fournier was concerned, science had been served and the case was closed. And the mother? Fournier told her what her daughter had revealed to him. But there the story ends. Fournier has no further interest, nothing to communicate to science. I confess to being haunted by that doll with the mobile eyes. What additional misery was in store for the child and her doll at the hands of that mother? Neither

Alfred Fournier

Fournier nor any of his colleagues were concerned with the effects of sexual abuse on the child. Fournier is, however, concerned with the welfare of accused men:

> An excellent and perfectly honorable man, father of a family, justly honored and absolutely incapable (I will gladly act as a guarantor) of any ignominious action, allowed himself to be caught up in a trap of this kind (p. 510).

The man had been accused of trying to rape a young girl. The girl and her family were poor and from the lower classes, hence, in Fournier's eyes, greedy. Moreover, they were of *déplorables antécédents*. The man was upper-class and rich, therefore trustworthy. Fournier tells us so explicitly: "All circumstances, both moral and material, argued in his favor." To Fournier's chagrin, the man agreed to pay the money demanded rather than be tried in court. Fournier is convinced he would have been proven innocent, but the man himself evidently had some doubts.

Tardieu had written that he doubted that vaginal discharge could be spontaneous, and that in his experience it was generally externally caused, that is, the result of a sexual assault. Fournier disagrees:

> For my part I have come across, in my practice, large numbers of vaginal inflammations which appeared in young children in an absolutely spontaneous manner, apart from any criminal violence, apart from any possibility of a sexual assault. For example, they appear in little girls who had not escaped the vigilant eye of their mothers for a single instant (p. 514).

But Fournier himself provided the case of an eight-year-old girl who also had never been away from the "vigilant eye" of her mother. This did not prevent her from becoming the victim of a vicious sexual attack, though it came from her own mother. But Fournier, even after himself presenting the case (and after reading Tardieu, who also cites such cases), is incapable of believing that such assaults by a mother constitute sexual abuse.

In the same address, Fournier quotes his friend Paul Brouardel, the dean of the Faculty of Medicine:

> Girls accuse their fathers of imaginary assaults on them or on other children in order to obtain their freedom to give themselves over to debauchery (p. 512).

Brouardel is the author of the other important article in this tradition. On June 11, 1883, he gave an address to the Société de Médecine Légale de France, subsequently published in the *Annales* (3rd ser., 10, pp. 60–71, 148–179), entitled "Les Causes d'erreur dans les expertises relatives aux attentats à la pudeur" (The Causes of Error in Expert Opinions with Respect to Sexual Assaults), dealing with the sexual abuse of children. The existence of this article, written at this time, shows that Brouardel was interested in this topic during the period that Freud was in Paris and not just in the last years of his life. The first half of the article deals almost exclusively with simulation. Brouardel provides the most elaborate account in the literature of the possible reasons why the little girl might lie about sexual seduction; it was later used by many other authors:

> The little girl has forged a tale, and is now impregnated with it; the pleasure she experiences in playing a role, in seeing herself surrounded with interest that is full of compassion, makes her unshakable in her affirmations. One often speaks of the candor of children. Nothing is more false. Their imagination likes to invent stories in which they are the hero. The child comforts herself by telling herself fantasies which she knows are false on every point. . . . This child, to whom one ordinarily paid only the most minor attention, finds an audience that is willing to listen to her with a certain solemnity

and to take cognizance of the creations of her imagination. She grows in her own esteem, she herself becomes a personage, and nothing will ever get her to admit that she deceived her family and the first people who questioned her. Her lie will be all the more difficult to unmask since the child lies without troubling herself over the improbabilities which one finds in her account (p. 63).

In Brouardel's book *Les Attentats aux moeurs*, his passion, his real interest, is reserved for his long chapter (pp. 52–72) on simulation. Therefore, it is reasonable to assume that he spoke on this topic to his audience at the morgue in Paris in 1885. He claims that of 100 complaints of sexual abuse of children, 60 to 80 are unfounded (p. 52). He describes the case given by Fournier, already cited, and says it is the most important one he has seen. At the end of his account appears a significant passage:

It can happen that the parents act in good faith, but that in their ignorance of infantile pathology they take simple inflammations of the vulva to be the result of criminal sexual assaults on their child. Panicked by findings that seem to her very grave and significant, the mother presses the child with questions and reaches, unconsciously, it must be added, the point where she suggests to the child an account which will then serve as the basis for the future accusations. Indeed, if the mother's ignorance is one of the elements of the slander, the other is the extreme suggestibility of the child.

Freud will adduce these very arguments, in later years, to explain his own error in believing his women patients.

Brouardel cites, as the one great advance made in recent years (Freud is not cited) toward the explanation of such phenomena, a series of 1905 articles by Dupré on *mythomanie*, pathological lying, which, in Brouardel's opinion and that of his colleagues, "is linked . . . to mental degeneration." He gives a case (p. 62) of a boy of nine whom he examined along with Paul Garnier (probably in the 1880s or 1890s; Garnier died in 1901)—"a little satyr," given to "monstrous perversions" with adults in terrifying orgies, according to the account of the boy himself. But Garnier and Brouardel were skeptical and discovered that his story was an invention— though not entirely. For, it turns out, it was the parents of the child who "handed over to his heated imagination these invented scenes." Brouardel explains that they did this out of an "unhealthy curiosity." He has still more to say about the supposed tendency of women to imagine they have been raped:

> Hysteria plays a considerable role in the genesis of these false accusations, either because of the genital hallucinations which stem from the great neurosis [hysteria] or because hysterics do not hesitate to invent mendacious stories with the sole purpose of attracting attention to themselves and [in an attempt] to make themselves interesting (pp. 64–65).

(Brouardel defends this same point of view in his 1883 article.)

Brouardel ends this, his most important chapter, and the only one that was destined to reverberate down to our own day, by expressing his interest in *"la psychologie de la victime"* (p. 71). He says of the medico-legal expert:

> He is not prohibited from acquainting the examining magistrate, from the very beginning, with the very special psychology of the *victims* and the people around them.

The italics are in the original. Who are these victims with a psychology so special that they create their own aggressors? They are, Brouardel continues, "pathological liars, hysterics who accuse [men of rape], or even simply children who have been depraved from an early age." But when rape did take place, and after all, it was Brouardel's professional duty to investigate primarily those cases where the rape was real, he took the position, later to be taken by Abraham and most of male society: "In general it is a question of women who are predisposed, and this is why one must carefully study the hereditary and personal antecedents of these people" (p. 96).

How, though, would Brouardel explain the seventeen knife wounds that one little girl received during her rape (in a case reported by Tardieu)? Surely they were not simulated psychosomatic wounds. Brouardel did not deny that such cases occurred (indeed, he cites this very case of Tardieu's on p. 129), but he seemed to take no theoretical interest in them, reserving his scientific ardor for cases in which he was satisfied the child was lying.

In November 1882, Dr. Claude Etienne Bourdin gave a paper to the Société Médico-psychologique with the revealing title "Les Enfants menteurs" (Children Who Lie).[37] In the second part of that article he tells the following story:

> A child was admitted to the hospital. He seemed to be six or seven years old. The physiognomy of this little boy expressed intelligence. He understood what was said to him, and obeyed the orders he was given, but he remained completely mute. This mutism lasted one year. During this entire time, the child was watched with particular care [to determine if it was feigned]. Neither his little friends, nor the nurses, nor the sisters were able to get anything else from him except signs. Nonetheless, one day a word escaped from the lips of the child. A nurse heard it. A conversation was established between the warden and the would-be mute boy. The child admitted that he knew how to speak as well as his little friends. He kept silent because his father told him he would kill him if he said a single word. In actual fact, this child never dared to reveal either the name or the address of his father and mother (p. 375).

Bourdin comments on this sad tale: "The information he provided on this subject . . . was recognized as almost entirely untrue." The child who lived in mortal fear and dared not speak was branded a liar. Already the victim of brutality, the child became the accused. For, as Bourdin states:

> Children are susceptible to cupidity, to hatred, to vengeance, to enmity, to jealousy especially, and, to state it bluntly, to almost all the passions that trouble the heart of the adult. One can, therefore, search for the source of their lies in the maze of passions; one is very likely to find it there (p. 378).

He advises:

> It is up to educators and particularly medical doctors to destroy the myth of the infallible sincerity of the child. This is a meritorious task in every respect (p. 384).

His conclusion:

> To conclude, I have yet to say some very sad words indeed, because it is necessary to strip from childhood the halo of sincerity with which it has been so unjustly crowned. To know the soul of the child, I followed the advice of an ancient source: "Speak," I said, "and act." The child answered. I listened to his words, and I judged his acts. From this double examination I came away with the absolute conviction that the child takes pleasure in lying, and that he knows how to use it skillfully in the interest of his evil instincts and his evil passions (p. 386).

A few years later, in 1887, Dr. Auguste Motet (b. 1832) wrote an article in support of Bourdin's thesis entitled "Les Faux Témoignages des enfants devant la justice" (False Testimony of Children before the Courts).[38] Motet says (p. 495) that he was inspired to do his work after observing the hysterics presented by Charcot. He states (p. 485) that the inventions of children and the lies of hysterics have much in common. This step, from the "lies of children" to the "lies of hysterical women," was to have a tragic effect on the history of psychological thinking in Europe. Bourdin (p. 380) had quoted an 1882 article by Vedie (*Annales médico-psychologiques*, 8, p. 239) to the effect that hysterical women lie and accuse, to which Bourdin added: "It seems to me that all psychiatrists agree with this opinion."

A posthumously published article entitled "Les Hystériques accusatrices" (Hysterical Women Who Accuse)[39] by Paul Garnier (1819–1901, chief physician of the hospital at police headquarters, author of *Masturbation à deux*), who had worked with Brouardel, follows this tradition and links sexuality, hysteria, and lying. A case he reports in great detail (pp. 345–361) is that of a tall, elegant, beautiful woman of twenty-two, Camille, who was intelligent and articulate, but, alas, a hysteric. Her father, Garnier assures us, was *"un homme fort honorable."* Thus when Camille accuses him of incest (p. 347), "the enormity of the accusation destroys its probability." Garnier comments that "obviously the incriminating tendency in her is primordial and fundamental" (p. 353). Garnier does not ask whether Camille's disturbances could have resulted from the reality of her accusations; instead he automatically assumes that her accusations are the result of her disturbances. Further proof, for him, is that she tells a panel of doctors investigating her that "my brother is the lover of my mother. He was already her lover when he was ten or twelve years old" (p. 357). And further: "My sister died of inanition, because nobody took care of her. For two years she was not allowed to leave the house" (p. 358). All these family "secrets" which Camille revealed to the panel (p. 361), "without any purpose, without any need," only provided further evidence of her hysteria. It is as if Garnier were saying: What Camille tells us could not possibly be true, and if it is true, then she has no business telling it to us. Either way she is crazy. Since she never ceased demanding that her father appear before a court of law (p. 361), "she was sent to [the insane asylum at] Sainte-Anne."

It was this tradition that was represented at the Salpêtrière by Charcot. The influence of this great teaching hospital weighed heavily with Freud, and Charcot's personal influence was even greater. Psychiatry and forensic medicine were at the time entirely separate fields. Tardieu and Brouardel, as legal physicians, did not engage in any form of therapy, least of all psychotherapy. Charcot, on the other hand, had an enormous reputation as a "healer." At that time, direct authoritative medical intervention held an appeal for Freud.

When Freud left Paris, no doubt both of the currents that he had been exposed to were active in his thinking. One tradition said that sexual assaults on children were frequent and that children seldom imagined them. The other said that rape was rare but children often imagined it.

The theoretical disagreement between Ambroise Tardieu, who argued that sexual traumas were only too real, and Alfred Fournier, who argued that they were fantasies, was not consequential so long as it was believed that these experiences had no psychological effect. When Freud joined the debate, he was clearly on the side of Tardieu. Over the years, however, Freud moved closer to the view held by Fournier, but with the difference that Freud believed the fantasies themselves had pathogenic psychological consequences. These issues are the elements of an unformulated yet fundamental debate. Freud's contribution added a critical dimension (the importance of fantasies) which then overshadowed the basic issue, which remains: Are sexual assaults rather than fantasies the real basis of illness? Or, put differently, are pathogenic sexual fantasies always based on real events? Freud's shift to a negative answer to both questions is not explicable in scientific terms. Historically, the material

I found in Paris set the stage for the drama that was to unfold in Vienna and illuminate Freud's preoccupation with these issues.

SUMMARY

UNTIL now there has been no information at our disposal that would permit historians to speculate about Freud's experiences in Paris. The little that was known of his personal and scientific contacts had not directed attention beyond Charcot and his influence on Freud with regard to hypnosis and current ideas about hysteria, ideas that Freud was destined to alter radically. But Freud had provided a hint of something more when he wrote: "While I was living in Paris in 1885 as a pupil of Charcot, what chiefly attracted me, apart from the great man's own lectures, were the demonstrations and addresses given by Brouardel." In the same year, an otherwise little-known book by Antonin Delcasse on cruelty toward children was published. In the preface to that book, Delcasse dedicates his work to Paul Brouardel, who, he explained, "often" showed his students what was otherwise a hidden and little discussed side of medicine: he performed autopsies on the bodies of children who had died as a result of abuse, often, Delcasse reminds the reader, at the hands of a parent. Thus although we cannot *prove*, in the strict sense of the word, that Freud, too, witnessed such autopsies at the Paris morgue, it seems very probable that he did, for there is no reason to assume that Brouardel would suddenly cease such demonstrations a few months after Delcasse wrote his book. The phrase that Freud used many years later (in 1913) to describe what he saw—

namely, things "of which science preferred to take no notice" —now makes sense.

Freud always claimed to have taken away from his years in Paris an interest in trauma as a causative agent in mental illness, something he learned from Charcot, even if by "trauma" Charcot meant something far less dramatic than a physical assault on a child by a parent. In discussing the seduction theory in 1914 (*S.E.*, 14, p. 17), Freud wrote: "Influenced by Charcot's view of the traumatic origin of hysteria, one was readily inclined to accept as true and aetiologically significant the statements made by patients in which they ascribed their symptoms to passive sexual experiences in the first years of childhood—to put it bluntly, to seduction." [Strachey's translation is incorrect. The German (*G.W.* 10, p. 55) reads: *Unter dem Einfluss der an Charcot anknüpfenden traumatischen Theorie der Hysterie war man leicht geneigt, Berichte der Kranken fuer real und ätiologisch bedeutsam zu halten, welche ihre Symptome auf passive sexuelle Erlebnisse in den ersten Kinderjahren, also grob ausgedrückt: auf Verführung zurückleiteten.* Freud is not saying that the patients ascribed their symptoms to seduction, but that *he* did so: "accounts of the patient which showed [me] that their symptoms can be traced back to . . . "] Given the new evidence just presented, it seems more likely that it was Freud's experiences at the Paris morgue that led to his later theoretical concepts about the origins of neurosis.

However, in 1896, when Freud first developed his traumatic theory of neurosis, he did not mention physical abuse, but was, rather, interested in sexual abuse. Now, although a sexual abuse is almost invariably a physical abuse as well (rape is always violent), a physical abuse is not invariably sexual. Is there any reason, then, to assume that Freud also witnessed the results of sexual abuse on a child at the Paris morgue? I think there is, though again, in the strictest sense of the word, we cannot *prove* it. My evidence is this: Ambroise Tardieu, predecessor to Paul Brouardel as professor of legal medicine at the Faculty of Medicine in Paris, devoted one third of his book *Les Attentats aux moeurs* to rape, and Tardieu tells us that of the 616 cases which he personally investigated, more than half, 339 to be exact, were cases of rape of children (primarily girls) under the age of eleven. Now, when Delcasse thanks Brouardel in his preface, he also mentions Tardieu and the fact that Brouardel is following in Tardieu's footsteps by investigating child abuse. Moreover, some of the cases that Tardieu gives (e.g., cases 41 and 48) are of the rape and murder of small children, in one case by a father. Both Brouardel and Tardieu were interested in physical and sexual abuse of children. Both men wrote books on the subject. Brouardel's book was published posthumously, in 1909, but represents his thinking during the very time that Freud was in Paris. This is clear from an influential article he wrote in 1883 about the legal aspects of the sexual abuse of children. It becomes ever more likely, the closer we examine the evidence, that Freud would have witnessed at least one autopsy of a sexually abused child. Certainly he would have heard discussion of this unusual topic, in which his teacher was so interested, both during the demonstrations and in the lectures by Brouardel that Freud said he attended.

I also learned that Freud owned both the book by Tardieu and the book by Brouardel on sexual abuse, including sexual abuse of children, and that he owned Bernard's book on the subject as well. I further found that in books in Freud's library by German authors (Krafft-Ebing, Moll, and others) on sexuality, Freud underlined passages in which some of Tardieu's and Brouardel's cases of sexual abuse are cited. Freud studied under Brouardel, the successor to Tardieu; he mentioned his demonstrations and lectures with respect and says that he learned things from him "of which science preferred to take no notice"; he underlined the names of Tardieu and Brouardel when he came across them in the German literature; and he owned their books.

If we add all these facts together: that Freud was impressed by something he saw at Brouardel's demonstrations in the Paris morgue; that Brouardel was known for his demonstrations of physically abused children; that Brouardel was interested in sexual abuse as well and wrote about both topics; that Tardieu, his predecessor, was also interested in both topics and wrote about them; and that Freud owned both of their books on these topics—then the hypothesis that Freud was exposed in Paris to material that would later come to play a major role in his theoretical thinking, though it is, strictly speaking, speculation, is speculation with a high degree of probability.

3 *Freud, Fliess, and Emma Eckstein*

> *Emma Eckstein was an early patient of my father's and there are many letters concerning her in the Fliess correspondence which we left out, since the story would have been incomplete and rather bewildering to the reader. I remember her vaguely and Mathilde remembers her well.*
> —UNPUBLISHED LETTER FROM ANNA FREUD TO
> ERNEST JONES, November 19, 1953; Jones Archives,
> London Institute of Psycho-Analysis

THE STORY OF AN OPERATION

BETWEEN 1894 and 1900, Wilhelm Fliess was Freud's closest friend and possibly the only person with whom Freud could discuss his newly emerging insights into the origins of mental illness. Fliess shared Freud's views on the importance of sexuality—i.e., masturbation, coitus interruptus, and the use of condoms—in the etiology of what were then called the "actual neuroses," primarily neurasthenia and certain physically manifested anxiety symptoms. But Fliess's interest was confined to physical symptoms with a physical etiology. As Freud's interest shifted to the neuroses proper—i.e., hysteria and obsessional neurosis—he began to seek their origins in psychological factors. The psychological aspects of illness did not interest Fliess, though this only became clear to Freud many years later. Their initial convergence of interest led to a collaboration the consequences of which were to resonate far beyond Vienna and would ultimately exert an influence on the way every psychother-

Sigmund Freud and Wilhelm Fliess in the 1890s

apist thought about the interaction between fantasy and reality.

Early in 1895 Fliess performed surgery on one of Freud's first analytic patients, Emma Eckstein (1865–1924). Emma Eckstein's name has been all but forgotten in the history of psychoanalysis, and had she not been mistakenly identified with the patient Freud called "Irma" in his discussion of the "dream-specimen" in *The Interpretation of Dreams*, she would not be remembered at all today.[1] She came from a prominent socialist family and seems to have been active in the women's movement in Vienna. When Emma Eckstein was about twenty-seven she entered analysis with Freud— several of her relatives said she was Freud's "first analytic patient" (see p. 245). That Freud was drawn to her is clear from the prominent place she occupies in his correspondence with Fliess. The passages concerning Emma Eckstein in the letters are, beyond question, the most passionate accounts Freud ever wrote about a patient. The exact nature of her complaints is unknown, but it appears that she suffered from stomach ailments and menstrual problems. She had difficulty walking, and spent much of her time (at least in later life) confined to her couch. Why Freud and Fliess decided that she needed an operation is not clear. Fliess had visited Freud in Vienna during Christmas of 1894, met Emma Eckstein, and suggested to Freud that she be operated on for her symptoms.

In Freud's copy of Fliess's 1902 book, *Über den ursächlichen Zusammenhang von Nase und Geschlechtsorgan* (On the Causal Connection between the Nose and the Sexual Organ),[2] there is a marked passage (p. 8) which reads:

> Women who masturbate are generally dysmenorrheal. They can only be finally cured through an operation on the nose if they truly give up this bad practice.

Emma Eckstein in 1895, before the operation

I believe that Freud marked this passage in later years because in his opinion it described the case of Emma Eckstein. She was, as we know from her own publications (see Appendix A), very much concerned with the then prevalent belief in the dangers of masturbation, something she undoubtedly discussed in her treatment with Freud. Her symptom of irregular or painful menstruation would have been attributed to masturbation, and when Fliess was brought in, he would certainly have recommended an operation on her nose, because of his belief that the nose and the sexual organs were intimately connected, and that sexual problems could be cured through nasal surgery.

If Freud's consent to such an operation seems puzzling, his idealization of Fliess as a great healer must be considered. Moreover, Freud, who had known Fliess since 1887, wanted a closer collaboration with him than he had so far been able to achieve.[3] Both men believed that sexual problems, and masturbation in particular, played a key role in the causation of neurotic illnesses. They also believed that displacements occurred often in such illnesses. Freud thought they were psychological displacements—i.e., shifting one's concern from a real problem to a harmless surrogate that could siphon off anxiety by obliterating any connection with the real source of anxiety. For Fliess, on the other hand, these displacements were purely physical: the problem was shifted from the vagina to the nose, and the only way to deal with such a problem was to intervene, physically, by operating on the nose. If Freud had told Fliess that Emma Eckstein's problems had to do with menstruation and that she masturbated, it would have been only natural for Fliess to suggest nasal surgery, *followed* by psychological treatment to prevent the recurrence of masturbation, as the only hope of curing her. This was certainly a revolutionary idea, one that would have appeared as bizarre to Freud's medical colleagues as his own views did. Perhaps the unorthodoxy of Fliess's methods encouraged Freud to believe they contained an unrecognized truth. In any event, he seems not to have hesitated in handing over Emma Eckstein to Fliess.

Max Schur was the first to quote from Freud's letters about the operation, but his evaluation was confined to the influence it had on Freud's dream of Irma's injection.[4] Because of the importance of this operation (it would affect Freud's views on the relative importance of fantasy and reality and his views on women and hysteria), it is worth telling the story in Freud's own words. In what follows I have used my translation[5] of Freud's letters to Fliess, introducing material Schur (and others, notably Ernest Jones) had not seen.[6] None of these letters was included in the published edition of the Freud/Fliess letters.

On January 24, 1895, in an unpublished letter, Freud tells Fliess, "Now only one more week separates us from the operation." Freud, in the same letter, complains that "my lack of medical knowledge once again weighs heavily on me. . . . I would not have dared to invent this plan of treatment on my own, but I confidently join you in it." A review of Fliess's publications indicates that this was Fliess's first major operation (his other interventions were confined to cauterization and cocainization of the nose), and Freud may well have been feeling hesitant, for he suggests, in the same letter, that Fliess work with Robert Gersuny, a well-known senior surgeon in Vienna.[7]

Fliess arrived in Vienna in the first week or two of February and operated on Emma Eckstein. He left soon thereafter.

Freud's first letter to Fliess after the operation is dated February 25, 1895, but concerns only a report of Fliess's work in the medical journal *Wiener allgemeine Zeitung*. There is no mention of Emma Eckstein. On March 4, 1895,

Freud writes Fliess about Emma Eckstein (in a letter published in part by Schur):

> Eckstein's condition is still unsatisfactory; persistent swelling, going up and down "like an avalanche"; pain, so that morphine cannot be dispensed with; bad nights. The purulent secretion has been decreasing since yesterday; the day before yesterday (Saturday) she had a massive hemorrhage, probably as a result of expelling a bone chip the size of a "Heller" [a small coin]; there were two bowlfuls of pus. Today we encountered resistance to irrigation; and since the pain and the visible edema had increased, I let myself be persuaded to call in Gersuny. (By the way, he greatly admired an etching of "The Isle of the Dead" [by Böcklin].) He explained that the access was considerably narrowed and insufficient for drainage, inserted a drainage tube, and threatened to break it [the bone?] open if that did not stay in. To judge by the smell, all this is most likely correct. Please send me your authoritative advice. I am not looking forward to new surgery on this girl.

In a later passage, apparently overlooked by Schur, Freud mentions having visited Josef Breuer (1842–1925; Freud's mentor and collaborator) "on Sunday evening and once again won him over—probably only for a short time—by telling him about the analysis of Eckstein, with which you are not really familiar either." Freud wished to win Breuer over to his views on the importance of sexuality in the neuroses, and thought he would do so by telling Breuer about Emma's case—i.e., by describing her sexual symptoms. This passage is thus the first hint that Emma's problems were of a sexual nature. The passage is also interesting in that Freud admits that he had turned his patient over to Fliess without first discussing her case with him in detail.

Freud then writes that the only other thing he can send

(*beilegen*; presumably there was an enclosure, subsequently lost) Fliess is "a small analogy to Emma's dream psychosis which we witnessed." It is not clear what a "dream psychosis" is, although it is probably some form of waking behavior which resembles dream behavior. Since the two men witnessed this together, Freud was present either at the operation or, more likely, when Fliess examined Emma for the first time.

Four days later (March 8, 1895) Freud wrote Fliess an important letter, published by Schur, which I reproduce here in its entirety:

Dearest Wilhelm:

Just received your letter and am able to answer it immediately. Fortunately I am finally seeing my way clear and am reassured about Miss Eckstein and can give you a report which will probably upset you as much as it did me, but I hope you will get over it as quickly as I did.

I wrote to you that the swelling and the hemorrhages would not stop, and that suddenly a fetid odor set in, and that there was an obstacle upon irrigation. (Or is the latter new [to you]?) I arranged for Gersuny to be called in; he inserted a drainage tube, hoping that things would work out once discharge was reestablished; but otherwise he was rather reserved.[8] Two days later I was awakened in the morning—profuse bleeding had started again, pain, etc. Gersuny replied on the phone that he was unavailable till evening; so I asked Rosanes[9] to meet me. We did so at noon. There still was moderate bleeding from the nose and mouth; the fetid odor was very bad. Rosanes cleaned the area surrounding the opening, removed some sticking blood clots, and suddenly he pulled at something like a thread, kept on pulling and before either one of us had time to think, at least half a meter of gauze had been removed from the cavity. The next moment came a flood of blood. The patient turned white, her eyes bulged, and she had no pulse. Immediately thereafter, how-

Paquet III

1895

(23 lettres)

X

1895

— 8 Janvier 1895

24 Janvier 1895

25 février 1895

Freud engage Fliess à une
publication et lui prêche la tolérance
avec le public, qui a d'abord mes travaux.

4 Mars 1895

8 Mars 1895

Fliess a laissé une compresse dans la
plaie de la tête de Melle Eckstein.
Freud le lui reffute et l'en console.
Il s'est lui-même trouvé mal à la
vue de la plaie saignante.

13-15-22-28 Mars 1895

Freud est déprimé : Melle Eckstein
semble perdue ! Il se repent de l'avoir
fait opérer par Fliess. Enfin elle est
sauvée ! Touchante conscience profession-
nelle.

*Marie Bonaparte's description of Freud's letters
to Fliess, February–March 1895*

ever, he again packed the cavity with fresh iodoform gauze and the hemorrhage stopped. It lasted about half a minute, but this was enough to make the poor creature, whom by then we had lying flat, unrecognizable. In the meantime—that is, afterward—something else happened. At the moment the foreign body came out and everything became clear to me, immediately after which I was confronted by the sight of the patient, I felt sick. After she had been packed, I fled to the next room, drank a bottle of water, and felt miserable. The brave Frau Doktor[10] then brought me a small glass of cognac and I became myself again.

Rosanes stayed with the patient until I arranged, via Streitenfels, to have both of them taken to Sanatorium Loew. Nothing further happened that evening. The following day, that is, yesterday, Thursday, the operation was repeated with the assistance of Gersuny; [the bone was] broken wide open, the packing removed, and [the wound] curetted. There was scarcely any bleeding. Since then she has been out of danger, naturally very pale, and miserable with fresh pain and swelling. She had not lost consciousness during the massive hemorrhage; when I returned to the room somewhat shaky, she greeted me with the condescending remark, "So this is the strong sex!"

I do not believe it was the blood that overwhelmed me—at that moment affects were welling up in me. So we had done her an injustice; she was not at all abnormal, rather, a piece of iodoform gauze had gotten torn off as you were removing it and stayed in for 14 days, preventing healing; at the end it tore off and provoked the bleeding. That this mishap should have happened to you; how you will react to it when you hear about it; what others could make of it; how wrong I was to urge you to operate in a foreign city where you could not follow through on the case; how my intention to do the best for this poor girl was insidiously thwarted and resulted in endangering her life—all this came over me simultaneously. I have worked it through by now. I was not sufficiently clear to think of immediately reproaching Rosanes at that time. This occurred to me only 10 minutes later; that he should immediately have thought: there is something inside; I shall not pull it out lest there be a hemorrhage; rather, I'll stuff it some more, take her to Loew, and there clean and widen it at the same time. But he was just as surprised as I was.

Now that I have thought it through, nothing remains but heartfelt compassion for my child of sorrow [i.e., Emma Eckstein]. I really should not have tormented you here, but I had every reason to entrust you with such a matter and more. You did it as well as one could. The tearing off of the iodoform gauze remains one of those accidents that happen to the most fortunate and circumspect of surgeons, as you know from the business with your little sister-in-law's anesthesia and the broken adenotome [an instrument for the removal of adenoids]. Gersuny said that he had had a similar experience and therefore he is using iodoform wicks instead of gauze (you will remember your own case). Of course, no one is blaming you, nor would I know why anyone should. And I only wish that you will arrive as quickly as I did at feeling sympathy, and rest assured that it was not necessary for me to restore my trust in you once again. I only still want to add that for one day I shied away from letting you know about it; then I began to feel ashamed, and here is the letter.

Besides this, other news really pales. As far as my condition is concerned, you are certainly quite right; strangely enough it is far easier for me to be productive when I have mild troubles of this kind. So now I am writing page after page of "The Therapy of Hysteria."

An odd idea of a different sort I shall entrust to you only after we have Eckstein off our minds. Here influenza is quite widespread, but not very intense. Your mama is not yet quite well either.

I shall soon write to you again, and, above all, report in detail on Emma E. Scientifically, otherwise quite desolate. Influenza has been eating up the practice of specialists. That it really took its toll on you I know. Just allow yourself a proper rest afterward. I am determined to do the same if it should strike me.

With cordial greetings,

your
Sigmund

This letter, which was omitted from the published edition of Freud's letters to Fliess, is critical for an understanding of subsequent events in Freud's intellectual life. Fliess had "mistakenly" left half a meter of surgical gauze in the cavity created by the removal of the turbinate bone in Emma's nose.[11] Freud wished to minimize the significance of this and to protect Fliess's reputation. He says that "no one is blaming you, nor would I know why anyone should." Yet Emma Eckstein had almost died, in what Freud calls a *Verblutungsszene* (a scene of bleeding to death). Had it not been for the swift intervention of other surgeons, she might well have died. Fliess's "mistake" could hardly be considered a trivial one.

Freud, who had initially wanted Gersuny to be involved in the operation (Fliess probably had objected), now called him in. If initially Gersuny had not thought that the operation was necessary, it is not surprising that he was now, as Freud says, "rather reserved." This reserve could only have escalated to censure once he became aware of the extent of Fliess's surgical carelessness. It becomes clear from a letter quoted below that Fliess realized this and was not as optimistic as Freud in thinking that nobody would blame him. He demanded (and did not get) a letter from the surgeons exonerating him. When, therefore, Freud says that "we had done her [Emma Eckstein] an injustice; she was not at all abnormal" (*sie war gar nicht abnorm gewesen*), he had a passing insight: the place to search for psychopathology in this case was in Fliess and in himself. It was "abnormal" of Freud to hand Emma Eckstein over to Fliess and it was "abnormal" of Fliess to operate at all and then to bungle the operation. Emma Eckstein's reaction—i.e., her hemorrhaging—was a completely normal response to surgical violence. Later Freud would retract this insight and would claim that Emma Eckstein's hemorrhages were hysterical in nature, the result of sexual longing. If Freud means that Emma Eckstein herself had not been "abnormal" prior to the operation, an even greater insight, then he and Fliess had no business subjecting her to a theory that was put into practice as a life-threatening operation. For it is one thing to hold "abnormal" views about the nasal origin of menstrual problems and quite another to test those theories by operative interventions for which one possesses neither the surgical knowledge nor the requisite skills.

The next reference to Emma Eckstein is from an unpublished letter dated March 13, 1895:

> Eckstein is finally doing well, as she could have done three weeks ago, if it had not been for the detour. It does speak well for her that she did not change her attitude toward either one of us; she honors your memory beyond the unwelcome accidentality [unerwünschte Zufälligkeit].

The detour (*Umweg*) Freud refers to must be Emma Eckstein's reaction to the operation — i.e., the hemorrhages — and not the operation itself, which took place around the 21st of February. This is the first hint that Freud will eventually blame Emma Eckstein for this response.

As for whether Emma maintained her respect for both men, Schur has a mysterious note to a passage on p. 67 of his book *Freud: Living and Dying* (New York: International Universities Press, 1972):

> That Fliess had a gift for impressing his friends and patients with the wealth of his biological knowledge, his far-reaching

imagination, and his unflagging faith in his therapeutic abilities can be concluded from the intense loyalty of his patients which was evident from Freud's correspondence with him. Even a patient who . . . suffered dangerous consequences from a grave "slip" committed by Fliess remained loyal to him *for the rest of her life* [emphasis added].

In the footnote Schur writes: "Personal communication." The source, however, could not be determined.

Freud continues the same letter on March 15 (a passage not quoted by Schur):

Surgically, Eckstein will soon be well, [but] now the nervous sequelae of the incident are starting: nightly hysterical attacks and similar symptoms which I must start to work on. It is now about time you forgave yourself the minimal oversight, as Breuer called it.

Whatever Breuer told Freud, and whatever reason Breuer had for saying it, what Fliess did could hardly be termed a "minimal oversight" (*das minimale Versehen*). Indeed, Max Schur, in his unpublished paper "The Guilt of the Survivor,"[12] writes:

The previously unpublished correspondence of these months revealed Freud's desperate attempts to deny any realization of the fact that Fliess would have been convicted of malpractice in any court for this nearly fatal error.

Freud has already begun to represent to Fliess and to himself that Emma Eckstein's problems originated with her, and not in the external world (in this case with two overzealous doctors). The powerful tool that Freud was discovering, the psychological explanation of physical illness, was being pressed into service to exculpate his own dubious behavior and the even more dubious behavior of his closest friend. Freud has begun to explain away his own bad conscience.

Freud continues the letter again on March 20:

Poor Eckstein is doing less well. This was the second reason for my postponement. Ten days after the second operation, after a normal course, she suddenly had pain and swelling again, of unknown origin. The following day, a hemorrhage; she was quickly packed. At noon, when they lifted the packing to examine her, renewed hemorrhage, so that she almost died. Since then she again has been lying in bed, tightly packed and totally miserable. Gussenbauer[13] and Gersuny believe that she is bleeding from a large vessel—but which one?—and on Friday they want to make an incision on the outside while compressing the carotid artery to see whether they can find the source. In my thoughts, I have given up hope for the poor girl, and am inconsolable that I involved you and created such a distressing affair for you. I also feel very sorry for her; I had become very fond of her.

With the most cordial greetings to you and Ida.

Your
Sigmund

One would naturally expect Freud to be "inconsolable" (*untröstlich*) for Emma Eckstein. In fact, he is inconsolable for Fliess, even though he says quite explicitly that he expects Emma to die (*ich habe die Arme in Gedanken verloren gegeben*).

In his next letter (not published by Schur), dated March 23, Freud writes:

I could not make up my mind to send off the letter before I could give you definite news about E. The operation was postponed to Saturday, [and is] just now over. It was nothing and nothing was done. Gussenbauer palpated the cavity and pronounced everything to be normal; [he] supposes the bleeding was only from granulation tissue; she is spared any disfigurement. They will continue to pack her [nose]; I shall try to keep her off morphine. I am glad that none of the bad expectations has materialized.

But it is not true that she was "spared any disfigurement."
According to Dr. Ada Elias, a distinguished pediatrician and
a favorite niece of Emma's, her features were permanently
marred: "As a result, her face was disfigured—the bone was
chiseled away, and on one side caved in."[14]

On March 28, Freud writes again:

> I know what you want to hear first: *she* is tolerably well;
> complete subsidence, no fever, no hemorrhage. The packing
> which was inserted 6 days ago is still in; we hope to be safe
> from new surprises. Of course, she is beginning with the new
> production of hysterias from this past period, which are then
> dissolved by me.

Presumably the "hysterias from this past period" refers to
her reactions to the operation, which, not surprisingly, were
strong.

The next letter was written on April 11, 1895:

> Gloomy times, unbelievably gloomy. Above all, this Eckstein
> affair, which is rapidly moving toward a bad ending. Last
> time I reported to you that Gussenbauer inspected the cavity
> under anesthesia, palpated it, and declared it to be satisfac-
> tory. We indulged in high hopes, and the patient was gradually
> recovering. [However,] 8 days [ago] she began to bleed, with
> the packing in place, something that had not been the case
> previously. She was immediately packed again; the bleeding
> was minimal. Two days [ago] renewed bleeding, again with
> the packing in place, and by then overabundantly. New pack-
> ing, renewed perplexity. Yesterday Rosanes wanted to ex-
> amine the cavity again; by chance a new hypothesis about the
> source of the bleeding during the first operation (yours) was
> suggested by Weil. As soon as the packing was partly re-
> moved, there was a new, life-threatening hemorrhage which
> I witnessed. It did not spurt, but it surged. Something like a
> [fluid] level rising extraordinarily rapidly, and then overflow-
> ing everything. It must have been a large vessel, but which

one and from where? Of course, one could not see anything and was glad to have the packing back in again. Add to this the pain, the morphine, the demoralization caused by the obvious medical helplessness, and the tinge of danger, and you will be able to picture the state the poor girl is in. We do not know what to do. Rosanes is opposed to the ligation of the carotid that was recommended. The danger that she will run a fever also is not far off. I am really very shaken [to think] that such a mishap [*Malheur*] could have arisen from the operation which was purported to be harmless.

The last line seems accusatory.

Fliess did not miss the overtones of this letter. For Freud's next letter to Fliess, dated April 20, 1895, is clearly written in response to a demand from Fliess for some sort of apology from Weil or a letter from Gersuny:

I did of course immediately inform Rosanes of your recommendations concerning E. At close range many things look different, for instance the hemorrhages; I can confirm that in their case there could be no question of biding one's time. There was bleeding as though from the carotid artery; within half a minute she would have bled to death. Now, however, she is doing better; the packing was gently and gradually removed; there was no mishap [*Malheur*]; she is now in the clear.

The writer of this is still very miserable, but also offended that you deem it necessary to have a testimonial certificate from Gersuny for your rehabilitation.

Freud uses the word *"Malheur"* again here, as he did in the letter of April 11, as if to say to Fliess: *this* time nobody slipped. Yet Freud goes on:

For me you remain the physician, the type of man into whose hands one confidently puts one's life and that of one's family —even if Gersuny should have the same opinion of your skills as Weil. I had wanted to pour forth my tale of woe and perhaps obtain your advice concerning E., but not reproach you with anything. That would have been stupid, unjustified, and in clear contradiction to all my feelings.

But unless we are missing a letter, this is the first time that Freud says openly to Fliess that somebody, in this case another surgeon, Weil, held a low opinion of his *"Kunst"* (art), a word which possibly encompasses more than just surgical skill.

On April 26 he writes that "she [Emma], too, my tormentor and yours, now appears to be doing well." And on April 27, "Eckstein once *again* is in pain; will she be bleeding next?" The question is not quite as rhetorical as it seems, for Freud is preparing the ground for a diagnosis of hysterical bleeding, as if to say: her pains are unreal, and the hemorrhages which may have appeared to come from your operation were in fact psychologically caused—they were hysterical in origin, deriving from repressed wishes, not unskilled surgeons. The last reference to Emma Eckstein that year is on May 25: "Emma E. is finally doing very well and I have succeeded in once again alleviating her weakness in walking, which also set in again."

FREUD AND FLIESS

THE story of Freud's seduction theory, its relation to Fliess's operation on Emma Eckstein, and the eventual renunciation of the theory by Freud, is intertwined with the story of Freud's relationship with Fliess. Freud met Fliess in 1887; he was to play the major role in Freud's intellectual, emotional, and scientific life over the next fifteen years, and possibly beyond.[15] Ernest Jones describes the friendship in the following passage:[16]

> We come here to the only really extraordinary experience in Freud's life. For the circumstances of his infancy, though doubtless important psychologically, were in themselves merely unusual but not extraordinary. Again, for a man of nearly middle age, happily married and having six children, to develop a passionate friendship for someone intellectually his inferior, and for him to subordinate for several years his judgment and opinions to those of that other man: this also is unusual, though not entirely unfamiliar. But for that man to free himself by following a path hitherto untrodden by any human being, by the heroic task of exploring his own unconscious mind: that is extraordinary in the highest degree.[17]

Nobody would disagree that Freud was enraptured with Fliess during the most important years of his scientific development. The precise influence that Fliess exercised on Freud through their meetings and letters is, of course, impossible to reconstruct, since we have only Freud's side of the correspondence; the letters from Fliess to Freud have never been found.[18]

At first it seemed, especially to Freud, as if the two men's thinking ran along parallel lines. On February 8, 1893, Freud sent Fliess a letter and a draft entitled "The Etiology of the Neuroses" (about the actual neuroses, primarily neurasthenia). It contains the first mention of an assault (*Attentat*), presumably sexual, on a patient of Freud's, which took place at the age of eight: "In a case of tormenting hypochondria which began at puberty, I was able to prove an assault in the eighth year of life." Freud does not, however, accord it any etiological or theoretical significance, saying that such "psychic traumas" are "only the precipitating cause" of periodic depressions. At Easter 1893, Freud visited Fliess in Berlin.

At some point after the Easter meeting, Fliess sent Freud a paper entitled "Die nasale Reflexneurose" (The Nasal Reflex Neurosis), which he intended to deliver at the 12th Congress for Internal Medicine in Wiesbaden, in June 1893. Freud comments on the paper in an undated letter to Fliess, written sometime between the Easter meeting and June:

> I think that you cannot avoid mentioning the sexual etiology of neurosis without tearing the most beautiful leaf out of the wreath. So do it immediately in a manner suitable to the circumstances. Announce the forthcoming investigations; describe the anticipated result as that which it really is, as something new; show people the key that unlocks everything, the etiological formula; and if in the process you give me a place in this by incorporating a reference such as "a colleague and friend," I shall be very glad rather than angry. I have inserted such a passage on sexuality for you, merely as a suggestion.[19]

In the work itself, published in the proceedings of the Congress,[20] it seems that Fliess took Freud's advice, and possibly incorporated what Freud wrote, in the following passage:

> For I admit to the expectation that [we] shall succeed in demonstrating: the etiology of neurasthenia proper, insofar as it can be differentiated from other *status nervosi* [nervous conditions], is to be found in *abusus sexualis,* in the misuse of the sexual function. I have joined forces with a colleague and friend for the purpose of proving this by a series of carefully analyzed observations of patients. You know that sexual abuse [e.g., masturbation and coitus interruptus] has always been cited among the causes of neurasthenia. In our view, this fact is the *specific* etiology of neurosis, either in the sense that this etiology by itself is sufficient to transform a healthy nervous system into a neurasthenic one, or in other cases that it represents the necessary precondition for the production of neurasthenia by other such noxae which by themselves are incapable of having this effect (p. 391).

At this point Freud was still interested in the pathogenic effects of masturbation, and was still looking to Fliess for a physical solution to the problem of neurasthenia. Fliess could incorporate Freud's views, and collaboration was still possible.

The book that emerged from Fliess's address was published in 1893 as *Neue Beiträge zur Klinik und Therapie der nasalen Reflexneurose* (New Contributions to the Theory and Therapy of the Nasal Reflex Neurosis).[21] Because nothing of Fliess's has been translated into English—even his German articles are difficult to obtain—and because of the importance of Fliess's influence on Freud, I have translated several key passages from his work. In the preface, dated November 1892, to the book just cited, Fliess makes a veiled reference to Freud (we know this from the correspondence) and repeats it on p. 3:

> My intention of making the [nasal] reflex neurosis the subject of a literary discussion is very recent and did not occur until a friend suggested it when I told him that this disease entity is a very common one.

Fliess is addressing this book to psychiatrists, and even says so explicitly on p. 4; no doubt this was at Freud's behest as a means of further cementing their collaboration, and demonstrating the usefulness of Fliess's views for Freud's specialization. There are 131 cases of "actual neuroses" reported in this book of 79 pages, and the treatment in every case is mild, i.e., non-surgical: cocaine to the nose, cauterization, and, at most, what Fliess calls *galvanokautische Behandlung,* i.e., treatment involving cauterization by means of a wire heated by a galvanic current. There is no evidence, in the cases given in the book, that Fliess performed major surgery, as he was to do in the case of Emma Eckstein. Clearly, however, Fliess considered the treatment he offered for "neurasthenia" to be revolutionary. He ends his book (p. 79) by saying that when his treatment is followed

> the immense multitude of "neurasthenics" who rush from doctor to doctor and from spa to spa, without success, and who make a mockery of our art by falling into the hand of quacks, will diminish. For a large proportion of so-called neurasthenics are nothing more than people suffering from the [nasal] reflex neurosis.

He believes (p. 3) that "this diagnosis in the future will become [a means of earning their] daily bread for physicians." On p. iii of the preface, Fliess says: "Frequently I succeeded, through using nasal therapy, in healing symptoms that the masters of the art of medicine had striven to cure in vain."

But at some point between writing this book, in 1893, and performing the operation on Emma Eckstein, early in 1895, Fliess had decided that more radical intervention was called for. To learn more about Fliess's views on the theme of masturbation, the nose, and neurosis during the time of his collaboration with Freud, we must turn to the last book that Fliess sent to Freud, which was published in 1902 but which represents Fliess's views from 1893 on (many of the cases date from 1893 to 1897), *Über den ursächlichen Zusammenhang von Nase und Geschlechtsorgan* (with a dedication: "To my dear Sigmund"). Here is the entire text of the passage (p. 7) which Freud marked in his private copy, and which no doubt provides the background for the conversations that the two men had in 1894 and 1895:

> The typical cause of neurasthenia in young people of both sexes is masturbation (Freud) . . . Naturally, bad sexual practices [masturbation, etc.] affect by no means only the nose; the nervous system is directly harmed. Still, the nose is regularly influenced by abnormal sexual satisfaction, and the consequences of this influence are not merely a very char-

acteristic swelling and sensitivity of the nasal "genital spots"; the entire symptom group of distant complaints [*Fernbeschwerden*] which I have described as "the nasal reflex neurosis" depends on this neuralgic alteration. And so it happens that this complex of painful spots, which is generally termed neurasthenic, can be removed through a treatment consisting of the use of cocaine, and the elimination of the pain lasts as long as the effect of the cocaine. They can be removed for a longer time through cauterization or electrolysis. But they return as long as the causes of the abnormal sexual satisfaction are in effect, and only cease when normal satisfaction finally takes over. Unmarried women who masturbate normally suffer from dysmenorrhea [painful menstruation]. In such cases, nasal treatment is only successful when they truly give up this aberration. Among the pains which derive from masturbation, I would like to emphasize one in particular, because of its importance: neuralgic stomach pain. One sees it very early on in the case of women who masturbate, and it is to be found among "young ladies" as frequently as masturbation itself.

Fliess goes on to say that this practice alters the left middle turbinate bone in its frontal third, and therefore he decided to call this spot the "stomach-ache spot." He continues by saying that hemorrhages from the nose are well known among women who masturbate (*die Epistaxis der Onanisten ist ganz bekannt*). This opinion had fateful consequences for Emma Eckstein. Fliess continues (p. 10):

I remember a patient who had been handed over to me by the Royal Gynecological Clinic because of massive uterine bleeding. All gynecological methods had failed in her case. The very moment that I removed the hypertrophic [overdeveloped] left middle turbinate bone, the uterine bleeding ceased completely. . . . It is to be noted that the middle turbinate bone seems to play a role precisely in the mechanism of uterine bleeding. Functional [i.e., neurotic] uterine bleeding is especially to be seen in women who masturbate. Here, as well, the way [of treating it?] is through the nose, as in the case for dysmenorrhea [caused by] masturbation.

In Fliess's major work, *Die Beziehungen zwischen Nase und weiblichen Geschlechtsorganen* (The Connections between the Nose and the Female Sexual Organs), published in 1897,[22] with an inscription to Freud that reads: *"Seinem teuren Sigmund—innigst dv"* (To my dear Sigmund—affectionately, the author), the last part of chapter 6 discusses these "stomach-ache spots" and the *"Dauererfolg durch Exstirpation jener Stelle"* (the lasting success through extirpation of these spots). The dates of the case histories make it clear that Fliess's views belong to the period of Emma Eckstein's operation. Here is an important passage from p. 108:

> The effect of masturbation on this organ [the nose] is by no means exhaustively described by the statement that the result is a change in the genital spots of the nose, certainly not if one understands the genital spots to be the lower turbinate bone and the *tuberculi septi,* as we have done so far for good reason. Another area of the nose undergoes a typical transformation as a result of masturbation, namely the middle turbinate bone on the left, primarily in its frontal third. . . . If one completely removes this segment of the middle turbinate bone on the left, which can easily be carried out with suitable bone forceps, the stomach pains can be permanently cured.

So between 1893 and 1897, Fliess had carried his nasal treatment a step further, and engaged in "daring" techniques. It is probable that the first person to be treated with this new technique was Emma Eckstein.

FREUD'S VIEWS ON SEDUCTION

IN an undated letter written by Freud to Fliess between April and June 1893, there is an important passage which was, curiously, omitted from the published version:

> I am not clear about the naval cadet. He confessed to masturbating already in the morning; did you establish that the attack followed directly upon a masturbatory excess? Certain fantasies about the possibility of suppressing the impulse to masturbate via the nose, to explain such impulses, to undo anesthesia and the like should remain only fantasies?

Presumably Fliess had as a patient a naval cadet who had some kind of (hysterical?) attack related to masturbation. It can be assumed that Fliess had written to Freud about the case, telling him that he intended to treat the young man by performing nasal therapy. Freud, in his response, seems to be telling Fliess something he would not risk telling him during their later and more intense friendship—namely, that the efficacy of "nasal treatment" was a fantasy of Fliess's, and perhaps a nose operation was not the best way to treat a problem connected with masturbation. From what we know of Fliess's later sensitivity to criticism, he would not have taken well to this challenge, even when put as a question, and this undoubtedly explains why, as we know from a passage in a letter of July 10, 1893, Fliess evidently declined Freud's earlier offer of collaboration on a book or article.

On May 30, 1893, Freud included in a letter to Fliess a passage in which, for the first time, he suggests to him the possibility of sexual seductions in early childhood. In the published edition of the Freud/Fliess letters, this passage is omitted without explanation. The omission is not indicated by ellipses in either the German or the English printed version of the correspondence, yet it consists of an entire postscript:

> I continue, because now I am writing more easily, to submit the following problem to you:
>
> Undoubtedly there exist cases of juvenile neurasthenia *without* masturbation, but *not* without the usual preliminaries of overabundant pollutions—that is, precisely as though there had been masturbation. I have only the following unproven surmises for the understanding of these cases:
>
>   1) Innate weakness of the genital and nervous systems
>   2) Abuse in the prepubertal period
>   3) Could it not be that organic changes of the nose produce the pollutions and thereby the neurasthenia, so that here the latter develops as a product of the nasal reflex noxa?
>
> What do you think and do you know something about it?

Since the word "abuse" (*Missbrauch*) cannot refer to masturbation (Freud is speaking here of "juvenile neurasthenia *without* masturbation"), it must refer to a "misuse" by another person, i.e., a sexual trauma, a seduction. In fact, in the entire *GW*, the word "*Missbrauch*" is used exclusively to refer to an externally caused sexual abuse, never to masturbation.

This is the first evidence we have that Freud was beginning to explore areas that were outside the realm of Fliess's interests. Whereas the psychopathology of masturbation permitted a collaboration between Freud and Fliess (Freud could encourage the patient to give up the practice, and Fliess could use his surgical skills to repair the "damage" already done), if the cause of illness lay in something hitherto ignored, a real trauma from the external world, there would be little reason for Fliess's medical intervention.

Moreover, the preponderance of the psychological factor

(both in the damage done and in the cure needed) would preclude any close collaboration. The physical and psychological explanations are fundamentally incompatible, though this seems not to have become apparent to either Freud or Fliess for some time. It is evident, however, that Freud was embarking on a new kind of search.

The letter which follows, dated August 20, 1893, was omitted from the published version of the Freud/Fliess correspondence. Unlike the other omitted letters and passages, however, Ernst Kris never saw it, and it was not excised after the transcript was made. I came across it in Freud's desk at Maresfield Gardens. The relevant passage, from the end of the letter, reads:

> For the rest, the etiology of the neuroses pursues me everywhere, as the Marlborough song follows the traveling Englishman. Recently I was consulted by the daughter of the innkeeper on the Rax; it was a nice case for me.

Fliess may not have perceived the implications of this important passage. A few months earlier Freud had sent him a draft with the title "The Etiology of the Neuroses," which referred to the "actual neuroses"[23] (neurasthenia, as opposed to the "psychoneuroses"—hysteria and obsessional neurosis), whose etiology, according to Freud, lay in masturbation. But in this letter Freud is no longer referring to masturbation and coitus interruptus (Fliess's *abusus sexualis*) as "the etiology of the neuroses," but is on the trail of something far more essential: childhood sexual seductions. For the "daughter of the innkeeper on the Rax" is none other than Katharina, whose story is told in *Studies on Hysteria*, which was not to be published until May 1895. (This is the only reference Freud makes to her outside of that book.)

This remarkable case history, written in a style unusual for the medical literature of the time, proceeds in dialogue form to reveal that Katharina had been sexually assaulted (Freud uses the words *nächtlicher Überfall*, literally a "nocturnal attack") when she was thirteen or fourteen. That her seducer was her own father, however, we learn only from a footnote that Freud added to the 1924 edition of the book:

> I venture after the lapse of so many years to lift the veil of discretion and reveal the fact that Katharina was not the niece but the daughter of the landlady. The girl fell ill, therefore, as a result of sexual attempts[24] on the part of her own father. Distortions like the one which I introduced in the present instance should be altogether avoided in reporting a case history.

Freud used the gifts of a novelist to say something that neither Fliess nor any of his medical colleagues, not even the French authors, had suspected. For there is no case history in the preceding medical literature which describes the consequences of a paternal seduction on the emotional life of a child. Thus, when Freud comments on the emotional relief that resulted from his conversation with Katharina, he says something completely new: "I hope this girl, *whose sexual sensibility had been injured at such an early age* [emphasis added], derived some benefit from our conversation. I have not seen her since" (p. 133).

Freud says explicitly (p. 132) that Katharina was suffering from hysteria, and not from an "actual" neurosis. So Freud had now applied his new etiological formula beyond neurasthenia to the psychoneuroses. He had, without knowing it, entered a realm where nobody was prepared to follow him.

In 1894, Freud was absorbed in collecting cases for his *Studies on Hysteria*, on which he was collaborating with his onetime mentor, Josef Breuer, and we know from other sources how reluctant Breuer was to publish it.[25] But nowhere is the reason for this reluctance more clearly revealed

Josef Breuer

than in another passage omitted from the published version of a letter, dated May 21, 1894, in which Freud writes to Fliess:

> Was not Marion Delorme a jewel?[26] She will not be included in the collection with Breuer because the second level [Stockwerk, i.e., of a building], that of the sexual factor, is not supposed to be disclosed there. The case history that I am writing now—a cure—is among my most difficult pieces of work. You will receive it before Breuer if you return it promptly. Among the gloomy thoughts of the past few months there was one, in second place, right after wife and children —that I shall no longer be able to prove the sexual thesis. After all, one does not want to die either immediately or completely.

This is the only source from which we learn that Breuer wanted Freud to omit "the sexual factor" from *Studies on Hysteria*. Breuer was not averse to recognizing the role of sexuality (here understood to mean masturbation and coitus interruptus) in the genesis of the "actual" neuroses.[27] But the deeper, more frightening thesis that hysteria was caused by sexual seductions in childhood was as repugnant to Breuer as it was to the rest of Freud's colleagues. So when Freud says here that he is afraid he might not be able to prove the "sexual thesis," he means that he might be prevented from proclaiming his new discovery that sexual violence against a child is the source of hysteria and obsessional neurosis. It is quite possible, then, that Freud altered the Katharina case for this book, by neglecting to identify her seducer as her father, at Breuer's request.

If one of Breuer's conditions for agreeing to joint publication was that this thesis of Freud's be omitted from the book, then some of the case histories take on a new meaning. For we can presume that Freud first wrote them with such sexual seductions in mind, then removed any mention of them, at Breuer's insistence. The following case history of Freud's treatment of a "lively and gifted girl" now makes sense:

> . . . I told her that I was quite convinced that her cousin's death had nothing at all to do with her state, but that something else had happened which she had not mentioned. At this, she gave way to the extent of letting fall a single significant phrase; but she had hardly said a word before she stopped, and her old father, who was sitting behind her, began to sob bitterly. Naturally I pressed my investigation no further; but I never saw the patient again (pp. 100–101).

It now seems possible that Freud is here depicting a scene where a young girl accuses her father of having raped her, upon which the man begins to sob, acknowledging his guilt. These passages in *Studies on Hysteria* are Freud's first published references to seduction and its importance.

The reading that Freud was doing precisely at this time was related to this subject. He had four copies of Krafft-Ebing's *Psychopathia Sexualis* in his personal library, the fifth edition (1890), seventh (1892), ninth (1894), and eleventh (1901). The ninth edition[28] is inscribed from Krafft-Ebing to Freud: "With friendly greetings to his colleague, Dr. Freud, from the author." This 1894 edition is the only one in Freud's possession that is annotated by him.

If we examine the passages that Freud marked,[29] it becomes clear that most of his notations have to do with the sexual abuse of children (though Krafft-Ebing himself held no theories about this). For example, on p. 375 of Freud's copy, there is a large check mark in the margin next to the following passage:

> Maids, in collaboration with their lovers, masturbated children who had been entrusted to them, performed cunnilingus on a seven-year-old girl, introduced turnips and potatoes into

her vagina and did the same to the anus of a two-year-old
boy![30]

This passage originally appeared in Ambroise Tardieu's *Les
Attentats aux moeurs*, which, as we have seen, Freud also
owned.[31]

Several influences were thus at work on Freud which encouraged his newly developed thesis about the importance
of sexual seductions: the memory of what he had seen and
read during his Paris stay, the reading he was doing cur-
rently, and the clinical work he was engaged in daily with
his patients (which we can read about in the published letters
to Fliess). Offsetting these influences was the disapproval of
his onetime friend and protector, Josef Breuer. But perhaps
nothing would have a greater effect on Freud than the attitude taken by Fliess on the subject, for Freud was now prepared to acknowledge publicly his scientific collaboration
with Fliess.

In a published letter to Fliess of August 29, 1894, Freud
refers to the "Migraine" of M., which Kris took to be a
reference to a work by Theodor Meynert. Actually, it is to
a book by Möbius on migraine that Freud reviewed in 1895,
though his review was not known to the editors of the *Standard
Edition*.[32] It contains, in fact, Freud's first published recognition
of Fliess's work. The last paragraph of that review reads as
follows:

> I would further like to emphasize a relationship—one that
> Möbius does not reject—between migraine and the nose . . .
> [which I mention because of my] intimate acquaintance with
> the work and the surprising therapeutic success of a researcher
> well known to the readers of this journal, Dr. W. Fliess in
> Berlin. According to Fliess, who went beyond his predecessor
> Hack in using cocaine as a diagnostic aid, in [adopting] the
> daring technique of modern therapy, and in [entertaining]
> viewpoints of general significance, the nose has to be accorded

a role in the pathogenesis of all headaches whatsoever as well as of migraine, not only in exceptional cases but rather as a rule. . . .

By this time Freud knew the exact nature of the new therapy: surgery—and perhaps that was why he characterized it with the German word *kühn* (daring). Thus, not only had Freud turned Emma Eckstein over to Fliess for an operation, but he was now openly acknowledging his admiration for Fliess as a physician, after the operation had taken place.

THE SEDUCTION OF EMMA ECKSTEIN

I have suggested that Emma Eckstein was the patient who provided Freud with the seduction theory, and my reasons for suggesting this will become apparent in what follows. But is there any documentary evidence that Emma Eckstein had herself been abused as a child? In "The Aetiology of Hysteria," written in 1896 while Emma was still a patient, Freud wrote (*S.E.*, 3, p. 199):

> If you submit my assertion that the aetiology of hysteria lies in the sexual life to the strictest examination, you will find that it is supported by the fact that in some eighteen cases of hysteria I have been able to discover this connection in every single symptom, and, where the circumstances allowed, to confirm it by therapeutic success. . . . These eighteen cases are at the same time all the cases on which I have been able to carry out the work of analysis. . . .

Freud certainly considered Emma a hysteric (cf. Schur's book, p. 80), and it is apparent, therefore, that Freud believed Emma Eckstein had been seduced as a child.

Additional information on this point lies in Freud's "Project for a Scientific Psychology," which he wrote in the autumn of 1895 (*S.E.*, 1, pp. 283–387). Section 4 of the "Project" (*S.E.*, 1, pp. 352–356) is an attempt to explain the origins of an apparently indecipherable symptom in a patient who is called Emma. Strachey, in his note to p. 353, writes: "Freud seems not to have mentioned this case elsewhere." This is because all references to this patient were omitted in the published version of Freud's letters to Fliess, and thus Strachey was not aware of them. (In the "Project," written for Fliess, Freud did not of course disguise the names of his patients.) The patient is, in fact, Emma Eckstein. Freud begins (Strachey's translation):

> Emma is subject at the present time to a compulsion of not being able to go into shops *alone*. As a reason for this, [she produced] a memory from the time when she was twelve years old (shortly after puberty). She went into a shop to buy something, saw the two shop-assistants (one of whom she can remember) laughing together, and ran away in some kind of *affect of fright*. In connection with this, she was led to recall that the two of them were laughing at her clothes and that one of them had pleased her sexually. [Strachey's translation is incorrect here. The German reads: *dazu lassen sich Gedanken erwecken,* which means "this leads one to surmise" and not "she was led to recall." The point is that the patient did not remember, Freud surmised.] . . . Further investigation now revealed a second memory, which she denies having had in mind at the moment of Scene I. . . . On two occasions when she was a child of eight she had gone into a small shop to buy some sweets, and the shopkeeper had grabbed at her genitals through her clothes. [Strachey has altered something here: Freud does not say "the shopkeeper," he says *"der Edle,"* "the high-minded man," that is, Freud is expressing with sarcasm his contempt for the act of the shopkeeper, no doubt in sympathy with Emma Eckstein herself.] In spite of the first experience she had gone there a second time; after the second time she stopped away [stayed away]. She now reproached herself for having gone there the

second time, as though she had wanted in that way to provoke the assault. In fact a state of "oppressive bad conscience" is to be traced back to this experience.

At the end of the section (p. 356) Freud concludes by saying:

Here we have the case of a memory arousing an affect which it did not arouse as an experience, because in the meantime the change [brought about] in puberty had made possible a different understanding of what was remembered. Now this case is typical of repression in hysteria. We invariably find that a memory is repressed which has only become a trauma by *deferred action*.[33] The cause of this state of things is the retardation of puberty as compared with the rest of the individual's development.

Freud has thus used the case of Emma Eckstein to explain repression. We do not know what Freud considered to be the root of Emma's problems. His theoretical position, often expressed, was that hysterical symptoms in latency (after the age of eight) or in adolescence almost invariably represent the effects of a much earlier sexual assault. No doubt he had reason to believe that Emma Eckstein had been abused in early childhood as well.[34]

Freud was at that time convinced that Emma Eckstein's memories were real. The word "scene" [*Szene*] as Freud uses it in this passage from the "Project" is beyond any question a reference to something that actually took place.[35] It was not until later that Freud would view such "scenes" as fantasies. This passage from the "Project" shows that in the aftermath of Emma Eckstein's operation, Freud was concerned with actual early events and traumas and their effects on the later emotional life of the victim.

THE FATHER AS SEDUCER

FREUD's new theory was first made public in the French journal *Revue neurologique* on March 30, 1896. His article was entitled "L'Hérédité et l'étiologie des névroses"[36] and begins with these words:

> I am addressing in particular the disciples of J.-M. Charcot, in order to put forward some objections to the etiological theory of the neuroses which was handed on to us by our teacher.

This paper contains the first published mention of the words "psychoanalysis" and "psychoneurosis." Freud reports carrying out "a complete psychoanalysis in thirteen cases of hysteria" (*S.E.*, 3, p. 152). "In none of these cases," Freud reports, "was an event of the kind defined above [seduction in childhood] missing. It was represented either by a brutal assault committed by an adult or by a seduction less rapid and less repulsive, but reaching the same conclusion." The word Freud uses, writing in French, to describe these assaults is *attentat: "Il était représenté ou par un attentat brutal commis par une personne adulte ou par une séduction moins rapide."* Freud returns, as it were, to his Paris days, in order to address his late teacher Charcot and remind him of *attentats aux moeurs*. It is as if he were asking: How could you have left this out in your teaching and in your theories? (For Charcot had been a great defender of *la famille névropathique*, the constitutionally tainted family, and of the unique importance of heredity in the etiology of neuroses.) Nor does Freud forget Fournier and the literature on children who lie:

> How is it possible to remain convinced of the reality of these analytic confessions which claim to be memories preserved

from the earliest childhood, and how is one to arm oneself against the tendency to lies and the facility of invention which are attributed to hysterical subjects?

The answer that Freud provides is as true today as it was then—namely, that the feelings evoked by such memories could not be the product of invention. Long-lost affects, which belonged to the original event and have been locked away for years, surface:

> The fact is that these patients never repeat these stories spontaneously, nor do they ever in the course of a treatment suddenly present the physician with the complete recollection of a scene of this kind. One only succeeds in awakening the psychical trace of a precocious sexual event under the most energetic pressure of the analytic procedure, and against an enormous resistance. Moreover, the memory must be extracted from them piece by piece, and while it is being awakened in their consciousness they become the prey to an emotion which it would be hard to counterfeit.

As we have seen, Freud repeats this same idea in "The Aetiology of Hysteria" in a passage quoted at the beginning of this book. Freud ends this paper by saying:

> I am convinced that nervous heredity by itself is unable to produce psychoneuroses if their specific aetiology, precocious sexual excitation, is missing (p. 156).

Freud submitted an even stronger paper to the *Neurologisches Zentralblatt*, "Weitere Bemerkungen über die Abwehrneuropsychosen" (Further Remarks on the Neuropsychoses of Defence),[87] on the same day; it was not published, however, until May 15, 1896. In this paper, Freud is, for the first time, skeptical about the effect of masturbation (which Fliess, along with many other authors, regarded as one source of hysteria).

Active masturbation must be excluded from my list of the sexual noxae in early childhood which are pathogenic for hysteria. Although it is found so very often side by side with hysteria, this is due to the circumstance that masturbation itself is a much more frequent consequence of abuse or seduction than is supposed (p. 165).

He notes that it is more common for girls to have been victims of sexual seductions, but Strachey's translation is misleading:

Furthermore, a path is laid open to an understanding of why hysteria is far and away more frequent in members of the female sex; for even in childhood they are more liable to provoke sexual attacks.

This implies that the girls are the ones who provoke the attacks, when in fact what Freud actually wrote (. . . *zu sexuellen Angriffen reizt*) was that it is the female sex which "stimulates [men] to sexual attacks." Strachey's version was to become the standard view, but it was not yet Freud's.

In this paper, as in the French paper and the "Project," Freud uses the word "scene" to mean a real event. In one case, he explains a night ceremonial of an eleven-year-old as an unconscious memory of a seduction—performed, not to repeat the seduction, but to *prevent* it (pp. 172–173 n.). Freud says the seductress was a servant girl. But Strachey comments (in a footnote to a passage in this paper, p. 164):

It may be remarked that in this published paper Freud does not mention the fact that with female patients the apparent seducer was so often their father.

At some time during 1895 or 1896, Freud had become convinced that the person most often guilty of the sexual abuse of young children (primarily girls) was the father. (In the published letter of September 21, 1897, to Fliess, Freud writes: "Then the surprise that, in all cases, the *father* [emphasis in original], not excluding my own, had to be accused of being perverse.") But Freud did not say this publicly. The taboo against speaking about this seems to have been handed down through the generations of analysts since Freud. Thus, the editors of *The Origins of Psychoanalysis*, Ernst Kris and Anna Freud, omitted from the letters written after September 21, 1897 (the date Freud supposedly gave up the seduction hypothesis) as well as earlier letters, those case histories in which a father seduced a child, thereby depriving posterity of the opportunity to judge or even become aware of the evidence Freud was finding in his clinical practice for his belief in the reality of early sexual traumas. The reason, presumably, for these omissions is that once Freud had given up this notion as a mistake, it would simply confuse future generations of analysts (and patients) to be given information dating to a time when Freud had not yet understood the all-powerful nature of fantasy. An important document in this respect is the following case history (from a letter of December 6, 1896) which was omitted from the published version:

A fragment from my daily experience: One of my patients, in whose history her highly perverse father plays the principal role, has a younger brother who is looked upon as a common scoundrel. One day the latter appeared in my office to declare, with tears in his eyes, that he was not a scoundrel but was ill, with abnormal impulses and inhibitions. By the way, he also complains, entirely as an aside, about what surely are nasal headaches. I direct him to his sister and brother-in-law, whom he indeed visits. That evening the sister calls me because she is in an agitated state. Next day I learn that after her brother had left, she had an attack of the most dreadful headaches—which she otherwise never suffers from. Reason: the brother told her that when he was twelve years old, his sexual activity consisted in kissing (licking) the feet of his sisters when they were undressing at night. In association, she recovered from the unconscious the memory of a scene in which (at the age of four) she watched her papa, in the throes of sexual excitement, licking the feet of a wet nurse. In this way she surmised that the son's sexual preferences stemmed from the father; that the latter also was the seducer of the former. Now she allowed herself to identify herself with him and assume his headaches. She could do this, by the way, because during the same scene the raving father hit the child (hidden under the bed) on the head with his boot.

The brother abhors all perversity, while he suffers from compulsive impulses. That is to say, he has repressed certain impulses which are replaced by others with compulsions. This is, in general, the secret of compulsive impulses. If he could be perverse, he would be healthy, like the father.

Even if he did not go so far as to publicly announce that the father was the guilty party, by 1896 Freud was willing to take a stand on the reality of seduction, as we have seen from his published writings during this period.

THE THEORY OF PERIODICITY

BUT during this same time, Fliess was moving in quite a different direction. It is important to examine some of his ideas from this period to learn how they contributed to Freud's final change of heart. For I believe that Fliess's views on the origin of neurosis were to affect Freud profoundly, causing him to adopt a totally new and skeptical attitude toward Emma Eckstein and her memories, and beyond that, to the majority of all his female patients from 1897 on.

Throughout their early relationship, Freud was convinced

that he and Fliess shared a common interest in the effects
of childhood sexuality and that they viewed masturbation
differently than did their colleagues. This is true, but in fact
their views were diametrically opposed to one another and
incompatible, though this was not clear to Freud.

In his 1897 book, *Die Beziehungen zwischen Nase und
weiblichen Geschlechtsorganen*, Fliess presents the case of
three-year-old Fritz L.:

> For one year the observant stepmother noticed that the little
> boy has very obvious feelings of shame, and is moreover quite
> clearly interested in the naked female body, touches it, etc.
> Since then he has *pavor nocturnus* [night terrors] and anxiety
> in the evening . . . that is almost always preceded by singultus
> [hiccups] one or two days earlier, along with erections (p. 192).

How does Fliess explain these observations? He says the
first attack of singultus came on October 11, the second on
February 26, and the third on May 28—138 days apart,
that is, 6 times 23, the "male period." "Female periods" of
28 days are also carefully observed in the little boy. A few
pages later on (p. 199), Fliess mentions Freud's "The Aetiology of Hysteria":

> Here too I would like to refer to Freud's works, which are
> pathbreaking and which provide us with new and totally unsus-
> pected insights into sexual relations and the effects of these
> on the nervous system.

But while he is apparently acknowledging Freud's work, he
negates his praise by announcing elsewhere in his book that
these manifestations of infantile sexuality are entirely spontaneous and proceed from biologically determined periods.
A person's sexual life, according to Fliess, consists in innate,
inborn, constitutional givens that differ from individual to
individual but are of no psychological significance and can-

not, by the very nature of his theories, be treated by psychological methods.

While a certain amount has been written about Fliess's
views recently,[38] the passages quoted below have not been
noted. Examining them will help us understand Freud's position. For example, as we shall see, Fliess told Freud that
Emma Eckstein's hemorrhages were determined by critical
dates in her biological life, in accordance with his new theory
of "periodicity." The height of his friendship with Freud
(1896 and 1897) coincides with the time during which
Fliess developed his theories about the influence of critical
dates in the life of the individual.

In the letters that Freud wrote to Fliess in 1896, omitted
from the published letters, periodicity comes to play a greater
and greater role. Freud is continually searching his own past
to find what Fliess called "*Termine*," critical dates. These
dates, according to Fliess, are always tied to 28 (the "female period") and 23 (the "male period") and numbers that
are in some way related to 28 and 23 (e.g., 5, the difference
between the two numbers). Fliess believed that all events
in a person's life are determined by these critical dates. Along
with this went a curious diagnostic megalomania. Fliess
thought that his theories gave him special powers that allowed him to predict a person's death:

> I have many times observed that the mother's last breath is
> taken at the exact same time as her daughter's monthly period
> sets in, even when the latter had no idea of the [impending]
> death. And, conversely, in cases of chronic disease which
> approached the final stage, I have been able to predict the
> dying day by tying it to such a day [menstruation]. "The
> mother will die on the day her daughter has her period." And
> then she died.[39]

In a letter of December 4, 1896, Freud had written to
Fliess: "My psychology of hysteria will be preceded by the

proud words: *Introite et hic dii sunt* [Enter, for here, too, are gods]."⁴⁰ Fliess later adopted this quotation for his own purposes when, in his 1919 book, *Vom Leben und vom Tod* (Of Life and Death),⁴¹ he speaks of a

> glimpse into that magnificent, simple order which ties death to life. It is the same order through whose rule the ages of entire generations to the very day are determined and which makes the birth of grandchildren dependent on the day of the death of a grandmother. To understand this order in detail, to trace its inescapable lawfulness, to recognize our dependence on its determination, will be the future task of research on life. Enter, here are gods (p. 59).

Freud used the Latin quotation to mean that although hysteria had not hitherto been considered worthy of a serious physician's interest, he was now proclaiming it so. Fliess knew that most medical specialists would regard as mere grandiosity his belief that he discovered, like Freud, a fundamental "secret of nature." As long as neither Freud nor Fliess was aware of the full implications of the other's research, they could share mottos and believe that they were both in the midst of discoveries that would shatter the ordinary boundaries of science. But in fact Fliess's views on periodicity deprived Freud's discoveries of any validity, and made all psychological efforts irrelevant. By the end of his life, Freud became aware of this fact.

On November 24, 1937, when Marie Bonaparte visited Vienna to show Freud the letters from him to Fliess which she had purchased, she discussed Fliess with him. She writes:

> If he held so tenaciously to the theory of periods which determine people's death, if he imagined it, it must be, Freud believes, because of his remorse over the death of his younger sister. She died of pneumonia as Fliess was finishing his medical studies. He reproached himself for possibly having cared

for her badly, or that she had been badly [cared for by others]. So if one died from a death [the date of which was] determined in advance, he could feel absolved.[42]

Indeed, Fliess says as much:

On the afternoon of March 24, 1899, my wife's sister, Melanie R., began to have labor pains, and six hours later her daughter Margaret was born. On the same afternoon my wife's period began, and, as we later learned, it was to be her last period [before becoming pregnant]. So one sister had continued the pregnant state of the other. This is more than a simple pattern. Behind it lies a hidden law of nature determining relationships. For if one continues 280 days from March 24, that is, 10 times 28, one comes to December 29, the very same date on which, 4 years earlier, my eldest son came into the world (December 29, 1895). And 20 years earlier, on December 29, 1879, my only sister became suddenly deathly ill with chills and died thirty hours later.[43]

Hidden behind this supposed mathematical objectivity lies a peculiar grandiosity, since Fliess considered himself to be the only person to have understood these great laws of nature. It is not surprising, then, that Freud would have been under considerable pressure either to recognize the same laws or to begin to distance himself from Fliess.

A case history from Fliess's 1897 book (*Beziehungen*, p. 191) alerts us to the explanations that he offered his patients. Mrs. N. was fifty-three years old. She had her last period on March 1, 1892, when she was forty-nine. On March 12, 1896, Fliess probed what was left of her left middle nasal concha, which had been removed earlier (most likely by Fliess himself). As he was carrying out this examination, she developed massive bleeding, which could only be stopped by a very tight packing. At the same time, tears mixed with blood came pouring out of her right eye. On the night of the 13th she had a bloody discharge from her vagina. Fliess

"explained" to her right away that the bleeding was vicarious
(*Die Blutung wurde sofort als vicariirende angesprochen*).
Proof: between March 1, 1892, and March 12, 1896, 1,472
days had elapsed, that is, 64 times 23, her male period.

Just as was to happen in the case of Emma Eckstein (see
p. 100), Fliess's immediate response to the hemorrhage was
to seek an explanation in terms of 28 and 23 rather than
in terms of what he had done to the patient. While Freud
could not go along with this in Emma's case without abandoning his scientific view, he, like Fliess (and no doubt for
the benefit of Fliess), turned his investigation away from the
operation, that is, away from an external source, and sought
the cause of the bleeding in Emma Eckstein herself. To
Emma Eckstein it would have been little comfort that Freud's
was the more sophisticated procedure. The truth is that the
source of her bleeding was to be found neither in series
of 23-day and 28-day cycles nor in hysterical longing, but
in an unnecessary operation which was performed because
of a *folie à deux* on the part of two misguided doctors.

Freud had the option to recognize this, confess it to Emma
Eckstein, confront Fliess with the truth, and face the consequences. Or he could protect Fliess by excusing what had
happened. But in order to do this, to efface the external
trauma of the operation, it would prove necessary to con-
struct a theory of hysterical lying, a theory whereby the
external traumas suffered by the patient never happened, but
are fantasies. If Emma Eckstein's problems (her bleeding)
had nothing to do with the real world (Fliess's operation),
then her earlier accounts of seduction could well be fantasies too. The consequences of Freud's act of loyalty toward
Fliess would reach far beyond this single case.

In the middle of 1896, Freud was faced, just as he was
in Paris, with conflicting points of view, this time directly
in his own clinical experience, and not just in the literature.

On the one hand, his patients told him their memories of traumas from their childhood; these he had no reason to disbelieve. Recognizing the psychological significance of events which he had already become familiar with in Paris, he published a series of fine clinical and theoretical essays embodying his new findings. On the other hand, one of the patients who were presenting him with evidence in this area had been severely injured by an operation that Freud had recommended and which was carried out by his closest personal friend and scientific colleague. The tension between these two sets of events, which on the surface did not seem irreconcilable, was bound to reach a breaking point. Freud would be forced to make a choice.

On April 16, 1896 (in a letter omitted from *The Origins of Psychoanalysis* but reproduced by Schur, as were the following two letters), Freud told Fliess that he had found

> a completely surprising explanation of Eckstein's hemorrhages—which will give you much pleasure. I have already figured out the story, but I shall wait before communicating it until the patient herself has caught up.

On April 26, Freud wrote again:

> First of all, Eckstein. I shall be able to prove to you that you were right, that her episodes of bleeding were hysterical, were occasioned by longing, and probably occurred at the sexually relevant times (the woman, out of resistance, has not yet supplied me with the dates).

It is clear from this passage that Fliess had told Freud that Emma Eckstein's bleeding after the operation had nothing to do with the gauze he left in her wound, but was hysterical, i.e., caused by her fantasies, and not by his inept medical care. The word Freud uses for "sexually relevant times" is *Sexualtermin*, Fliess's notion that sexual events are tied to special dates. The dates of the bleeding are what seem to have most interested Fliess.

On May 4, Freud provides the explanation:

As for Eckstein—I am taking notes on her history so that I can send it to you—so far I know only that she bled out of *longing*. She has always been a bleeder, when cutting herself and in similar circumstances; as a child she suffered from severe nosebleeds; during the years when she was not yet menstruating, she had headaches which were interpreted to her as malingering and which in truth had been generated by suggestion; for this reason she joyously welcomed her severe menstrual bleeding as proof that her illness was genuine, a proof that was also recognized as such by others. She described a scene, from the age of 15, when she suddenly began to bleed from the nose when she had the wish to be treated by a certain young doctor who was present (and who also appeared in the dream). When she saw how affected I was by her first hemorrhage while she was in the hands of Rosanes, she experienced this as the realization of an old wish to be loved in her illness, and in spite of the danger during the succeeding hours she felt happy as never before. Then, in the sanitarium, she became restless during the night because of an unconscious wish to entice me to go there, and since I did not come during the night, she renewed the bleedings, as an unfailing means of rearousing my affection. She bled spontaneously three times, and each bleeding lasted for four days, which must have some significance. She still owes me details and specific dates.

Freud is eager to be able to supply Fliess with the dates that would finally absolve him of any responsibility for Emma Eckstein's bleeding. There is an important shift in Freud's use of the word "scene." It has begun to take on connotations of fantasy; it is connected with "wish fulfillment," not just with real events. The shift will soon be completed.

The next letter (unpublished) about Emma Eckstein appears not to have been noticed by Schur. Freud writes to Fliess on June 4, 1896:

> Eckstein's significant dates unfortunately cannot be obtained because they were not recorded at the sanitarium. Her story is becoming even clearer; there is no doubt that her hemorrhages were due to wishes; she has had several similar incidents, among them actual [*direkte*] simulations, in her childhood. Incidentally, she is doing exceedingly well.

Freud is attempting to rationalize the aftermath of the operation, in which Emma Eckstein nearly bled to death. The operation itself has receded far into the background; it was only a minor incident. The true cause of Emma Eckstein's hemorrhaging was not the gauze that was left in her nose, but a wish to have Freud by her side. Evidence for this is that she suffered from nosebleeds in childhood. How Emma Eckstein could have "simulated" a massive hemorrhage is difficult to understand.

Fliess seems to have written to Freud telling him that he suspected Emma's hemorrhages did not stem from a physical cause, but were "psychosomatic." By attempting to obtain Emma's "significant dates," Freud is tacitly accepting Fliess's supposition. The theory of hysterical bleeding could more easily be accommodated to Fliess's theories than could the recognition of the true source of Emma's bleeding. Fliess believed that Emma's abdominal and menstrual symptoms were related to the genital spots in the nose. Removing those spots would remove the symptoms. Yet if the operation had really been needed, as Fliess thought, then surely Emma Eckstein should now be cured, and there would be no need for Freud to see her again, or any other patient for that matter, since all their symptoms could be relieved by nasal treatment. Could Freud believe that he was seeing Emma Eckstein now merely to treat her for her hysterical reaction to the operation? Perhaps. But Fliess had not decided to operate on Emma Eckstein because of hysterical bleeding. The bleeding, even by Freud's account, was a product of the operation, not its causal antecedent. Yet there is no word, here, about the operation itself. It seems to have been completely forgotten, "wished away," to use one of Freud's own terms.

THE WITCH MUST DIE

> . . . *these poor women were forced by*
> *bitter torture to confess what they*
> *never did; innocent blood was spilled*
> *through hard-hearted butchery; and*
> *through a new alchemy, human blood*
> *was transformed into gold and silver.*
> —CORNELIUS LOOS (1546–1595)

> *Once torture has begun the game is*
> *won. The witch must confess, the witch*
> *must die. And whether she confesses*
> *or not, it amounts to the same thing,*
> *for once a woman has been brought into*
> *the prison, she is guilty, whether she*
> *has been brought there rightly or*
> *wrongly.*
> —FRIEDRICH SPEE (1591–1635)

ON January 17, 1897, Freud wrote to Fliess and, in a passage omitted from the published letters but included by Schur, mentioned Emma Eckstein: "Emma has a scene where the *Diabolus* sticks pins into her finger and puts a piece of candy on each drop of blood." When Freud had used the word "scene" in his 1896 papers, he was referring to a real event. But now his usage has changed. Max Schur writes about this passage:

> The use of the word "scene" here . . . is very significant. We know from Freud's correspondence with Fliess that he still believed in the "seduction etiology" of hysteria. However, in the published portion of this letter and the preceding one he clearly describes what he later called fantasies. This holds true for Emma's "scenes." It would therefore seem that Emma was one of the first patients who offered Freud a clue to the crucial realization that what his patient had described to him as actual seduction episodes were fantasies. As we know, this realization opened the way to the discovery of early infantile sexuality and its manifestations in infancy.[44]

The letter in which this passage occurs is the first letter that Freud wrote to Fliess on the subject of witchcraft. There he states:

> What would you say, by the way, if I told you that my brand-new theory of the early etiology of hysteria was already well known and had been published a hundred times over, though several centuries ago? . . . But why did the devil who took possession of the poor things invariably abuse them sexually and in a loathsome manner? Why are their confessions under torture so like the communications made by my patients in psychological treatment?

The answer to this question is important. Freud does not provide it. For it very much matters whether one says that the reason the devil invariably abuses the witch sexually is that this is a fantasy on the part of the witch, originating in a childhood wish to be possessed by the father, or whether one says that this is a distorted memory of a real and tragic event that is so painful it can only be recalled via this subterfuge. Schur is right: the hint that Freud throws out in this letter is that the witches *invented* the seductions out of longing. Similarly, Emma Eckstein associates blood with the devil and (sexual) pleasure. Freud continues his letter to Fliess with an astonishing sentence: "As far as the blood is concerned, you are completely without blame!"

A week later, on January 24, 1897, Freud again wrote to Fliess (a passage published by Schur) about witches, blood, and sexuality in a passage about Emma.

> Imagine, I obtained a scene about the circumcision of a girl. The cutting of a piece of the *labia minora* (which is still shorter today),[45] sucking up the blood, following which the child was given a piece of the skin to eat.

Again, by "scene" Freud means a fantasy, thereby providing Fliess with evidence that Emma was a hysteric who invented traumas. The point of insisting on this is to demonstrate to Fliess that his conduct of the operation was completely blameless: Emma hemorrhaged because she was filled with fantasies. Freud continues:

> An operation once performed by you was affected by a hemophilia which originated in this way.

In other words: Emma would have hemorrhaged no matter what was done to her. Fliess was not to blame. Freud went even further, for his mind was taken up with the question of the fantasy nature of sexual seductions:

> I dream, therefore, of a primeval devil religion whose rites are carried on secretly, and *I understand the harsh therapy of the witches' judges* [emphasis added].

Freud is implying here that the Sabbats were *real* events (part of a ritualized religion in which sexual perversions were acted out). He seems to be saying: The torture and the murder of the witch are understandable, for the judges were attempting to curtail a heinous cult.

Unpleasant chains of associations are set off: if Fliess is

the judge, and Emma is the witch, then Freud, as observer, suddenly understands why Fliess had to be so harsh in his punishment of her—she was, during the operation, secretly enacting her own ritual, using Fliess's operation as a kind of somatic compliance—she bled, not in response to Fliess, but in response to her own private, internal theater of fantasy. So, if she nearly bled to death, it was not because of Fliess but because of her own perverse imagination.

4 Freud's Renunciation of the Theory of Seduction

LETTERS TO FLIESS

FROM 1894 through 1897, no subjects so preoccupied Freud as the reality of seduction and the fate of Emma Eckstein. The two topics seemed bound together. It is, in my opinion, no coincidence that once Freud had determined that Emma Eckstein's hemorrhages were hysterical, the result of sexual fantasies, he was free to abandon the seduction hypothesis. Freud's preoccupation with seduction seemingly came to an abrupt end on September 21, 1897, upon the writing of a remarkable letter to Fliess. Ernest Jones's account of this letter (1, p. 292) is dramatic:

> Up to the spring of 1897 Freud still held firmly to his conviction of the reality of childhood traumas, so strong was Charcot's teaching on traumatic experiences and so surely did the analysis of the patient's associations reproduce them. At that time doubts began to creep in although he made no mention of them in the records of his progress that he was regularly sending to his friend Fliess. Then quite suddenly, he decided to confide to him "the great secret of something that in the past few months has gradually dawned on me." It was the awful truth that most—not all—of the seductions in childhood which his patients had revealed, and about which he had built his whole theory of hysteria, had never occurred. The letter of September 21, 1897, in which he made this

announcement to Fliess is perhaps the most valuable of that valuable series which was so fortunately preserved.[1]

No other letter that Freud wrote has called forth such a response. Hardly any major historian of psychoanalysis has failed to comment on it in detail.[2] Because of the critical place it occupies in the history of Freud's thinking, this letter deserves to be quoted at length:

Dear Wilhelm:

Here I am again, arrived yesterday morning, refreshed, cheerful, impoverished, at present without work, and, having settled in again, I am writing to you first.

And now I want to confide in you immediately the great secret of something that in the past few months has gradually dawned on me. I no longer believe in my *neurotica* [theory of the neuroses]. This is probably not intelligible without an explanation; after all, you yourself found what I was able to tell you credible. So I will begin historically [and tell you] from where the reasons for disbelief came. The continual disappointment in my efforts to bring any analysis[3] to a real conclusion; the running away of people who for a period of time had been most gripped [by analysis]; the absence of the complete successes on which I had counted; the possibility of explaining to myself the partial successes in other ways, in the usual fashion—this was the first group. Then the surprise that in all cases, the *father,* not excluding my own, had to be accused of being perverse—the realization of the unexpected frequency of hysteria, with precisely the same conditions prevailing in each, whereas surely such widespread perversions against children are not very probable. (The [incidence] of perversion would have to be immeasurably more frequent than the [resulting] hysteria because the illness, after all, occurs only where there has been an accumulation of events and there is a contributory factor that weakens the defense.) Then, third, the certain insight that there are no indications of reality in the unconscious, so that one cannot distinguish between truth and fiction that has been cathected with affect. (Accordingly, there would remain the solution that the sexual fantasy invariably seizes upon the theme of the parents.) Fourth, the consideration that in the most deep-reaching psychosis the unconscious memory does not break through, so that the secret of the childhood experiences is not disclosed even in the most confused delirium. If one thus sees that the unconscious never overcomes the resistance of the conscious, the expectation that in treatment the opposite is bound to happen to the point where the unconscious is completely tamed by the conscious also diminishes.

I was so far influenced [by this] that I was ready to give up two things: the complete resolution of a neurosis and the certain knowledge of its etiology in childhood. Now I have no idea of where I stand because I have not succeeded in gaining a theoretical understanding of repression and its interplay of forces. It seems once again arguable that only later experiences give the impetus to fantasies, which [then] hark back to childhood, and with this, the factor of a hereditary disposition regains a sphere of influence from which I had made it my task to dislodge it—in the interest of illuminating neurosis.

If I were depressed, confused, exhausted, such doubts would surely have to be interpreted as signs of weakness. Since I am in an opposite state, I must recognize them as the result of honest and vigorous intellectual work and must be proud that after going so deep I am still capable of such criticism. Can it be that this doubt merely represents an episode in the advance toward further insight?

It is strange, too, that no feelings of shame appeared, for which, after all, there could well be occasion. Of course I shall not tell it in Dan, nor speak of it in Askelon, in the land of the Philistines, but in your eyes and my own, I have more the feeling of a victory than a defeat (which is surely not right). . . . I vary Hamlet's saying: "To be in readiness": To be cheerful is everything! I could indeed feel quite discontent. The expectation of eternal fame was so beautiful, as was that of certain wealth, complete independence, travels, and lifting the children above the severe worries which robbed me of my youth. Everything depended upon whether or not hysteria would come out right. Now I can once again remain quiet and modest, go on worrying and saving. A little story from my collection occurs to me: "Rebecca, take off your gown, you are no longer a *Kalle* [bride]."[4]

Despite the many commentaries this letter has received from psychoanalysts, it is still bristling with obscurities. The objections Freud raises in the letter to the reality of the sexual abuse of children sound like those raised earlier by his colleagues, critical of the theory from the beginning. Freud had answered those objections in the three 1896 papers on seduction referred to in the last chapter, the three papers in which Freud establishes his belief in the reality of childhood seduction, providing evidence and answers to possible objections, the very objections that Freud raises in this letter. The letter symbolizes the beginning of an internal reconciliation with his colleagues and with the whole of nineteenth-century psychiatry. It is as if Freud were standing before his colleagues at the Society for Psychiatry and saying: "You were right, after all—what I thought was true is nothing but a scientific fairy tale."

The idea that Freud made a decisive and permanent decision about seductions, that they were, by and large, unreal, the fantasies of hysterical women, has become standard in psychoanalytic thought.[5] Marie Bonaparte, when she bought Freud's letters to Fliess, was the first to record this opinion. She kept a notebook about the letters, giving brief summaries of the contents of each. These summaries are remarkably objective and accurate. With one exception, I did not find a single misrepresentation of Freud's remarks in the letters. That single exception is her comment on the letter of September 21, 1897, which shows yet again how deeply

*Correspondance
de Freud
à Fliess

acquise par moie Bonaparte
de R... Stahl
le 12 février 1937*

*remise à R. Stahl
pour moi par la veuve de Fliess*

*Correspondance lue par moi au l'automne
de Freud, en 1937.*

**Title page of Marie Bonaparte's notebook in which
she describes Freud's letters to Fliess**

charged with emotion the topic is for all analysts. For Marie Bonaparte writes: *"Freud a percé à jour le 'mensonge' des hystériques. La séduction regulière par le père est un 'fantasme.'"* (Freud dragged into the light the "lie" of hysterics. The frequent seduction by the father is a "fantasy.") In fact, as we can see from reading the letter, Freud did not say that this was a lie, yet this is how it was to be understood by generations of psychoanalysts.

For example, Ernst Kris, who, along with Anna Freud, made the selection of Freud's letters to Fliess for publication, wrote in his introduction to the volume:

> In the spring of 1897, in spite of accumulating insight into the nature of infantile wish-phantasies, Freud could not make up his mind to take the decisive step demanded by his observations and abandon the idea of the traumatic role of seduction in favour of insight into the normal and necessary conditions of childish development and childish phantasy life. He reports his new impressions in his letters, but does not mention the conflict between them and the seduction hypothesis until one day, in his letter of September 21st, 1897 (Letter 69), he describes how he realized his error (p. 29).

In explanation of this important step, Kris writes in a note (p. 216):

> He had drawn near to the Oedipus complex, in which he recognized the aggressive impulses of children directed against their parents, but had still remained faithful to his belief in the reality of the seduction scenes. It seems reasonable to assume that it was only the self-analysis of this summer that made possible rejection of the seduction hypothesis.

Kris is correct: Freud had altered the direction of his thinking. Earlier, he had recognized the aggressive acts of parents against their children—for seduction was an act of violence. Now Freud had a new insight, that children had aggressive impulses against their parents; cf. *Origins*, p. 207: "Hostile impulses against parents (a wish that they should die) are also an integral part of neuroses." Indeed, why should children not wish for vengeance for a crime committed against them? If the seductions had actually taken place, these "aggressive impulses" would have been healthy signs of protest. But once Freud had decided that these seductions had never occurred, that the parents had not done anything to their children in reality, then these "aggressive impulses" replaced seduction in Freud's theories. An act was replaced by an impulse, a deed by a fantasy. This new "reality" came to be so important for Freud that the impulses of parents against their children were forgotten, never to surface again in his writings. It was not only the aggressive acts of a parent that were attributed to the fantasy life of a child; now aggressive impulses too belonged to the child, not the adult.

In a letter in response to my view that Freud was wrong to abandon the seduction hypothesis, Anna Freud wrote to me (September 10, 1981):

> Keeping up the seduction theory would mean to abandon the Oedipus complex, and with it the whole importance of phantasy life, conscious or unconscious phantasy. In fact, I think there would have been no psychoanalysis afterwards.

This is the standard view—that if Freud had not given up his seduction theory, he would never have become aware of the power of internal fantasy, and would not have been able to go on to make the discoveries he did, including the Oedipus complex, leading to the creation of psychoanalysis as a science and a therapy. Of course, nobody can know what would have happened had Freud not abandoned the seduction hypothesis. What we can know for certain, however, is that the view adopted by Anna Freud and almost all other analysts is deeply engrained. In fact, supporting this view seems to have been so crucial to the maintenance of psycho-analytic theory that Anna Freud and Ernst Kris were willing to deprive Freud of his own doubts in the matter. In the "Editors' Note" at the beginning of *The Origins of Psycho-analysis*, signed by Marie Bonaparte, Anna Freud, and Ernst Kris, the authors write:

> The selection was made on the principle of making public everything [though this word was not in the original German edition] relating to the writer's [Freud's] scientific work and scientific interests and everything bearing on the social and political conditions in which psycho-analysis originated; and of omitting or abbreviating everything publication of which would be inconsistent with professional or personal confidence.

The truth is, however, that Freud had not been allowed his voice. Anna Freud and Ernst Kris were so convinced that they had understood what Freud meant that they expunged from the public record evidence to the contrary: *for the un-edited letters provide evidence that Freud was not convinced that he had done the right thing.*

In an unpublished letter dated December 12, 1897, three months after he supposedly abandoned his theory, Freud writes:

> My confidence in the father-etiology has risen greatly. Eckstein treated her patient deliberately in such a manner as not to give her the slightest hint of what will emerge from the unconscious, and in the process obtained, among other things, the identical scenes with the father. By the way, the young girl is doing beautifully.

Although the wording is somewhat obscure, there can be no doubt about the meaning of this passage: Emma Eckstein is treating a woman in analysis. She is using Freud's method, and has thereby come upon "identical scenes with the father," that is, the same "scenes" (here used in Freud's old sense, to mean genuine memories) that Freud himself elicited from his patients, memories of being sexually assaulted by the father.

Moreover, Freud says that Emma Eckstein treated the patient in such a manner that she carefully avoided any form of suggestion, precisely the error that Freud believed he himself had fallen into. Freud probably instructed Emma Eckstein to be certain that she *not* suggest scenes of seduction to the patient, but wait to see what material emerged. What then emerged convinced Freud that he had been correct to believe in the "father-etiology." And by "father-etiology," Freud must mean the source of neurosis that lies in actions on the part of the father, i.e., sexual attacks on the daughter. (Freud uses the term in this fashion elsewhere.[6])

This letter is, therefore, a postscript to the earlier letter of September 21, 1897. It is as though Freud were telling Fliess: I was too hasty, I believe I was right to think that seductions occur and can be remembered in analysis. Moreover, I believe I was right to think that the source of illness can be traced to such events. *And yet Ernst Kris and Anna Freud omitted this passage from the published letters.* According to the "official" history, Freud abandoned the seduction hypothesis in September 1897. Here is a letter from December 1897 in which Freud states, unambiguously, that now he has changed his mind again. There is no doubt that Anna Freud and Ernst Kris's view, that this was a mistaken pause along the road to truth, came ultimately to be shared by Freud himself. Freud did, eventually, renounce the seduction hypothesis as wrong. But he should be allowed his own voice, his own doubts, his own slow pace.

Furthermore, Freud did not reach this position of doubting his wisdom in renouncing the seduction theory for no reason at all. He provides us with clinical evidence for his

hesitations. Yet this critical clinical evidence, too, was removed from the record. For example, later that month, on
December 22, 1897, he sent Fliess a case history which
allows us a rare glimpse into his clinical material on
seduction:

The following little scene which the patient claims to have
observed as a three-year-old child speaks for the intrinsic
genuineness of infantile trauma. She goes into a dark room
where her mother is carrying on [*ihre Zustände abmacht?*]
and eavesdrops. She has good reason to identify with that
mother. The father belongs to the category of men who stab
women, for whom bloody injuries are an erotic need. When
she was two he brutally deflowered her and infected her with
gonorrhea, so that her life was in danger as a result of the loss
of blood and vaginitis. The mother *now* stands in the room
and screams: "Rotten criminal, what do you want from me?
I will have no part of that. Just whom do you think you have
in front of you?" Then with one hand she tears off her clothes
while with the other hand she presses them against her body,
making a funny impression. Then, with her features distorted
with rage, she stares at a spot in the room, covers her genitals
with one hand and pushes something away with the other.
Then she raises up both hands, claws at the air and bites the
air. While screaming and cursing she bends over backwards,
again covers her genitals with one hand, then falls forward so
that her head almost touches the floor, finally falls over backwards quietly to the floor. Afterwards, she wrings her hands,
sits down in a corner with her features distorted with pain
and weeps.
    Most notable to the child is the scene where the mother
is standing bent forward. She sees that the toes are strongly
pointed *inward*. When the girl is six to seven months old (!!)
the mother is in bed almost bleeding to death as a result of
an injury inflicted by the father. At the age of sixteen she
again sees the mother bleeding from the uterus (carcinoma),

which brings about the beginning of her neurosis. The neurosis breaks out one year later when she hears of an operation for hemorrhoids. Can it be doubted that the father forces the wife into anal intercourse? Can one not recognize in the fit of the mother the separate phases of this assault, first the effort to get at her from the front, then the pressing down from behind and the penetration between her legs, which forces her to turn her feet inward? Finally, how does the patient know that in fits one usually performs the part of both persons (*self*-mutilation, *self*-murder) as in this case where the woman tears off her clothes with one hand, like the assailant, and with the other holds on to them, as she did then?

Have you ever seen a foreign newspaper which went through Russian censorship at the border? Words, entire phrases and sentences obliterated in black, so that the rest becomes unintelligible. Such Russian censorship occurs in psychoses and produces the apparently meaningless deliria.

A new motto: What have they done to you, poor child?

But now, enough of my filthy stories.

Freud is reporting to Fliess additional clinical evidence, from his own practice, that seductions occur, and, moreover, that these seductions are not minor sexually tinged acts (which they were later to be categorized as, e.g., bathing a child), but are frightening, violent, explosive scenes which can affect the victim's entire later life. In addition, Freud hints here, with his comment about censorship, that such events cause gaps in memory, so that what is left appears unintelligible, as the symptoms in a psychosis. The original scene is symbolized in the symptoms, which are nothing less than the signposts of memory, pointing back to the original reality.

Freud seems to be moved by the suffering of his patient (either she or the mother was psychotic, or both), and he proposes to Fliess that from now on the motto of psychoanalysis should be: "What have they done to you, poor

Last page of Freud's letter to Fliess, December 22, 1897, with the quotation from Goethe

child?" This is a line from a poem by Goethe, from his novel
Wilhelm Meisters Lehrjahre (1795–1796), and is put in
the mouth of the strange, androgynous character Mignon.
She sings a song to Wilhelm Meister that begins: "Do you
know the country where the lemon trees flower, and the
golden oranges glow in the dark foliage . . ."[7] The sympathy
Freud shows for the suffering of this patient was not permitted to stand. This passage was omitted from the published
letters, and Freud's motto, along with it, was removed from
the record.

THE PUBLIC RENUNCIATION OF THE
SEDUCTION THEORY

THE earliest published reference to Freud's altered views on
the origins of neurosis has gone unnoticed by historians. It
is contained in a letter Freud wrote to the Munich psychiatrist Leopold Löwenfeld (1847–1923). Löwenfeld was a
well-known psychiatrist and prolific writer on medical and
neuropsychiatric topics. Freud refers to him several times
in his published writings (e.g., *S.E.*, 16, p. 245; *S.E.*, 10, p.
221) and in fact included two of his own papers—"Freud's
Psycho-Analytic Procedure" and "My Views on the Part
Played by Sexuality in the Aetiology of Neuroses" (*S.E.*, 7)
—in books written by Löwenfeld. In 1904 Löwenfeld published *Die psychischen Zwangserscheinungen* (Psychic Obsessions)[8] with a preface dated 1903, which gives evidence
of a lively correspondence between Freud and Löwenfeld
during the years 1900–1903, the critical period for Freud's
change of heart about the seduction hypothesis. On p. 296

Leopold Löwenfeld

of that work, Löwenfeld discusses Freud's views on seduction:

> I refrain at this point from discussing in any detail the complicated processes which, according to the author, supposedly take place between the initial infantile sexual factor and the onset of obsessional ideas, in view of the fact that Freud, according to communications made to me, changed his views on a number of points over the years, and it is not known to me at this moment to what extent he still holds to his views published in 1896 . . . [but] with respect to the modifications made to the above-mentioned views of the author [Freud] in the course of the years, I believe that I may mention here that he no longer attributes to infantile sexual experiences the same meaning with respect to compulsion neurosis as he did earlier. According to the current views of the author, the symptoms of compulsion neurosis do not originate directly from real sexual experiences, but from fantasies which attach themselves to these experiences. The latter accordingly form important intermediary links between memories and pathological symptoms. *"As a rule it is the experiences of puberty which have a harmful effect. In the process of repression these events are fantasied back into early childhood, following the pathways of sexual impressions accidentally experienced during the illness or arising from the [sexual] constitution."* (Letter from the author.). . . . This modification does not change the basic tenets of the theory.

There is a further quotation from Freud (p. 297 n.):

> At the present Freud summarizes the essence of his theory in the following two sentences:
> a) Psychic obsessions always originate in repression.
> b) Repressed impulses and ideas from which the resulting obsession arises stem quite generally from the sexual life.

Since this is not a quotation from one of Freud's early papers, I believe that it, too, is from a letter, and in fact summarizes

Freud's position from the period of around 1902. In fact, it is the only word we have from Freud during this important period.

These two previously unknown passages by Freud aid our understanding of Freud's shift in direction. He has now precisely reversed his earlier theory. In the 1896 papers, he postulated that the experiences of puberty were harmful because they repeated, or stirred up, unconscious memories of early traumatic events. The adolescent experiences were unconsciously repressed (or even consciously suppressed) because they were reminiscent of earlier, far more painful ones. But here he is saying that the early childhood traumas turn out to be fantasies which are conjured up as a defense against fully experiencing the events of adolescence. The psychological motives for repression have been removed, leaving the sexual constitution as the only explanation. The "neurotic" adolescent does not want to acknowledge her own sexual desires, and in order to cover them up, she "invents" sexual tales of seduction from her early childhood. She does this propelled by her sexual constitution, and not out of defense, i.e., in order to escape painful memories from her past. Sexual constitution was not a term that Freud employed in the 1896 papers. From now on it would come to dominate much of his thinking about women and sexuality. This becomes apparent in one of his most famous books, *Three Essays on the Theory of Sexuality*.[9]

Three Essays can be thought of as the theoretical conclusion of the "insights" Freud had gained from treating Emma Eckstein and Dora,[10] an extended rebuttal of his 1896 papers. What Freud now (p. 170) calls a "constitutional disposition" begins to play an increasing role in his theoretical thinking. He talks of the "excessive intensity of . . . the sexual instinct" (p. 170) and the "innate strength of the tendency to perversion" (p. 170).

Sexual assaults such as Freud described them in the 1896 papers have been entirely relegated to the fantasy life of the child, or to the lies of hysterical women. The corresponding "truth" is now called an "excess of parental affection":

> It is true that an excess of parental affection does harm by causing precocious sexual maturity and also because, by spoiling the child, it makes him incapable in later life of temporarily doing without love or of being content with a smaller amount of it. One of the clearest indications that a child will later become neurotic is to be seen in an insatiable demand for his parents' affection. And on the other hand neuropathic parents, who are inclined as a rule to display excessive affection, are precisely those who are most likely by their caresses to arouse the child's disposition to neurotic illness (p. 223).

Three Essays also contains Freud's first published reference to his abandonment of the seduction hypothesis (apart from the letter to Löwenfeld quoted above). Freud writes (p. 190):

> I cannot admit that in my paper "The Aetiology of Hysteria" (1896) I exaggerated the frequency or importance of that influence [seduction], though I did not then know that persons who remain normal may have had the same experiences in their childhood, and though I consequently overrated the importance of seduction in comparison with the factors of sexual constitution and development.

In a footnote to this passage in *Three Essays*, Freud writes:

> Havelock Ellis (1913 [1903] Appendix B)[11] has published a number of autobiographical narratives written by people who remained predominantly normal in later life and describing the first sexual impulses of their childhood and the occasions which gave rise to them. These reports naturally suffer from the fact that they omit the prehistoric period of the writers' sexual lives, which is veiled by infantile amnesia and which can only

be filled in by psycho-analysis in the case of an individual who has developed a neurosis. In more than one respect, nevertheless, the statements are valuable, and similar narratives[12] were what led me to make the modifications in my etiological hypotheses which I have mentioned in the text.[13]

Freud is stating here that in reading the case histories given by Havelock Ellis in the appendix to his 1903 volume, *Analysis of the Sexual Impulse*,[14] he learned that someone can be seduced in childhood and yet remain comparatively normal in later life. Since Freud had believed that these early sexual experiences were traumatic, and led to later neurosis, this kind of information, if correct, would have important consequences for his theories. Indeed, in this note Freud says that narratives similar to those in Ellis's book led him to give up his seduction hypothesis. Since this is the case, and given the historic importance of this step for the later history of psychoanalysis and psychotherapy in general, it is only natural that one would wish to take a closer look at Ellis's book.

Ellis, in the preface to the 1903 edition of his book, writes:

> In an Appendix will be found a selection of histories of more or less normal sexual development. Histories of gross sexual perversion have often been presented in books devoted to the sexual instinct; it has not hitherto been usual to inquire into the facts of normal sexual development.[15]

This undoubtedly struck Freud as true. The German authors that Freud mentions as authorities on "the sexual aberrations" (p. 135) in the beginning of *Three Essays* (Krafft-Ebing, Moll, Möbius, Löwenfeld, etc.) do not provide case histories of normal sexual development. Freud's own theories, of course, were based exclusively on people who had sought his help. Here, then, was Freud's first significant encounter with a point of view different from the one he had espoused in 1896 but dealing with the same material. It could hardly fail to arouse his interest.

Phyllis Grosskurth, in her recent study of Ellis, has some harsh yet justified comments about his case histories:

> The highly eccentric nature of the organization of the *Studies* is a reflection of its amateur basis and of a descriptive empirical approach to the subject. . . . His citation of vague authorities—"a friend," "a correspondent," "a woman who enjoys the confidence of many women"—is ridiculous. Even Krafft-Ebing was far more sceptical of the reliability of the case accounts in his case-histories, and Kinsey, who was to owe much to Ellis, devised methods of circumventing lies or exaggerations.[16]

Only one of the twelve case histories (six more were added to the second edition, but none of those added deals with seduction) involves a sexual seduction of a child, and, indeed, not at all the kind of sexual seduction that Freud had in mind when he wrote about his own case histories in his letters to Fliess (as we saw from the two cases quoted in the preceding chapter), or when he spoke about seduction in the 1896 papers.

The first case in Ellis's book tells of the seduction of a nine-year-old boy by a servant girl, written in the third person:

> T. was nine when he interrogated a servant girl of sixteen about babies and their origin. She laughed and said that one day she would tell him how children came. One Sunday this servant took T. for a country walk and initiated him in sexual intercourse, telling him he was too young to be a father, but that was the way babies were made. The girl took T. into a field, saying she would show him how to do something which would make him "feel as though he was in heaven," informing him that she had often done this with young men. She then succeeded in causing an erection and instructed him how

to act. . . . The girl took the masculine position and embraced him with great passion. T. can recall the expression on the girl's face, the perspiration on her forehead, and the whispered query whether it had pleased him. The embrace lasted for about ten minutes, when the girl said it had "done her good . . ." After this episode T. began to speculate about sexual matters. . . .

This is the *only* account of a sexual seduction that occurs in the case histories. Indeed, in all the seven volumes of *Studies in the Psychology of Sex* there is no discussion of seduction or its effects. For the rest, the case histories are rather pathetic and sad accounts, primarily by men, of their struggles with masturbation, of their shame at having had sexual thoughts early in life, and of adolescent explorations. There is nothing in this book by Ellis that could possibly support or refute Freud's 1896 thesis. Ellis's work is wholly irrelevant to the seduction hypothesis. How, then, can we explain the fact that Freud specifically cites this book by Ellis as a major reason for abandoning the seduction hypothesis?

I believe I have an answer to this puzzle, though it is somewhat speculative. It seems to me that Freud had not read this book by Ellis at all. In a footnote to the Dora case (p. 51), Freud praises a book by Iwan Bloch, *Beiträge zur Aetiologie der Psychopathia Sexualis* (Contributions to the Etiology of Sexual Pathology), which was published in 1902 and 1903.[17] Though not mentioned in the Trosman and Simmons catalogue of Freud's library, this book is in the collection at Maresfield Gardens in London, and was marked by Freud. On p. 13 (vol. 1), Freud marked the following passage:

> Many of the autobiographical statements and descriptions of sexual perverts taken by Krafft-Ebing too trustingly, clearly reveal the influence of fantasy. Thereby the true state of affairs is frequently falsified in a clearly recognizable manner.

Bloch is criticizing Krafft-Ebing for not giving due credit to fantasy, the very complaint that Krafft-Ebing had implicitly made against Freud when he called his paper a "scientific fairy tale." On p. 175, Freud checked the following passage:

> We would like to impress on all parents, doctors, and teachers the warning of Rétif de La Bretonne, who certainly knew, "Parents, if you have children, beware of the morals of your servants."[18]

The reference is to the possibility that servants will sexually seduce children in their care. On the next page is the passage which solves our mystery:

> The large role played by seduction in the sexual life even of healthy people is very significant. Havelock Ellis recently provided the anamneses of five such cases.[19]

The passage is not marked, but since Freud had marked a passage on seduction on the preceding page it is almost certain that he read it. However, it seems that Bloch himself had not seen the article by Havelock Ellis, but only a review of the article. The review appeared in the *Monatshefte für praktische Dermatologie* (33, no. 12, December 15, 1901) on pp. 627–628, signed Hopf, Dresden, and it discusses Havelock Ellis's article "Die Entwicklung des Geschlechtstriebes" (The Development of the Sexual Instinct) from the *American Journal of Dermatology and Genitourinary Diseases* (no. 5, September 1901, pp. 176–188; continued in the November issue, pp. 266–281). In fact, this article is simply a reprint from the *Alienist and Neurologist* (22, no. 3, July 1901, pp. 501–521), a fact that Bloch was not aware of. There can be no doubt that Bloch takes his remarks about seduction from the review by Hopf, for he cites the same (inexact) reference that Hopf does, and more important, Bloch does not give any detail from the article

by Ellis that is not given by Hopf (though Hopf's citations
are very brief). Furthermoıe, except for certain omissions,
Bloch gives the cases in Hopf's words, not in the words of
Ellis. Moreover, Bloch (1, p. 177 n.) cites Hopf's review
but does not indicate that his information comes, not from
the article itself, but from Hopf's review. Bloch was himself
a dermatologist, and in fact a review by him is included in
the same issue of the *Monatshefte* (33, p. 50), which shows
that he knew this volume. It was Bloch who added the
comments about the importance of sexual seduction. This
is not part of Ellis's original article or of Hopf's review.
The title of Ellis's article, "The Development of the Sexual
Instinct," is appropriate, since Ellis is concerned with learn-
ing about the early history of people's sexual lives. He
does not single out seduction, and is not, in fact, concerned
with it in the article. Nor does Ellis say it played any particular role in the sexual history of the five cases he gives.
This is entirely Bloch's interpretation of the article, based,
not on the original article itself, but, as I have shown, on a
review of the article. Freud seems to have seen neither Ellis's
original article nor the review by Hopf, but only Bloch's
interpretation of this review. Freud would thus have given
up his major discovery partly on the basis of a comment
derived from an account in a review of an article which he
had never seen.[20]

It should be noted that on the same page marked by Freud
(1, p. 175), Bloch says that little girls are liars and that they
often unjustly accuse servants of sexually molesting them.
In vol. 2 (p. 258) Bloch complains that schoolgirls have
sexually corrupted perfectly moral young teachers. Freud
does cite the appendix to Ellis's 1903 book, rather than the
1901 article on which it is based, so it is not impossible that
Freud drew from the article precisely the same conclusions
that Bloch did. But since these conclusions are by no means .

obvious, nor are they the ones indicated by Ellis himself, such a coincidence strikes me as improbable, and I believe that Freud in fact based his comments on Bloch because Bloch's observations were necessary to him, not because they represented new evidence or new facts he had overlooked.

Freud's first explicit rejection of the seduction hypothesis appeared in a book written by Löwenfeld, *Sexualleben und Nervenleiden* (Sexual Life and Neurosis).[21] At Löwenfeld's request, in 1905 Freud wrote a short piece that was incorporated in the book, entitled "My Views on the Part Played by Sexuality in the Aetiology of Neuroses" (*S.E.*, 7, pp. 270–279), in which he writes:

> At that time my material was still scanty, and it happened by chance to include a disproportionately large number of cases in which sexual seduction by an adult or by older children played the chief part in the history of the patient's childhood. I thus overestimated the frequency of such events (though in other respects they were not open to doubt). Moreover, I was at that period unable to distinguish with certainty between falsifications made by hysterics in their memories of childhood and traces of real events (p. 274).

Thus, although Freud concedes that *some* seductions were real, the theoretical importance of seduction, which Freud now called an "accidental influence," was greatly diminished:

> Accidental influences derived from experience having thus receded into the background, the factors of constitution and heredity necessarily gained the upper hand once more (p. 275).

In explaining why he has come to this new view, Freud gives the same reason as in *Three Essays*:

> Further information now became available relating to people who had remained normal; and this led to the unexpected finding that the sexual history of *their* childhood did not nec-

essarily differ in essentials from that of neurotics, and, in particular, that the part played by seduction was the same in both cases (p. 276).[22]

This "further information" is probably a reference to the work of Havelock Ellis, examined above. In any event, it is curious that Freud does not reveal the source of this new information which has had such important theoretical consequences for him. There was no way an impartial reader could investigate the matter for himself, since Freud does not give any reference. On such a crucial matter, one would expect Freud to provide a detailed commentary. His reticence is disquieting.

Is Freud's essay, apart from these difficulties, entirely sincere? I quote again: "I thus overestimated the frequency of such events [seductions]" (p. 274). Yet in the same year (1905), Freud wrote in *Three Essays*: "I cannot admit that in my paper 'The Aetiology of Hysteria' (1896) I exaggerated the frequency or importance of that influence [seduction]" (p. 190). These statements cannot both be true.

In Freud's first fully articulated account of his changing views on fantasy vs. reality, "On the History of the Psycho-Analytic Movement (1914; *S.E.*, 14, p. 17), he writes:

On the way [to the creation of psychoanalysis], a mistaken idea had to be overcome which might have been almost fatal to the young science. Influenced by Charcot's view of the traumatic origin of hysteria, one was readily inclined to accept as true and etiologically significant the statements made by patients in which they ascribed their symptoms to passive sexual experiences in the first years of childhood—to put it bluntly, to seduction. [Strachey's translation is incorrect. For a corrected translation, see p. 52.] When this etiology broke down under the weight of its own improbability and contradiction in definitely ascertainable circumstances, the result at first was helpless bewilderment. Analysis had led back to these infantile sexual traumas by the right path, *and yet they were not true* [emphasis added]. The firm ground of reality was gone. At that time I would gladly have given up the whole work, just as my esteemed predecessor, Breuer, had done when he made his unwelcome discovery [about love and transference in the case of Anna O.]. Perhaps I persevered only because I no longer had any choice and could not then begin at anything else. At last came the reflection that, after all, one had no right to despair because one has been deceived in one's expectations; one must revise those expectations. If hysterical subjects trace back their symptoms to traumas that are fictitious, then the new fact which emerges is precisely that they create such scenes in *fantasy*, and this psychical reality requires to be taken into account alongside practical reality. This reflection was soon followed by the discovery that these fantasies were intended to cover up the autoerotic activity of the first years of childhood, to embellish it and raise it to a higher plane. And now, from behind the fantasies, the whole range of a child's sexual life came to light.

With this sexual activity of the first years of childhood the inherited constitution of the individual also came into its own. . . . The last word on the subject of traumatic etiology was spoken later by Abraham, when he pointed out that the sexual constitution which is peculiar to children is precisely calculated to provoke sexual experiences of a particular kind — namely traumas.

The last comment is curious. It is a misreading of a 1907 paper by Karl Abraham, "The Experiencing of Sexual Trauma as a Form of Sexual Activity."[23] The point of Abraham's paper is not that children *in general* have a sexual constitution calculated to provoke sexual traumas, but that *certain* children are seductive, desire the seduction, provoke it, and, the tone suggests, deserve it. Abraham says:

I arrived at the conclusion that their sexual development was precocious and their libido itself quantitatively abnormal, and that their imagination was prematurely occupied with sexual matters to an abnormal degree. This idea can now be expressed more definitely. We can say that children belonging to this category show an abnormal desire for obtaining sexual pleasure, and in consequence of this undergo sexual traumas (p. 54).

The point of view taken by Abraham is contrary to a psychological one. For example, he writes:

For a child *disposed* to hysteria or dementia praecox . . . undergoes the trauma in consequence of a tendency in its unconscious. If there is an underlying unconscious wish for it, the experiencing of a sexual trauma in childhood is a masochistic expression of the sexual impulse. . . . It is a remarkable thing that a child who has experienced a sexual trauma should keep it secret from its parents. . . . A girl of 9 years was enticed by a neighbour into a wood. She followed him quite willingly. He then attempted to rape her. It was only when he had almost or quite [?][24] attained his purpose that the child succeeded in getting free. She hurried home but said nothing about what had happened; nor did she ever speak about it afterwards to her family . . . [she] had allowed herself to be seduced. She had followed the neighbour into the wood and allowed him to go a long way in carrying out his purpose before she freed herself from him and ran off. It is not to be wondered at that this child kept the occurrence secret (pp. 51–53).

Strange that it never occurs to Abraham to seek another explanation for her secrecy. Perhaps the child feared her parents would have taken her confession as a fantasy and beaten her for inventing stories.

If this is the "last word," as Freud says, then it is a frightening one.

In his *Introductory Lectures on Psycho-Analysis* (1916; S.E., 16, p. 370), Freud writes: ". . . if in the case of girls who produce such an event [seduction] in the story of their childhood their father figures fairly regularly as the seducer, *there can be no doubt either of the imaginary nature of the accusation* [emphasis added] or of the motive that has led to it." And he continues: ". . . up to the present we have not succeeded in pointing to any difference in the consequences, whether phantasy or reality has had the greater share in these events of childhood."

Freud is saying that whether seduction actually took place or was only a fantasy does not matter. What matters, for Freud, are the psychological effects, and these effects, Freud states, are no different where the event is a real one or imagined. But in actuality there is an essential difference between the effects of an act that took place and one that was imagined.

To tell someone who has suffered the effects of a childhood filled with sexual violence that it does not matter whether his memories are anchored in reality or not is to do further violence to that person and is bound to have a pernicious effect. A real memory demands some form of validation from the outside world—denial of those memories by others can lead to a break with reality, and a psychosis. The lack of interest in a person's store of personal memories does violence to the integrity of that person.

Freud's statement, however, was not taken by psychoanalysts at face value; in fact, psychoanalysts have always shown a greater interest in the fantasy life of a patient than in real events. Freud shifted the interest of psychoanalysis to the pathogenic effects of fantasies, putting less emphasis on the pathogenic effects of real memories in repression. The ideal analytic patient has come to be a person without serious traumas in his childhood. Analysis, it is felt, is not equipped to deal with patients who have suffered real and serious emotional injury in childhood. This is undoubtedly true, but the more important question is why this has come to be true, and whether it is an inevitable outcome of Freud's shift of interest from real seductions to fantasies. Because these are serious questions, the answers to which make a real difference in the lives of many people, it is important that we be informed of all the possible reasons why Freud made his shift. While I would describe this shift as a loss of courage, I do not believe that this judgment provides an explanation. Perhaps we will never have a single explanation for why Freud shifted his interest from real traumas to fantasies, but I believe that the historical documents allow us to come much closer to an answer than has been possible until now.

FREUD'S ISOLATION

WE have already seen the roles played by the case of Emma Eckstein and Freud's close relationship with Fliess in this shift. Freud could not have remained close to Fliess if he had not been willing to change his emphasis from what really happened to Emma Eckstein to her fantasies. The real operation and its ill effects, and the real seduction, had to cede place to "bleeding out of longing" and the *wish* to be seduced. But perhaps Freud's shift of interest to wishes and fantasies was motivated, at least in part, by still other factors.

Freud suffered emotional and intellectual isolation as long as he held to the reality of seduction. Freud felt his isolation most following the meeting of April 21, 1896, when he first publicly announced the seduction theory. ("I felt as though I were despised and universally shunned."[25]) Freud had hoped that Breuer, after collaborating with him on *Studies on Hysteria*, would gradually alter his views on the sexual etiology of the neuroses. This did not happen. On the contrary, Breuer joined the ranks of those who believed Freud was losing his grip on reality, as we see from an unpublished passage in a letter from Freud to Fliess of March 1, 1896, in which he writes of Breuer that

> our personal relationship, externally reconciled, casts a deep shadow over my existence here. I can do nothing right for him and have given up trying. According to him, I would daily have to ask myself whether I am suffering from moral insanity or *paranoia scientifica*.

Condemnation was not confined to Breuer and Freud's colleagues. Freud had been timid enough in *Studies on Hysteria* when it came to discussing the effects of real seduction. But the book did speak about the importance of sexual life in the origin of the neuroses, and this alone was enough to provoke others to reject Freud's ideas, as is shown by the reviews. The German psychiatrist Adolf von Strümpell, in his review of *Studies on Hysteria* for an influential psychiatric journal, *Deutsche Zeitschrift für Nervenheilkunde*, complains bitterly of Freud's invasion of the private sexual life of the patient.[26] He claims that what Freud and Breuer discovered were only the "fantasies and invented tales" typical of hysterics. Conrad Rieger was even more forceful and unpleasant in his comments on "Further Remarks" in *Centralblatt für Nervenheilkunde Psychiatrie und gerichtliche Psychopathologie*, where he writes:

> I cannot believe that an experienced psychiatrist can read this paper without experiencing genuine outrage. The reason for this outrage is to be found in the fact that Freud takes very seriously what is nothing but paranoid drivel with a sexual content—purely chance events—which are entirely insignificant or entirely invented. All of this can lead to nothing other than a simply deplorable "old wives' psychiatry."[27]

The medical community was offended by Freud. Breuer had now abandoned him. Löwenfeld, who had initially shown some interest, certainly more than other psychiatrists, seems to have attempted to persuade Freud to abandon the seduction hypothesis. As long as he held to the seduction theory, Freud was alone.

Where was Freud to turn for support? As we saw in chapter 2, in France Freud could look to a large medico-legal literature in support of the factual aspects of his work. Such events, the French literature made clear, do happen, and far more often than anyone but the legal physician is in a position to recognize. But the climate seems to have been different in Vienna. Eduard von Hofmann, professor of legal medicine at the University of Vienna from 1875 to 1897[28] (during the period of Freud's emerging views), had written an obituary of Tardieu in 1879 in which he took issue with him for being naïve in his book on *attentats aux moeurs*. Yet Hofmann also said that "this work alone would have been sufficient to assure the fame of the name of Tardieu in legal medicine."[29] In 1888, Hofmann wrote an influential article (which Freud certainly saw—he had mentioned this issue to Fliess) in the very first issue of the *Wiener klinische Wochenschrift* about the case of a twenty-year-old servant, to determine whether or not she had been sexually attacked by her employer.[30] Hofmann decided against the girl, primarily on the grounds that she had already had sex, and that she was strong and could have defended herself. His conclusion is significant for us:

> . . . It must be mentioned that in the case of the neurosis known as hysteria (which takes on many forms) it is common knowledge that it frequently entails a pathological tendency to lie and exaggerate as well as an inability to faithfully retell [an event]. This reveals itself in a partiality for sexual accusations.

But the work on seduction most often referred to by Freud's German colleagues (especially by Krafft-Ebing, but also by Bloch and others) was Johann Ludwig Casper's *Klinische Novellen zur gerichtlichen Medicin* (Clinical Stories from Forensic Medicine), published in Berlin in 1863.[31] Casper had warned against the lies and general unreliability of children. Indeed, on the very first page of the book he speaks of the "outright lies" of children who accuse adults of rape. In one case he speaks of a thirteen-year-old who had a

> shocking confrontation with her father, whom she had accused of incest and who, according to all the circumstances, was innocent, and used a way of speaking and expressions in her outrageous accusation that are simply not to be repeated (p. 14).

The German medico-legal literature was thus more strongly identified with the current represented by Fournier in Paris than it was with the other tradition in the French literature.[32] Freud could find no support there.

In accepting the reality of seduction, in believing his patients, Freud was at odds with the entire climate of German medical thinking. Moreover, the acceptance of external trauma from such an unexpected source (the family) also cast doubts on yet another bulwark of traditional medicine: the primacy of constitutional factors. Indeed, as long as Freud believed in seduction, he would have to reject the conventional explanations of mental illness in terms of heredity (*la famille névropathique*, as the French called it). Freud's independence in 1895 and 1896 was brought home to me when, in London, I examined his copy of Löwenfeld's *Pathologie und Therapie der Neurasthenie und Hysterie* (Pathology and Therapy of Neurasthenia and Hysteria).[33] On p. 20 n., Löwenfeld writes: "Bouveret makes a special point of noting that in a considerable number of neurasthenics whom he saw, 'there could be found no trace whatever of nervous heredity.' " Freud penciled in the margin: "Bravo!"

THE SEDUCTION OF ROBERT FLIESS

FREUD believed, for many years, that he had found at least one person who would support him in his views when everybody else in the scientific community shunned him, and that was Wilhelm Fliess. We have seen several reasons why Fliess would not have been receptive to Freud's theory of seduction. Nevertheless, Freud continued to write to Fliess about his new discoveries. He was the one person to whom Freud was willing to tell everything he knew about the evidence slowly emerging from his clinical practice supporting the reality of seductions and their psychological impact. We have no way of investigating Fliess's response, though this response was bound to affect Freud profoundly. I have found evidence, however, not previously suspected, that Robert Fliess (1895–1970), Wilhelm Fliess's son, believed that his father had sexually molested him, and this at precisely the time Freud was writing to Fliess about seduction.[34] If true, it casts an entirely new light on the relationship between the two men.

The final volume of the Psychoanalytic Series that Robert Fliess had been engaged in all his professional life appeared in 1973 as *Symbol, Dream, and Psychosis*. This volume constitutes an eloquent and intelligent plea for the return of Freud's early seduction theory to modern-day psychoanalytic practice. The heart of the book is an exposition of Robert

Fliess's conviction that Freud made a mistake when he abandoned the seduction hypothesis. He also explains why seductions are so often denied by analysts, and shows how deep amnesia reaches and how difficult it is to undo. His thesis is that *all* severe neurotics have been sexually seduced or otherwise traumatized in early childhood by a psychotic (but often perfectly socially adjusted) parent, and in the process are violated, humiliated, and damaged. Moreover, he believes this happens at a very early age, before the age of four (cf. p. 218 of *Symbol, Dream and Psychosis*). The irony is that Freud propounded this very thesis to Robert Fliess's father in 1896 and 1897. Could something have happened to Robert Fliess around that time?

In the first volume of his series, *Erogeneity and Libido: Addenda to the Theory of the Psychosexual Development of the Human*, published in 1956, Robert Fliess writes (foreword, p. 17) about the "unbelievable frequency of the ambulatory psychosis," and he defends, there, the reality of the memories of severe aggression and sexual seductions: "The amnesia removal uncovers, much more frequently than Freud's writings lead one to expect, *memories* of which there can be no doubt [wrongly printed as "of which there can be doubt"[35]] as to their authenticity." In a footnote to this passage Robert Fliess writes:

> The appearance of Freud's biography compels me further to append a remark that I would not otherwise make. However, the initiative is no longer mine. In the first volume of his biography Jones gives a description of my father that enables the psychiatric reader to make his own diagnosis. Some of these readers, perhaps defending themselves against acknowledging the above-mentioned incidence in their own families, may therefore be tempted to dismiss what I have observed as a form of projection. For their benefit: following Freud's

Wilhelm Fliess's son, Robert Fliess, age six

advice to the analyst to re-enter analysis, I have clarified the picture of my father in two expert and thorough analyses, the last in middle age with Ruth Mack Brunswick; and I have had an extended conversation with Freud himself about his onetime friend.

What are the implications of this passage? Robert Fliess is saying that it is in bad taste to discuss serious defects in one's parents in print, but since Jones has already described his father Wilhelm in such a fashion that an experienced diagnostician will know the mental disease he was suffering from, there is no point in not acknowledging it. What is this disease? Not, in fact, paranoia (which would be the diagnosis drawn from the hint that Jones provides), because that is not relevant to what Robert Fliess is discussing; nor would he expect the reader to defend himself against the possibility of such a disease existing in his own family. What Robert Fliess unquestionably is referring to is psychosis in that particular form which interested him: ambulatory psychosis. The ambulatory psychotic is, to the external world, a normal person, possibly even a great scientist (there is every reason to believe that Robert Fliess admired his father's medical achievements well into adult life). No one (with the possible exception of his most intimate family, who would have every reason to deny it) would suspect that the person is suffering from a psychosis that invades his sexual life. Robert Fliess goes on to say that one might be tempted to dismiss what he has observed as a form of projection, that is, as an invention, a fantasy. But Fliess explains that he did not fantasize these seductions or beatings; they actually happened. When he says that he "clarified the picture" of his father, he must mean that the picture he had finally managed to put together of his father as a child abuser, or molester, was accurate. In telling us that he had an extended conversation with Freud himself about Wilhelm Fliess, Robert

Fliess apparently meant that Freud accepted what he had to tell him about his father as true.

The assumption that Robert Fliess is talking about a seduction in this passage is supported by another statement on the preceding page:

> There is no place here to deal with the inexhaustible subject of the psychoses; I can therefore say only in passing that the child of such a parent becomes the object of defused aggression (maltreated and beaten almost within an inch of his life), and of a perverse sexuality that hardly knows an incest barrier (is seduced in the most bizarre ways by the parents, and, at his or her instigation, by others).

Robert Fliess tells us explicitly in this passage that a psychotic adult both beats and seduces the child. Indeed, the case histories that Robert Fliess gives in his last book are in support of this.

I think it is clear from this earlier book, taken in conjunction with the later volume, that *Robert Fliess believed that his father had sexually seduced him when he was a young child*. Now, if it is true that Wilhelm Fliess was seducing or otherwise harming his own child at the same time that Sigmund Freud was on the track of his greatest discovery, one that could not be acknowledged in scientific circles or given any theoretical credence (even though it had been mentioned earlier in the French and German medico-legal literature), then we see here one of the poorest matches in the history of intellectual discoveries. Freud is communicating his newly gained insights to the one person least prepared to hear them, because of the profound significance these theories held for that person's own life. Freud was like a dogged detective, on the track of a great crime, communicating his hunches and approximations and at last his final discovery to his best friend, who may have been in fact the criminal.

CONCLUSION

FRANK Sulloway, in his recent influential book *Freud: Biologist of the Mind* (p. 191), champions the view that Fliess had discovered infantile sexuality either before Freud or at the same time, and that he was a major influence on Freud's views on the subject. He writes:

> Wilhelm Fliess's discoveries on the subject of infantile sexuality bring me to the second question concerning Freud's debt to him. If the spontaneous, Fliessian conception of infantile sexual development proved in the end so fruitful for understanding neurotic phenomena, why did Freud ever develop his own antithetical seduction theory of neurosis? . . . In fact, it was only two years later, in the fall of 1897, that Freud finally gave up his seduction theory; and only then did he replace this erroneous notion with the spontaneous conception of infantile sexual life championed by Fliess.

On the next page Sulloway writes:

> Fliess's influence therefore consisted, in part, of his independent pursuit of a genetic, spontaneous, and biological conception of human sexual development that only became fully relevant to Freud and psychoanalysis when the seduction theory finally collapsed.

Inadvertently, Sulloway has put his finger on a crucial issue: it is true that, for Freud, all non-traumatic forms of sexuality were irrelevant to subsequent neurosis, as long as he believed in seduction. For Fliess, this was never the case. The two men, curiously, were never closer in their views than when their friendship finally collapsed. Sulloway is correct: Freud became more like Fliess than he was prepared to admit. But Sulloway is wrong to believe (cf. p. 205), with the majority of analysts, that this was the real triumph of psychoanalysis. It was the beginning of its end.

The strange fact is that no author of this time directly refuted Freud's major contributions relating to the effects of seduction in childhood on a person's later life. Löwenfeld, for example, superior in many respects to his psychiatric colleagues, nevertheless consistently missed the point of Freud's 1896 papers, though he was preoccupied with them and wrote about them seriously. There is no scientific criticism of the thesis, only disavowal and disgust. If Freud found this silence perplexing, he finally decided to identify with it. *Studies on Hysteria* and *The Interpretation of Dreams* are revolutionary books in ways that no subsequent book written by Freud would be. True, he enabled people to speak about their sexual lives in ways that were impossible before his writings. But by shifting the emphasis from an actual world of sadness, misery, and cruelty to an internal stage on which actors performed invented dramas for an invisible audience of their own creation, Freud began a trend away from the real world that, it seems to me, is at the root of the present-day sterility of psychoanalysis and psychiatry throughout the world.

5 *The Strange Case of Ferenczi's Last Paper*

AFTER Fliess, Sándor Ferenczi (1873–1933) was for more than twenty years Freud's closest analytic friend (Freud often addressed him as "dear son"). Until the last years of his life, Ferenczi was a loyal pupil, loved by many analysts, a constant source of papers, ideas, encouragement, and inspiration to younger analysts. But in the last few years of his life, Ferenczi began developing in a direction that alarmed Freud. In a series of three papers that uncannily parallel Freud's three 1896 papers, Ferenczi began to believe more and more strongly that the source of neurosis lay in sexual seductions suffered by children at the hands of those closest to them. This culminated in a paper, "Confusion of Tongues,"[1] his last (included below as Appendix C in a new English translation), that was, in many respects, the twin to Freud's "The Aetiology of Hysteria."

The story of this paper, how it came to be written and how Freud and his colleagues reacted to it, was told by Jones in the third volume of his biography of Freud. Because Jones had been in analysis with Ferenczi, and had come to dislike him, this account was not necessarily reliable. But there were, unfortunately, no other sources to turn to for more information, until, in my search for documents relating to Fliess, Anna Freud took me to her father's desk in Maresfield Gardens. I found there a series of unpublished letters that cast a new light on Jones's account and offer a far more reliable version of what actually happened between Freud and Ferenczi.

Portrait of Ferenczi by Olga Dormandi, ca. 1926

FERENCZI'S UNPUBLISHED DIARY AND

THE "CONFUSION OF TONGUES"

BETWEEN July and October 1932, Ferenczi kept a personal day-by-day account of his analyses.[2] The main themes of this diary, which has not yet been published, are the prevalence of trauma (primarily sexual seduction) in the childhood of his patients and Ferenczi's previously unknown experiments with mutual analysis. In every case discussed in these pages, Ferenczi traces the neurosis to sexual abuse suffered in childhood (which he believed to be far more common than anyone was prepared to believe) and focuses his concern on the distortions in the personality that ensue. In response to a question from a patient as to why she cannot remember having been raped, but dreams of it incessantly, Ferenczi answers (July 30, 1932):

> I know from other analyses that a part of our being can "die" and while the remaining part of our self may survive the trauma, it awakens with a gap in its memory. Actually it is a gap in the personality, because not only is the memory of the struggle-to-the-death effaced, but all other associatively linked memories disappear . . . perhaps forever.

Ferenczi had returned to Freud's earliest insights, while putting a different interpretation on many later analytic concepts. For example, he maintained (July 24, 1932) that the Oedipus complex could well be "the result of real acts on the part of adults, namely violent passions directed toward the child, who then develops a fixation, not from desire [as Freud maintained], but from fear. 'My mother and father will kill me if I don't love them, and identify with their wishes.'" Ferenczi never dared show this diary to Freud.

The paper he read before the 12th International Psycho-Analytic Congress is a somewhat milder distillation of these views. Yet the ideas he expressed in the paper met with the strongest disapproval by every leading analyst of the day. Ferenczi's tenacious insistence on the truth of what his patients told him would cost him the friendship of Freud and almost all of his colleagues and leave him in an isolation from which he never would emerge.

Ferenczi's paper, "Confusion of Tongues," is one of those rare publications that show unmistakable signs of having been written by someone in a state of emotional turmoil which opens access to truths that are otherwise unavailable. The main focus of Ferenczi's paper is the reality of sexual assaults on young children. In his paper Ferenczi states (my translation[3]):

> Above all, my previously communicated assumption, that trauma, specifically sexual trauma, cannot be stressed enough as a pathogenic agent, was confirmed anew. Even children of respected, high-minded puritanical families fall victim to real rape much more frequently than one had dared to suspect. Either the parents themselves seek substitution for their lack of [sexual] satisfaction in this pathological manner, or else trusted persons such as relatives (uncles, aunts, grandparents), tutors, servants, abuse the ignorance and innocence of children. The obvious objection that we are dealing with sexual fantasies of the child himself, that is, with hysterical lies, unfortunately is weakened by the multitude of confessions of this kind, on the part of patients in analysis, to assaults on children.

Ferenczi explains that the child's desire for tenderness can be exploited by an adult's need for sexual gratification at any price. The child cannot refuse, because he (she) is helpless and paralyzed by fear. The child brings to bear instead a pathogenic defense mechanism that Ferenczi was the first to name: identification with the aggressor.[4] The guilt that the parent ought to feel but does not is then introjected by the child (the act is perceived as wrong, but there is nobody else to take responsibility for it except the child victim).

Furthermore, Ferenczi explains, the parent who denies what he has done, or denies its harmful effects, often becomes physically abusive toward the child (projecting the wickedness onto the child). A seduction is generally followed by violence, suggesting to the child a connection between sexuality and violence, with disastrous effects on the child's ability to love later in life. As a defense the child sinks into a dream or trance state in which it is easier to misperceive the quality of the aggression. The child's need to deny altogether what has happened severely loosens her hold on reality. She (or, more rarely, he) becomes ashamed, the victim of the unconscious remorse of the parent that is expressed in violent anger toward the child.

Seduction, then, is a form of hatred, not love. The child will often become extremely depressed after such an incident. The consequence for the abused child is that his or her own sexuality will remain undeveloped or will assume perverted forms. The child may well become psychotic (which is a defense not dissimilar to the original trance state, a protected but lonely hiding place). Another consequence, unrecognized before, even by Freud, is that

> The sexually violated child can suddenly bring to fruition under the pressure of traumatic exigency all future faculties which are virtually preformed in him and are necessary for marriage, motherhood and fatherhood, as well as all feelings of a mature person. Here one can confidently speak of *traumatic* (pathologic) *progression or precocity* in contrast to the familiar concept of regression. It is only natural to think of fruit that ripens or becomes sweet prematurely when injured by the beak of a bird, or of the premature ripening of wormy fruit. Shock can cause a part of the person to mature sud-

denly, not only emotionally *but intellectually as well*. I remind
you of the typical "dream of the wise baby" singled out by
me so many years ago, in which a newborn child or infant
in its cradle suddenly begins to talk, indeed teaches wisdom
to all the family.[5] Fear of the uninhibited and therefore as
good as crazy adult turns the child into a psychiatrist, as it
were. In order to do so and to protect himself from the dangers coming from people without self-control, he must first
know how to identify himself completely with them.

Ferenczi continues:

In addition to passionate love and passionate punishments
there is a third way of binding the child to oneself and that is
the terrorism of suffering. Children have the compulsion to
smooth over all kinds of disorders in the family, that is to
say, to take onto their tender shoulders the burdens of all
others; naturally, in the final analysis, not out of pure unselfishness but to regain the lost peace and the tenderness that is
part of it.

Perhaps never before had anyone spoken for the abused
child with such sympathy and eloquence. The ideas that
Freud had propounded to a skeptical medical world in his
1896 papers were here repeated, but expanded through the
knowledge gained by analysis in the years after 1896.

It is as if Ferenczi were demonstrating to the analytic
world how psychoanalysis could have developed had Freud
not abandoned the seduction hypothesis. But since Freud *had*
abandoned that theory, the paper was a major break with
the direction psychoanalysis had taken from the time of its
inception to the present. This shift in direction was not lost
on the analysts who heard the paper.

Ferenczi was not yet sixty when he attended the 12th
International Psycho-Analytic Congress held in Wiesbaden
in September 1932 (the last he was to attend). Ferenczi
opened the Congress with his paper. Freud was too sick to

attend, but many of the leading analysts of the time were there: Anna Freud, Federn, Alexander, Jekels, Jones, de Groot, Brunswick, Simmel, Hárnik, Bonaparte, Sterba, Reik, Balint, Deutsch, Rado, Weiss, Odier, Glover, Roheim, Menninger, de Saussure.[6] Their response to the paper was uniformly negative. These senior analysts, the "bearers of the ring," were of the opinion that views such as those expressed in the paper should not be circulated more widely than was absolutely necessary, that the dissemination of such views constituted a danger to society.

As long as Ferenczi was alive, nothing could be done to prevent the paper from being published in German. But the much larger circulation that the paper would receive by appearing in English in the *International Journal of Psycho-Analysis* was a problem that concerned many analysts, particularly Jones. It was well known that the majority of analysts, even then, did not know German and had no access to literature not translated into English. During a visit to America in 1926, Ferenczi had delivered a paper before the American Psychoanalytic Association on present-day problems in psychoanalysis in which he began by saying:

> Perhaps one of the chief handicaps which may prevent the American members of our movement from contributing to psychoanalytic knowledge and research through their own original works, is due in great measure to the fact that only after considerable time are they able to acquaint themselves with European literature in translated form.[7]

It is clear, therefore, that Ferenczi would have wanted his Congress paper translated into English as soon as possible. In fact, Jones wrote to Ferenczi and told him that he had translated the paper into English, and that it would appear in the *International Journal of Psycho-Analysis*. Ferenczi, in an unpublished letter (in English) to Jones, dated March

22, 1933, writes: ". . . I thank you for wanting to publish my Congress paper in the English Journal." Ferenczi never learned that Jones was being insincere and did not have the courage to tell Ferenczi his real view. Emboldened, however, by Ferenczi's death in May of that year, Jones wrote to Freud on June 3, in an unpublished letter (Jones Archives, London):

> . . . It is about Ferenczi's Congress paper that I am now writing. Eitingon did not wish to allow it to be read at the Congress, but I persuaded him. I thought at the time of asking you about its publication in the *Zeitschrift*. I felt he would be offended if it were not translated into English and so asked his permission for this. He seemed gratified, and we have not only translated it but set it up in type as the first chapter in the July number. Since his death I have been thinking over the removal of the personal reasons for publishing it. Others also have suggested that it now be withdrawn and I quote the following passage from a letter of Mrs. Riviere's[8] with which I quite agree: "Now that Ferenczi has died, I wondered whether you will not reconsider publishing his last paper. It seems to me it can only be damaging to him and a discredit, while now that he is no longer to be hurt by its not being published, no good purpose could be served by it. Its scientific contentions and its statements about analytic practice are just a tissue of delusions, which can only discredit psychoanalysis and give credit to its opponents. It cannot be supposed that all *Journal* readers will appreciate the mental condition of the writer, and in this respect one has to think of posterity too!" I therefore think it best to withdraw the paper unless I hear from you that you have any wish to the contrary.

We do not have Freud's response, but presumably he agreed, for Jones wrote to A. A. Brill (1874–1948), the powerful and conservative American psychoanalyst, on June 20, 1933 (unpublished):

To please him [Ferenczi] I had already printed his Congress paper, which appeared in the *Zeitschrift,* for the July number of the *Journal,* but now, after consultation with Freud, have decided not to publish it. It would certainly not have done his reputation any good.

Brill responded to Jones on August 11, 1933 (unpublished):

I fully agree with you about the publication of his paper. The less said about this whole matter, the better.

It is evident from this exchange that it was Freud's wish as well to see the paper suppressed. The lack of loyalty toward a former friend and the rapid move to strangle ideas contrary to accepted doctrine are distressing.

The proofs were destroyed, and an English translation was not published for another sixteen years—until Michael Balint translated the paper and published it in the *International Journal of Psycho-Analysis* in 1949.[9]

In order to understand why this paper was so disliked and so feared, we must examine the relationship between Freud and Ferenczi and Ferenczi's developing technique.

FERENCZI'S DEVELOPING TECHNIQUE

A number of authors have written about Ferenczi's experiments with technique and I do not wish to repeat this easily available information.[10] Freud himself hinted that Ferenczi's innovation had something to do with the relationship between the two men. Jones writes that "the time the two men passed together in Sicily [in 1910] was fateful for their subsequent relationship. Since the bond between them was the most im-

portant Freud was to forge in his later years, it is necessary
to mention briefly the beginning of their difficulties."[11] Jones
continues:

> As I well know from many intimate talks with him, he [Fer-
> enczi] was haunted by a quite inordinate and insatiable long-
> ing for his father's love. It was the dominating passion of
> his life and was indirectly the source of the unfortunate
> changes he introduced into his psycho-analytic technique
> twenty years later, which had the effect of estranging him from
> Freud (though not Freud from him). His demands for in-
> timacy had no bounds. There was to be no privacy and no
> secrets between him and Freud.

How Jones could know whether such a childhood longing
was "inordinate" is a mystery. Nor is it true that Freud was
not estranged from Ferenczi, as the material quoted in this
chapter demonstrates. Jones then quotes a letter that Freud
wrote to Ferenczi on October 6, 1910,[12] after the trip: "I
am not the psycho-analytical superman that you construed
in your imagination, nor have I overcome the countertransference."[13] Jones goes on to quote one of Freud's rare references to his early relationship with Wilhelm Fliess, in a letter
to Ferenczi on October 6, 1910:

> You not only noticed, but also understood, that I *no longer*
> [emphasis in original] have any need to uncover my person-
> ality completely, and you correctly traced this back to the
> traumatic reason for it. Since Fliess's case, with the over-
> coming of which you recently saw me occupied, that need has
> been extinguished. A part of homosexual cathexis has been
> withdrawn and made use of to enlarge my own ego. I have
> succeeded where the paranoiac fails.

In the letters to Fliess, Freud's need to uncover his personality completely is evident, and clearly clashed with Fliess's
greater personal reserve. The more Fliess withdrew from him,

the greater was Freud's urge to rescue the friendship by displaying his innermost life to Fliess. Fliess had already decided to withdraw from Freud in 1900, but did not ever directly reveal this to him. (See W. Fliess, *In Eigener Sache* [In My Defense] [Berlin: Emil Goldschmidt, 1906], p. 16). No doubt it was this unspoken rejection that hurt Freud, for he could never confront it directly. By his own telling, it took Freud many years to overcome the hurt he experienced, and he was not about to enter another such relationship with Ferenczi.

Ferenczi responded to Freud's letter with a six-page letter, which has not been published, in which he complains about the lack of intimacy during their travels. Ferenczi asks Freud: "Do you not in fact believe that I intuit that you have some magnificent secret?"[14] Ferenczi had obviously wanted Freud to reveal to him more of his inner life, and in particular the details of his relationship with Fliess (which Ferenczi must have envied). The "magnificent secret" Ferenczi mentions probably referred to some aspect of this relationship. Possibly Ferenczi believed that Freud had been in love with Fliess, or even that he had had a homosexual relationship with him. In any event, the secret that Ferenczi hints at seems to have been sexual in nature. In the same letter, Ferenczi also revealed to Freud that he had a dream about him in which Freud appeared naked. Ferenczi, who had already spoken of unconscious homosexual longings, interpreted the dream as "the longing for absolute, equal openness." Freud's response to this letter, in which he tells Ferenczi that his dreams at the time "were concerned entirely with the Fliess affair," has been quoted above (note 15, chapter 3).

No doubt Ferenczi was intrigued by Freud's earlier closeness to Fliess and must have pressed him for details of the relationship. In his response of October 12, Ferenczi tells Freud:

In addition I have an interesting case of neurotic stool-incontinence in the case of a certain Schlesinger, an engineer, who is an intimate friend of Dr. Fliess. He intends to find out about psychoanalysis from Fliess. I am curious to see what he answers.

There is no further mention of Fliess, but Ferenczi seems to have at least partially identified with Freud and Fliess's early interest in masturbation. For in 1912 Ferenczi published some remarks about Fliess in his contribution to a discussion on masturbation (my translation):

The discoveries of Fliess on the relationship between the nose and the genitals should also not be forgotten. The vasomotor overexcitation which results from masturbation causes chronic disturbances in the erectile tissue of the mucous membrane of the nose. These create in their wake various forms of neuralgia and functional disturbances. In some cases of neurasthenia caused by masturbation, cauterization of the genital points of the nose appreciably improved the condition. Research on a large number of cases should be carried out in this area.[15]

Ferenczi, in his early years as an analyst, seems to have believed what all other analysts believed about fantasy and reality. In 1912 he wrote, in a letter to James Jackson Putnam, the American psychiatrist and early follower of Freud:

As far as Kollarits' comments [?] are concerned, I can enlighten you in a few words. I know for certain that Kollarits has no knowledge of psychoanalytic literature, except for my Hungarian essays and perhaps Freud's Five Lectures. He himself has *never* done *analysis*. The source of his attitude toward the etiology of the neuroses can easily be guessed on the basis of his naive pronouncements on the subject: he believes everything his patients say and takes their utterances to be statements of fact.[16]

It is true that Ferenczi also began, early on, experimenting with psychoanalytic technique. At first the experiments consisted of demanding greater "abstinence" from his patients, ordering them to give up certain pleasures (especially masturbation) in order to heighten the tension in the analytic sessions, which it undoubtedly did, and bring to light material otherwise unavailable. In Ferenczi's middle period, during the 1920s, he wrote a series of controversial papers about his psychoanalytic technique, which were collected and published in English in 1926,[17] and were reviewed by Edward Glover:

> . . . a number of analysts temporized in the hope of getting some authoritative guidance from Freud himself . . . but the only authoritative comment we have had from Freud has been that all efforts to accelerate materially analytic treatment have come to nothing. "The best way to shorten treatment," he says in "Die Frage der Laienanalyse," "is to carry it out correctly."[18]

Freud himself seems to have taken a benevolently skeptical interest in Ferenczi's experiments. At this time, neither Freud nor any other analyst thought any the less of Ferenczi for these adventures in technique.

But at some point in his analytic practice Ferenczi became convinced that the analytic setting was fraudulent. The analyst behaved with neutrality, but actually felt something quite different. These feelings, especially when they were negative, were not conveyed to the patient. This, Ferenczi felt, was hypocrisy. Moreover, he noticed that his patients were very sensitive to this hypocrisy, and try as he might to conceal his real feelings, patients invariably uncovered them. This sensitivity to genuine emotional states began to preoccupy Ferenczi more and more (the diary discusses it at length). He speculated on why his patients were so sensitive to issues of truth and honesty. Slowly it dawned on Ferenczi that all his patients had been severely damaged. The love his patients had hoped for as children had not been forthcoming. What was this lack of love? Ferenczi thought, at first, that the child wished for oedipal gratifications it could not receive. Ferenczi shared the orthodox view of the pathogenic power of desire, that people fall ill from wishes they cannot fulfill. His response was to try to provide patients with the love they had not received as children (a no doubt impossible undertaking). I learned from Dr. Jeanne Lampl-de Groot, who saw one of Ferenczi's woman patients after his death, that Ferenczi sat the patient upon his lap and stroked her like a child.[19] Clara Thompson, who had been one of Ferenczi's analysands, reports how he gave a patient (probably her) a doll for comfort.[20]

Freud's attitude toward these breaks with classical technique is apparent from a charming letter he wrote to Ferenczi, which Jones quotes:[21]

I see that the differences between us come to a head in a technical detail which is well worth discussing. You have not made a secret of the fact that you kiss your patients and let them kiss you; I had also heard that from a patient of my own. Now when you decide to give a full account of your technique and its results you will have to choose between two ways: either you relate this or you conceal it. The latter, as you may well think, is dishonorable. What one does in one's technique one has to defend openly. Besides, both ways soon come together. Even if you don't say so yourself it will soon get known, just as I knew it before you told me.

Now I am assuredly not one of those who from prudishness or from consideration of bourgeois convention would condemn little erotic gratifications of this kind. . . . Picture what will be the result of publishing your technique. There is no revolutionary who is not driven out of the field by a still more radical one. A number of independent thinkers in matters of technique will say to themselves: why stop at a kiss? which after all doesn't make a baby. And then bolder ones will come along who will go further to peeping and showing—and soon we shall have accepted in the technique of analysis the whole repertoire of demiviergerie and petting-parties, resulting in an enormous increase of interest in psychoanalysis among both analysts and patients. The new adherent, however, will easily claim too much of this interest for himself, the younger of our colleagues will find it hard to stop at the point they originally intended, and God the Father Ferenczi gazing at the lively scene he has created will perhaps say to himself: maybe after all I should have halted in my technique of motherly affection *before* the kiss.

Freud seems in this response to have kept the discussion at a purely objective, friendly, and rational level. In the letter as published by Ernest Jones, there are no ellipses to indicate that anything has been omitted from it. However, I had the opportunity of seeing the original letter, and, in fact, Jones omitted a crucial sentence. He translates a later passage from the letter:

In this warning I do not think I have said anything you do not know yourself. But since you like playing a tender mother role with others, then perhaps you may do so with yourself. And then you are to hear from the brutal fatherly side an admonition. That is why I spoke in my last letter of a new puberty, a Johannis impulse, and now you have compelled me to be quite blunt.

But the last sentence really makes no sense without the passage Jones omitted:

According to my memory the tendency to sexual playing about[22] with patients was not foreign to you in pre-analytic times, so that it is possible to bring the new technique into relation with the old misdemeanors. That is why I spoke in my last letter of a new puberty . . .

Freud has remembered something that had come up in Ferenczi's analysis, some twenty years earlier—that he had a tendency to sexually exploit his medical patients. The significance of the preceding portions of the letter, the ones that Jones quoted, is now altered. For the entire tone of the letter is different from what one might have supposed from the published version. Freud is not, in fact, displaying humor or attempting to remonstrate gently with his old friend. Freud's analytic stance was bound to wound Ferenczi, and undoubtedly succeeded.

Ferenczi replied (unpublished) on December 27, 1931:

I consider your fear that I will develop into a second Stekel[23] unfounded. "The sins of youth," misdemeanors, if they are overcome and analytically worked through, can make a man wiser and more cautious than people who never went through such storms. My extremely ascetic "active therapy" [i.e., abstinence] was surely a cautionary device against precisely such tendencies, which is why it took on, in its exaggeration, the character of an obsession.

Ferenczi goes on to say: "Now, I believe, I am capable of creating a mild, passion-free atmosphere, suitable for bringing forth even that which had been previously hidden."

At about this time, late in 1931 (possibly earlier), Ferenczi began his experiments with what he called "mutual analysis," as a means of correcting the hypocrisies inherent in the analytic setting. Ferenczi never published anything on this subject—it would have been unacceptable to Freud—but his diary provides details. Ferenczi seems to have begun mutual analysis by confessing to certain patients his own problems when they overlapped with problems of the patient. Thus when one of his patients had a dream (cited in the diary) of a powerful man with a tiny penis, Ferenczi was convinced that the dream was a transference dream that related to him and was instigated by his own (unstated) concerns about the size of his penis. He confessed to this same patient that he actually had continual anxiety about the size of his penis. Whatever the drawbacks of this technique (and Ferenczi discusses them in some detail in the diary), possibly this was what enabled his patients to begin talking about the real traumas of their childhood.

It was at this time (1931–1932) that Ferenczi began to develop an interest in the real traumas suffered by his patients in childhood. One patient in particular, with whom mutual analysis seems to have gone further than with any other (it is not clear, from the diary, how many patients Ferenczi treated with mutual analysis, and how formal the mutuality was, whether Ferenczi actually lay on the couch, how often, whether he paid his patient, and whether he allowed himself complete freedom in his associations), seems to have played a major role in Ferenczi's developing ideas at this time. That patient was Elizabeth Severn, a name not previously known to the analytic literature.

Elizabeth Severn appears frequently in Ferenczi's diary. The portrait of her that Dr. Judith Dupont sent me was painted in 1926, by Olga Dormandi (Olga Székely-Kovács), Dr. Dupont's mother. Olga Dormandi sailed to America in the fall of 1926, on the same ship as Ferenczi. Ferenczi had analyzed her mother, Vilma Kovács, and had known the entire family for a long time.

According to the diary, Mrs. Severn, who at the time was a dancer,[24] was in analysis with Ferenczi in Budapest at some point before 1926. I was not able to find out much about her. I do not know, for example, whether she had any formal training as an analyst or psychologist, but Ferenczi seems to have accepted her as an analytic pupil. In his 1931 paper

Portrait of Mrs. Elizabeth Severn
by Olga Dormandi, ca. 1926

"Child Analysis in the Analysis of Adults,"[25] Ferenczi wrote about her as follows:

> Our colleague, Elizabeth Severn, who is doing a training-analysis with me, once pointed out to me, when we were discussing this amongst a number of other subjects, that I sometimes disturbed the spontaneity of the fantasy-production with my questions and answers.

In his 1929 paper "The Principle of Relaxation and Neocatharsis"[26] he writes:

> In every case of neurotic amnesia, and possibly also in the ordinary childhood-amnesia, it seems likely that a psychotic splitting off of a part of the personality occurs under the influence of shock. The dissociated part, however, lives on hidden, ceaselessly endeavouring to make itself felt, without finding any outlet except in neurotic symptoms. For this notion I am partly indebted to discoveries made by our colleague, Elizabeth Severn, which she personally communicated to me.

From these comments it appears possible that Mrs. Severn was the first person to spark Ferenczi's interest in real traumas.

In the 1931 article (p. 136) in which he thanks Mrs. Severn, he records a dialogue:

> Quick, quick! What shall I do? They have wounded my child! There is no one to help. He is bleeding to death. He is scarcely breathing. I must bind up his wound myself. Now, child, take a deep breath or you will die. Now his heart has stopped beating! He is dying! He is dying!

Possibly inspired by Mrs. Severn, Ferenczi used twilight states and dreams to reconstruct early traumas, availing himself of the insight that these states reproduced the very states which the child had entered as a refuge from having to suffer the full force of the real attacks. The events were too terrifying to be consciously remembered, but the obscure memories of these twilight states and the images of the dreams pointed to real events.

In his posthumously published article "Gedanken über das Trauma" (Thoughts on Trauma),[27] Ferenczi recounts the dream of a patient that allows us to ascertain how he came to use such dreams to reconstruct real childhood traumas:

> A young girl (child?) lies at the bottom of a small boat, nearly dead and white. Above her a gigantic man, crushing her with his face. Behind them in the boat stands a second man, whom she knows. The girl is ashamed that this man witnesses what takes place. The boat is surrounded by enormously high, steep mountain cliffs, so that no one can look in from anywhere.

For Ferenczi this is a re-enactment of an early seduction scene, in which a child is seduced by a man while another man (her father possibly) looks on without doing anything to protect her. The original assault, which must have taken place in secret, is translated into a dream-image (in the dream nobody could see it). The details are authentic pictorial representations of original events too painful to be remembered consciously but which could be reproduced in the relative safety of a dream. This is an original and revolutionary use of dream technique, one anticipated by Freud in 1899 in *The Interpretation of Dreams*, but never further elaborated (possibly because it belonged to the period of his faith in the seduction theory).

It may well be that Mrs. Severn helped Ferenczi face the full reality of these traumas. Her book, *The Discovery of the Self: A Study of Psychological Cure* (London: Rider & Co., Paternoster House, n.d.), is a curious work, written in a pious, mystical manner, unprofessional and unscholarly, but nevertheless with a certain admirable ability to recognize the suffering of a child. According to Mrs. Severn, Ferenczi developed his technique from her instructions. On p. 95 she writes:

> I will speak in the next chapter of the importance of trauma in general, in the production of all neuroses. I wish here to emphasize the difference between the accepted psycho-analytic mode of treatment, which is purely dissecting in nature and which places its reliance chiefly on the mental grasp or "reconstruction" the patient can gain of his past; and a method which having found the trauma or specific cause of the illness, does not scorn to "play mother" or be Good Samaritan to the injured one, and which encourages the full reproduction of the emotions and feeling-tone of the traumatic period or events *under different and better circumstances.* It takes more time, it takes more patience, and it takes above all an emotional capacity or "gift" on the part of the analyst, who unless he can do this, is not a true "physician of the soul."

In a footnote to this passage, she writes: "This addition to, or alteration in, psycho-analytic technique has since been adopted by Ferenczi, and is the basis of his so-called 'Relaxation-principle.' "

On the other hand, on p. 125, she writes:

> The importance of *trauma* as a specific and almost universal cause of neurosis, *was first impressed upon me by Ferenczi* [emphasis added], who, probing deeply, had found it present in nearly all his cases. He thus resurrected and gave new value to an idea which had once, much earlier, been entertained by Freud, but which was discarded by him in favour of "phantasy" as the explanation of the strange tales or manifestations given by his patients. . . . Experience has convinced me, however, that the patient does not "invent" but *always tells the truth* [emphasis in the original], even though in a distorted form: and further, that what he tells is mostly of a severe

and specific injury, inflicted on him when he was young and helpless.

Her case histories are badly presented, but at least two of the dreams recorded by her are worth repeating. In the case of a young actress, she uncovered a violent sexual seduction by the grandfather, who lived in an idyllic setting in the country. The woman had a recurrent nightmare (cf. p. 148) which consisted of her going back to their country house, seeing the little schoolhouse, the road, and suddenly her grandfather's car. But inside, it "is full of mutilated children, there are dozens of little girls with their bodies and legs all cut, they are bleeding, they are smashed to pieces. I cannot bear it." The second part of the dream is the actual re-enactment of the seduction in a barn and of her screaming to her mother for help. Another case (reported on pp. 153–157) tells of a child drugged by her father and then violently raped. She dreamt she attended her own funeral as a child, was conveyed to her grave, and found she was the only mourner, which is a remarkable representation of her helplessness and loneliness and a powerful indictment of her mother's acquiescence in the partial murder of the child.

However Ferenczi came to believe in the reality of childhood traumas, whether through his mutual analyses or from Mrs. Severn or simply by listening in a new way to his patients, one fact is evident: *it is Ferenczi's ideas about trauma that made him unacceptable to Freud, and not his experiments with technique.*

Although Ferenczi was the actual founder of the International Psycho-Analytic Association, he had never been its president (the first president was Jung, followed by Abraham, Eitingon, and Jones), though he very much wished to be. Freud's unpublished letters to Ferenczi reveal that he told Ferenczi he did not want Eitingon to serve a second term, or Jones to become president, but wished that Ferenczi at last would become the president of the association he founded.

In an unpublished letter of May 12, 1932, Freud writes:

I am sorry that you find it so easy to deprive yourself of the presidency. I would like to insist on it for you. It is undeniable that in the last years you have withdrawn into isolation once again, something you had so brilliantly overcome when you were the Budapest leader and teacher. Taking over the presidency of the International would have the effect of a forced cure on you, to bring you back to society and to move you to take up the appropriate role of leader that is due you. . . . *But you must leave the dream-island on which you are living with your fantasy children, and once again take part in the struggle of men* [emphasis added].

"Phantasiekinder" (fantasy children) is ambiguous: it can refer to the children of one's imagination, but it can also refer to the fact that Ferenczi "adopted" fantasies and thought of them as real. The word "fantasy" turned into a weapon against Ferenczi. "The struggle of men" is an unkind hint that Ferenczi's withdrawal was an "effeminate" and weak response. Ferenczi, in Freud's opinion, by allying himself with the hurts of the child, was behaving in an unmanly fashion. It was a comment that wounded Ferenczi.

He replied, in an unpublished letter, on May 19, 1932:

Dear Professor:

I must honestly confess that although I have often expressed myself concerning my present activities with words like "dream-life, daydreams, puberty crises," etc., this does not actually mean that I have complete "insight into my illness" [i.e., that I acknowledge that I am ill]. In reality I have the feeling that out of the relative confusion much that is useful will develop, in fact has already done so. So I can't really see the presidency as a forced cure for a disease which I cannot acknowledge really to be one. I honestly believe that I am doing something not entirely useless by continuing with my present work. If you believe that this work can be brought into harmony with what would be expected of the president of a society, and if I can, as you assure me is the case, count on the active help of Anna and the two vice-presidents, then I would consider it an honor to become the president of a society in the foundation of which I took part and in the activities of which I for so long played an active role.

A brave postscript, which undoubtedly did not please Freud, followed on May 22:

P.S. to my last letter: it will interest you to know that in our group lively debates are taking place on the female castration complex and penis envy. I had to confess that in my practice they did not play the large role that one would, theoretically, have expected. What are your experiences? Venice, as always, is lovable. I am living in the Hotel Danieli. Your Ferenczi.

Ferenczi's views on female sexuality were undergoing radical changes in the light of his discoveries about the sexual traumas so many women had been subjected to in childhood (he discusses these emerging views in the unpublished diary).

Freud's displeasure at this turn of events was communicated to Ferenczi from many sides. Finally, Ferenczi wrote Freud on August 21, 1932, in an unpublished letter, of his decision not to serve as president:

After a long, torturous hesitation I have decided not to seek the presidency. In addition to the reasons I have already given you, there has since arisen the following circumstance: in the course of my attempts to make my analyses deeper and more effective, I have drifted into critical and self-critical channels which in some respects seem to require not merely additions but also corrections to our practical and in part also to our theoretical views. Now I have the feeling that such a mental state is not appropriate to the dignity of a president whose chief concern should be the conservation and consolidation of gains already made. My inner feeling tells me that it would not even be honest for me to occupy this position.

Freud's (unpublished) response was sent on August 24, 1932:

I have, in the interest of all concerned, very much regretted your rejection [of the presidency]. Your argument does not convince me. As long as the alterations in technique and in theory which you propose to introduce are not fundamental enough to oblige you to found a new variety of analysis, you do not need to avoid the presidency in its normal form. But I am far from wishing to influence you. You yourself must know best what is going on inside you.

But Freud had never been sincere in urging Ferenczi to accept the presidency. For when Jones was elected president (because Ferenczi had withdrawn his candidacy), Freud wrote him, on September 12, 1932 (unpublished):

Dear Jones:
Thank you for your first letter as president. I felt bad that Ferenczi's obvious ambition could not be satisfied, *but it really was not in doubt for even a single moment that only you could possibly take over the International* [emphasis added].

Freud knew that Ferenczi himself had decided not to run for president, but does not have the courtesy to Ferenczi to tell this to Jones. No doubt Jones would have been less pleased by Freud's flattery if he had been in a position to see what Freud, in an unpublished letter, had written a week earlier to Max Eitingon, then president of the International:

Jones is hardly a happy prospect for the future.[28]

FREUD'S LAST MEETING WITH FERENCZI

AND THE WIESBADEN CONGRESS

A few days before the Congress, Ferenczi passed through
Vienna on his way from Budapest to Wiesbaden to read his
paper aloud to Freud, who was too ill to attend the Congress.
It was the last time the two friends were to see each other.

The exact date of this meeting between Freud and Ferenczi
is unfortunately not ascertainable, though I believe it took
place on August 30.[29] This becomes critical in the light of
an unpublished letter that Freud wrote to Eitingon on August
29, 1932:

> He must not be allowed to give the paper. Either another one
> or none. He does not seem disinclined now to be chosen as
> president. Whether he can still be chosen [for president] by all
> of you after these revelations is another question. Our behavior
> will depend, in the first place, on whether he agrees to the
> postponement [of his Wiesbaden paper] as well as on the
> impression that he makes on all of you in Wiesbaden.

The critical question is whether this letter of August 29
was written *before* Freud had seen Ferenczi or after. It is
critical because if Freud wrote it before their meeting, then
he was writing about a paper *he had not yet read*.[30] I believe
that Freud had not yet seen the paper and that the meeting
took place the next day, on August 30. Freud sent a telegram
to Eitingon on September 2, 1932 (published by Jones but
with the crucial first four sentences omitted). The whole
telegram reads: "Ferenczi read me his paper. Harmless.
Dumb. Otherwise he is inaccessible. The impression was un-
favorable." Freud would not have sent this telegram if he

had read the paper before he wrote the letter to Eitingon on August 29.

Jones (3, p. 184) reports the actual meeting:

> Without a word of greeting, Ferenczi announced on entering the room: "I want you to read my Congress paper." Halfway through Brill came in and, since Ferenczi and he had recently talked over the theme, Freud let him stay, though he took no part in the talk. Freud evidently tried his best to bring about some degree of insight [in Ferenczi], but in vain.

A. A. Brill, whom both Freud and Ferenczi disdained, was the official representative of the by then powerful American Psychoanalytic Association (he was strongly opposed to allowing non-medical people to train as analysts). He was on hand for the reading of the paper possibly so that he could lend the support of the Americans to Eitingon's and the others' attempts to suppress Ferenczi's paper at the Congress. Ferenczi was hurt by this turn of events, as he told Freud.[31] Brill later reported the meeting to Jones (in an unpublished letter of June 6, 1933):

> I told the Professor that I urged Ferenczi not to give out his new ideas for the present . . . that I urged him to wait and told the Professor that he should do the same thing when he saw Ferenczi, to which the Professor said: "What is the use? It has to come out sooner or later."

Freud told Brill the story of the old Jew who promises a Polish baron that he will teach the baron's dog to talk within three years. "Why not, after all," he told his closest friend, for "in three years either the baron will be dead, or the dog, or me." Freud meant, presumably, that he and Ferenczi would soon be dead and the world would not care.

Ferenczi, after the meeting, wrote to Freud, in an unpublished letter, on September 27, 1932:

The second unpleasant surprise [after Brill's presence] was your demand that I refrain from publication. I still cannot see how my presentation could possibly hurt either me or psychoanalysis.

Freud responded to Ferenczi, in an unpublished letter, on October 2, 1932:

The request that you should not publish for one year was made primarily in your interest. I did not want to give up the hope that you would yourself come to recognize in further work the technical incorrectness of your results. You seemed to promise this to me, but I naturally relieve you of your promise and waive, perforce, any influence over you, which in any event I do not really possess. I no longer believe that you will correct yourself, the way I corrected myself a generation ago.

Jones's account of the Congress itself tells us how reluctant the senior analysts were to allow Ferenczi to read his paper. Jones (3, p. 185) writes:

At the Congress itself a delicate question arose. Freud thought the paper Ferenczi had prepared could do his reputation no good and begged him not to read it. Brill, Eitingon, and van Ophuijsen went further and thought it would be scandalous to read such a paper before a Psycho-Analytic Congress. Eitingon therefore decided to forbid it firmly. On the other hand I thought the paper too vague to leave any clear impression, for good or bad—which it turned out to be—and that it would be so offensive to tell the most distinguished member of the Association, and its actual founder, that what he had to say was not worth listening to that he might well withdraw altogether in dudgeon.

Unpublished letters give us some insight into the depth of the distaste that Ferenczi's paper evoked. In a fawning and even cowardly letter, Jones wrote to Freud on September 9,

1932, immediately after the Congress (the letter is in the Colchester Archives):

Dear Professor:

I seize the first peaceful moment to write to you. In the first place will you allow me to express my sympathy over the difficulty that has arisen with your oldest and dearest analytical friend. I know that you will not be tempted to copy the old Kaiser (*"mir bleibt . . ."* [?]) because your calibre is too tough, and you are surrounded both by affection and by followers whose acceptance of the unconscious is unbreakable. Nevertheless, how painful it must be I can imagine. To Eitingon it came as a shock of surprise, to you probably less so. To me not at all, for I have followed Ferenczi's evolution (including the pathological side) closely for many years, and knew it could only be a question of time before this dénouement arrived. Abraham and I drew him forcibly back from the precipice at the Rank time, and lately Rickman's regular reports of his analysis showed me clearly the direction things were going. His exceptionally strong need of being loved, together with the repressed sadism, are plainly behind the tendency to ideas of persecution. My reaction was therefore very simple: first the cause, then everything to keep him with us. The first excluded the possibility of his being President— in that I agreed with the firm attitude of Eitingon and von Ophuijsen. But the second made me oppose both these two and also Brill. They wanted at all costs that Ferenczi be asked to withdraw his *Vortrag* [paper] and to postpone as long as possible the expression of his ideas—to avoid scandal. On the contrary I insisted that there would be less scandal if we kept it inside the *Vereinigung* [Association] and that we were quite strong enough to digest the ideas ourselves without harm coming. It would have fed the pathological ideas to have told him that his *Vortrag,* etc., was too wicked to be presented to us, and that might end in his publicly withdrawing from the *Vereinigung.* I gained my point, and so far as I can judge the advice was successful, for Ferenczi, finding himself welcomed and listened to, visibly expanded and day by day identified himself ever more with the interests and plans, business, etc., of the *Vereinigung;* he felt himself one of us, which is what I intended and which I am confident will do us no harm. He is, I am afraid, a sick man—also physically—and the impression he made was very pathetic.[32] To me personally he was affectionate, and I think I was able to help both him and his wife. It is terrible—but also unprofitable—to make comparisons with the brilliant past. One can only accept the facts, do the little possible to help, and again learn how one underestimates the difficulties in the way of retaining a full acceptance of the reality of the unconscious; most people seem to have a limit to their power in this respect.

Freud, in an unpublished letter (from the Colchester Archives) dated September 12, 1932, responded by saying:

Ferenczi's change of direction is certainly a highly regrettable event, but there is nothing traumatic about it. For the last three years I have been observing his increasing alienation, his inaccessibility to warnings about the incorrectness of his technique, *and what is probably the most decisive* [emphasis added], a personal animosity against me, for which I certainly gave even less occasion than in earlier cases. Except, perhaps, for the fact that I am still here. Unfortunately the regressive intellectual and affective development seems to have had, in his case, a background of physical decline. His clever and good wife conveyed to me that I should think of him as a sick child.

FERENCZI'S DEATH

JONES'S account of Ferenczi's last days implies that both he and Freud remained close and loyal to Ferenczi to the end, that they both endured with mature resignation a fate that could not be avoided. Jones (3, p. 188) writes:

> In America some former pupils of Ferenczi's, notably Izette de Forest and Clara Thompson, have sustained a myth of Freud's ill-treatment of Ferenczi. Phrases such as Freud's "enmity," "harsh and bitter criticism," have been used, and he is said to have pursued Ferenczi with hostility. Freud's correspondence, and also my personal memories, leave no doubt that *there is no truth whatever* [emphasis added] in this story, although it is highly probable that Ferenczi himself *in his final delusional state* [emphasis added] believed in and propagated elements of it. Freud's only feelings at his friend's self-absorbed withdrawal were of sadness and regret, while his attitude toward what he and all the rest of us regarded as Ferenczi's errors of regression was that of a friend who until it was plainly hopeless did what he could in the endeavour to save him from them.

But the truth was rather different. Here is Jones's account (3, p. 190) of Ferenczi's final days:

> The mental disturbance had been making rapid progress in the last few months. He related how one of his American patients, to whom he used to devote four or five hours a day, had analysed him and so cured him of all his troubles. Messages came to him from her across the Atlantic—Ferenczi had always been a staunch believer in telepathy. Then there were the delusions about Freud's supposed hostility. Towards the end came violent paranoia and even homicidal outbursts,[33] which were followed by a sudden death on May 24. That was the tragic end of a brilliant, lovable and distinguished personality, someone who had for a quarter of a century been Freud's closest friend. The lurking demons within, against whom Ferenczi had for years struggled with great distress and much success, conquered him at the end, and we learnt from this painful experience once more how terrible their power can be. I of course wrote to condole with Freud over the loss

of our friend, "of that inspiring figure we all loved so much. I am more glad than ever that I succeeded at the last Congress in keeping him within our circle." Freud replied: "Yes, we have every reason to condole with each other. Our loss is great and painful; it is part of the change that overthrows everything that exists and thus makes room for the new. Ferenczi takes with him a part of the old time; then with my departure another will begin which you will still see. Fate. Resignation. That is all."

This is the version of history that Jones recorded for public consumption. It does not remotely correspond to the truth. Perhaps, however, Ferenczi believed the protests of Jones that Freud still cared for him deeply. He seems more perplexed than angry at what was happening to him.

It took a great deal of courage for Ferenczi to stand with his patients and recognize that what had happened to them was not fantasy but the terrible truth. He knew that such courage would cost him his standing in the analytic world. But he did not know that Freud would so easily turn away from him. Their last meeting was a sad ending. After the Congress, Ferenczi took a trip to the South of France, to try to recover his physical and emotional balance, but it was no use. In an unpublished letter to Freud, written on September 27, 1932, Ferenczi wrote to say that the final meeting upset him deeply:

Dear Professor:
  You can measure the depth of my shock by the length of time it has taken me to react to our conversation in Vienna before the Congress. Unfortunately, with me, such things are always connected to physical complaints, so that my trip through Baden-Baden to the South of France was and is really a *"voyage de lit à lit."*

Ferenczi in Groddeck's sanatorium in Baden-Baden at the end of his life

On March 29, 1933, Ferenczi wrote to Freud of a nervous
breakdown (*nervöser Zusammenbruch*). On May 24, 1933,
he died.

Then came the obituaries by the very men who had turned
away from him when he was alive. Jones, in his obituary,
published in the *International Journal of Psycho-Analysis,*
the same journal which had just destroyed the proofs of
Ferenczi's last paper, wrote:

> Of his more personal attributes I do not find it easy to speak,
> for he was one of my nearest and dearest friends. His kind-
> liness was unfailing and showed the genuine nature of his
> charm and loveableness.[34]

Was this a fantasy or simply a lie? Was the hypocrisy that
Jones and Freud and all the other senior analysts offered the
public in their writing about Ferenczi the real world as opposed to the world of Ferenczi's "imagination," in which
children suffered tortured lives at the hands of brutal parents?
Max Eitingon—the same Eitingon who a few months earlier
had refused to have his scientific integrity compromised by
allowing Ferenczi to read his paper—gave his epitaph at a
special meeting of the Berlin Psychoanalytic Society:

> Ferenczi writes very beautifully, most often clearly, lucidly.
> His style is generally flawless. His writing is interesting and
> has unique appeal, and is very personal, as though he were
> speaking. His lectures were generally among the highlights of
> our congresses.[35]

Even more disturbing is the fact that Freud was no more
prepared than his colleagues to allow the public any glimpse
into his real feelings about Ferenczi or the real reasons for
his dislike of Ferenczi's 1932 paper. His obituary of Ferenczi[36] is no less hypocritical than the others'. Freud writes

that "it is probable that some time in the future there will really be a 'bio-analysis' as Ferenczi had prophesied, and it will have to cast back to the *Versuch einer Genitaltheorie* [Attempt at a Theory of Genitality]."[37] Freud here singles out for praise Ferenczi's most dubious work (in a dubious prophesy), contrasting it with Ferenczi's later work, which is in reality his one great achievement:

> After this summit of achievement, it came about that our friend slowly drifted away from us. On his return from a period of work in America he seemed to withdraw more and more into solitary work, though he had previously taken the liveliest share in all that happened in analytic circles. We learnt that one single problem had monopolized his interest. The need to cure and to help had become paramount in him. He had probably set himself aims which, with our therapeutic means, are altogether out of reach to-day. From unexhausted springs of emotion the conviction was borne in upon him that one could effect far more with one's patients if one gave them enough of the love which they had longed for as children. He wanted to discover how this could be carried out within the framework of the psychoanalytic situation; and so long as he had not succeeded in this, he kept apart, no longer certain, perhaps, of agreement with his friends. Wherever it may have been that the road he had started along would have led him, he could not pursue it to the end. Signs were slowly revealed in him of a grave organic destructive process which had probably overshadowed his life for many years already. Shortly before completing his sixtieth year he succumbed to pernicious anemia. It is impossible to believe that the history of our science will ever forget him.

Possibly, but the history of psychoanalysis certainly tried to forget Ferenczi's views. "Sexual playing about with patients" becomes transformed here, for public consumption, into "unexhausted springs of emotion." It is not that I admire Ferenczi's sexual conduct with patients (though at least it was not a deliberate and selfish attempt to exploit them). But I find it curious that Freud could tolerate this technique as long as Ferenczi held standard psychoanalytic views. It became insupportable to Freud only when Ferenczi (for whatever reasons) began to pay closer attention to real traumas. Moreover, as we see from Freud's obituary of Ferenczi, he was not prepared to let the public know any of this background. Instead he altered the true history to create a more palatable version of Ferenczi's past, one that reflected better on one of the founders of the psychoanalytic association, whether to protect the memory of his once cherished friend or to protect the profession of psychoanalysis (for it would not be instructive for the public to know Ferenczi's true story).

FERENCZI'S "ILLNESS"

THESE obituaries and the subsequent published comments by Freud, Jones, and others do not represent the real feelings of these analysts toward Ferenczi. The letters which I found in Freud's desk and in the Jones and Colchester Archives in England make clear what these men really thought. Four days after Ferenczi died, Freud, in an unpublished letter dated May 29, 1933, wrote Jones:

The loss was certainly not new; for years Ferenczi was not with us, in fact, not even with himself. One more easily gets an overview now of the slow process of destruction to which he fell victim. His organic symptoms in the last two years were a pernicious anemia which soon resulted in severe motor disturbances. Liver therapy improved his blood but had no influence on the other. In the last few weeks he could no longer walk or stand up. At the center was the conviction that I did not love him enough, that I did not want to recognize his works, and also that I had badly analyzed him. His innovations in technique were connected to this, since he wanted to show me how lovingly one must treat one's patients in order to help them. In fact, these were regressions to the complexes of his childhood, the chief pain of which was the [alleged] fact that his mother had not loved him, a middle child among eleven or thirteen others, passionately or exclusively enough. He would himself become a better mother, and in fact found the children he needed. Among them was a suspect American woman, to whom he devoted four or five hours a day (Mrs. Severn?) [so in original]. When she left he believed that she could influence him through vibrations sent across the ocean. He said that she analyzed him and thereby saved him. (So he played both roles, was both the mother and the child.) She seems to have produced in him a *pseudologia phantastica,* since he believed her accounts of the most strange childhood traumas, which he then defended against us. In these disorders was snuffed out his once so brilliant intelligence. But let us preserve his sad exit as a secret among ourselves.

Jones responded on June 3, 1933, in an unpublished letter that I found in the Jones Archives in London:

It was distressing to hear of the bad time that poor Ferenczi must have gone through, but I hear from Roheim that the end was unexpectedly sudden and without suffering. Presumably there was degeneration of the spinal cord which sometimes accompanies pernicious anemia. I will of course keep secret what you told me about the American lady, but I am afraid the paranoia is public news: *it was sufficiently obvious to all analysts from his last Congress paper* [emphasis added].

When Jones writes that "the paranoia is public news" he is referring first of all to Freud's claim that Ferenczi was suffering from a *pseudologia phantastica*. This is a psychiatric term, which the German medical dictionary *Pschyrembel* (s.v.) defines as the "invention of experiences that are just fairy-tales." Freud is stating that Ferenczi's belief in the reality of Mrs. Severn's memories of childhood traumas demonstrates that he suffered from this "disease." Jones agrees with Freud and adduces further proof: Ferenczi's Congress paper, "Confusion of Tongues," was evidence that Ferenczi was paranoid, because in that paper he said that what his patients remembered from their early childhood were not inventions; the traumas were real. Freud and Jones agreed that this act of faith on Ferenczi's part was paranoid. Such events, Jones and Freud insisted, had never taken place in reality but were only fantasies of Ferenczi's patients.

In an unpublished letter to Eitingon written on August 28, 1933, Freud reveals the true reason for his disappointment with Ferenczi:

> His source is what patients tell him when he manages to put them into what he himself calls a state similar to hypnosis. He then takes what he hears as revelations, *but what one really gets are the fantasies of patients about their childhood, and not the [real] story. My first great etiological error also arose in this very way* [emphasis added]. The patients suggest something to him, and he then reverses it. I have insisted for years that he regressed to his earlier neurosis as he grew older.

What Freud states here explicitly is that memories of seduction (and, by extension, of real traumas) are not memories at all, but fantasies. Since Ferenczi had told Freud, during his analysis, that one of the great traumas of his childhood had been the fact that he *was* unloved (as opposed to the *feeling* that he had been unloved), it is very likely that Freud would have regarded this memory of Ferenczi's as a fantasy and not a reality. Freud could not know whether Ferenczi's patients "imagined" their traumas, any more than he could know whether Ferenczi imagined his trauma. Ferenczi, in fact, wrote to Groddeck on December 25, 1921, in a letter just released:

> *It is certain* [emphasis added] that as a child I received from my mother too little love and too much severity. . . . Sentiments and caresses were unknown in our family. Feelings such as modest [?] respect for parents, etc., were all the more jealously cultivated. From such an education, could anything other than hypocrisy be the result? The most important thing was to keep up appearances, to keep "evil habits" hidden away. It is thus that I became an excellent student and a secret masturbator.[38]

Even more important, Freud tells Eitingon that Ferenczi should not believe his patients, for "what one really gets are the fantasies of patients about their childhood, and not the [real] story [or history]." Yet how can Freud know what did or did not happen to Ferenczi's patients in their childhood? Unless of course he had made the decision that nothing had ever happened to anybody, and that any belief to the contrary was the product of imagination or, even worse, of paranoia. Freud never met Mrs. Severn. How can he know, as he writes to Jones, that "her accounts of the most strange childhood traumas" are not true accounts? When he accuses her of having produced in Ferenczi a *pseudologia phantastica*, that is, a belief in bizarre tales or lies, he is returning to the views of nineteenth-century psychiatry, that whenever a patient tells of something inherently repulsive or upsetting (to the physician's idea of social order), that "story" is attributable to a disease, *pseudologia phantastica*. The German and French nineteenth-century psychiatrists wrote about *pseudologia phantastica* in children, the peculiar need to accuse their parents of strange crimes, that is, sexual assaults. Even *Pschyrembel* mentions the accusations by children of sexual assaults as coming under the aegis of this "illness."

Nor is there any evidence that Ferenczi felt Mrs. Severn "could influence him through vibrations sent across the ocean." What Ferenczi wrote, in his diary, was that the analysis of Mrs. Severn had sensitized him to certain aspects of telepathy. And in fact Ferenczi produced the only intelligent explanation of telepathy I have ever seen. Ferenczi says that "mediums" and other people who claim to be clairvoyant (though undoubtedly Ferenczi was less skeptical than I am, and believed them) have been forced into a kind of hypersensitivity from childhood. That is, they have been the victims of such cruelty on the part of their parents that in order to survive they had to develop a remarkable sensitivity to determine what their parents were really feeling, so that they could avoid their murderous rage. The senses of a medium are more developed than other people's senses out of dire necessity. To protect themselves, they learned to see what other people avoided seeing.

Freud felt that Ferenczi was paranoid to believe his patients (and his own memories) when they said that parents could be cruel and sexually violent to their children. Jones agreed with Freud: ". . . it was sufficiently obvious to all analysts from his last Congress paper." Because Ferenczi told the assembled analysts that these things really happened, that children were often the victims of sexual abuse, were often beaten and destroyed as human beings, and that it was incumbent on analysts to find some means of dealing with such suffering instead of denying it, he was considered paranoid. It was a high price to pay for telling the truth.

CONCLUSION

JONES, referring to Ferenczi's paper in his obituary notice, wrote: "Ferenczi showed unmistakable signs of mental regression in his attitude towards fundamental problems of psycho-analysis." And in his book *Free Associations: Memoirs of a Psycho-Analyst*, Jones writes:

> During his final illness Ferenczi lost most of his old cheerfulness and vitality, became heavy, depressed and ungracious, withdrew from his friends, and—most serious of all—allowed his scientific judgment to be gravely deflected.[39]

In my opinion Jones and the others wrote as they did about Ferenczi because they were seeking Freud's approval. By "regression" Jones means that Ferenczi returned to Freud's early views on seduction. Had Freud told the analysts that Ferenczi's Congress paper was brilliant and profound, they might have agreed. Their view of Ferenczi was filtered through Freud's eyes.

Jones would have us believe that the case history of Sándor Ferenczi was easy to tell, the truth available to all. But the letters I found reveal a more complex and unpleasant story. Jones wrote a history that would support Freud's version of the history of the psychoanalytic movement, not one that sought the truth. The great names of the history of psychoanalysis do not fare well in the cold light of these documents.

The real disappointment, however, is Freud himself. The distortions of Jones, Brill, Eitingon, and others do not matter so much. But what happened to Freud that he could so resolutely, so coldly turn his back on the man who had been his most beloved pupil and colleague?

Ferenczi in his 1932 paper had repeated the essence of Freud's 1896 paper "The Aetiology of Hysteria" and went further by investigating the defenses that people develop to ward off the knowledge of their childhood wounds. Ferenczi's paper is a response to Freud's abandonment of the seduction theory, for it asserts that a real trauma can itself give rise to horrible fantasies—that these fantasies derive from a real event, they do not replace it. People fall ill from what happened to them, not from what they imagine happened to them. It was as if Ferenczi were telling Freud: "You lacked the courage to stay with the truth and defend it. The movement that grew up around you is a product of this cowardice. I will not be part of it. I will not break faith with what I know to be true." And that is what happened; Ferenczi died, but he did not recant.

I believe this is what so disappointed Freud about Ferenczi, that he knew a truth and, unlike Freud, would not give it up. This seems to be what Ferenczi himself thought. For in his diary (May 1, 1932), he reveals an unknown side of Freud:

I remember certain remarks that Freud made in my presence, evidently counting on my discretion: "Patients are riffraff" (*Gesindel*). I believe that Freud originally truly believed in analysis; he followed Breuer with enthusiasm, occupied himself passionately and devotedly with helping neurotic patients (lying on the floor for hours when necessary next to a person in a hysterical crisis[!]), but he must have been first shaken, then sobered by certain experiences more or less the way Breuer was upon the relapse of his patient and as a result of the problem of countertransference which suddenly opened up before Breuer like an abyss. In Freud's case, this corresponds to the discovery of the mendacity of hysterics. Since this discovery, Freud no longer likes sick people. He returned to loving his orderly, cultured superego. Further proof that this is so is Freud's dislike of and expressions of disapproval directed at psychotics and perverts, in fact with respect to anything that is too abnormal . . .[40]

Ferenczi is here referring to Freud's disappointment when he became convinced that the "scenes" of seduction which he had originally believed to be true were lies. But there was no reason to be disappointed, for nobody had lied to Freud. The disappointment is Freud's own inability to believe his patients, for they were telling him the truth. The lies came from Freud and the whole psychoanalytic movement. Ferenczi, in 1932, was the one man who would have no part of this lie.

The following fragment is the only indication that Ferenczi knew that his dispute with Freud would hasten his death. It comes from the unpublished diary that Ferenczi kept during the last few months of his life.

OCT. 10, 1932

The moment I realized that not only could I not count on the protection of a "higher power" [Freud], but on the contrary, would be destroyed by this indifferent power as soon as I went my way instead of his, I developed pernicious anemia [lit. "blood-crisis"]. The insight which this experience led me to, was that I was only courageous (and capable of achievement) as long as (unconsciously) I leaned on this power, so that really I was never a "grown-up." Scientific achievements, marriage, disagreements with strong colleagues — all of this was only possible under the protection of the idea that I could, under all circumstances, depend on my father-surrogate. Was it this identification with the "higher power," this instantaneous formation of a superego, the support that in the past kept me from total collapse? Is the only possibility of my continued existence the giving-up of the greater part of my own self in order to carry out the will of this "higher power" (as if it were my own)?

Just as I must now build new red blood-cells, so, too, if I can, must I create a new character-basis for myself, giving up the old one as false and unreliable? Am I faced with the choice, at 59, of dying, or refurbishing myself? On the other hand, does it make any sense to do nothing but live the life (or will) of another person? Is not this life nearly a death? If I risk this life, do I lose much? Who knows? . . . I have just this minute received a friendly personal letter from Jones. . . . I cannot deny that even this pleased me. For I felt abandoned by my colleagues . . . , all of whom had too much fear of Freud to be objective in a dispute between Freud and me or even to show me any personal sympathy.

CONCLUSION

BETWEEN 1897 and 1903, Freud came to believe that the case of his early patient Emma Eckstein was typical: most (though not all) of his women patients had deceived themselves and him. Their memories of seduction were nothing more than fantasies, or memories of fantasies—they were products of the Oedipus complex, part of normal childhood sexuality.

The new world that opened up to Freud with this "discovery" was a remarkable one and permitted him to make a large number of genuine discoveries that have retained their value over the years: the sexual and emotional passions of childhood, the reality of the unconscious, the nature of transference and resistance, repression, unconscious fantasies, the power of unconscious emotions, a need to repeat early sorrows, and so on.

The question whether psychoanalysis could have emerged had Freud retained his earlier belief that the memories of his patients were real, not fantasies, is hardly peripheral to the practice of psychoanalysis (and perhaps to the practice of psychotherapy in general, since most therapies are based, openly or implicitly, on Freudian theory). Psychoanalysts, beginning with Freud himself, agree that the abandonment of the seduction theory was the central stimulus to Freud's later discoveries. The original existence and the persistence of psychoanalysis are, by universal agreement, linked to the abandonment of the seduction theory. The preceding chapters have been concerned with the influences that came to bear on Freud, leading him away from the initial and unpopular insights he gained concerning the reality of abuse, physical and sexual, of children. I adduce a large number of new facts that were unknown before, or simply unnoticed, to support my opinion that Freud gave up this theory, not for theoretical or clinical reasons, but because of a personal failure of courage. I do not think that Freud ever made a conscious decision to ignore his earlier experiences or that he ever recognized what he did as a failure of courage. No doubt he believed he was doing the right thing, and the difficult thing, when he shifted his attention from external trauma to internal fantasy as the causative agent in mental illness. But that does not mean it represents the truth.

In fact, in my opinion, Freud had abandoned an important truth: the sexual, physical, and emotional violence that is a real and tragic part of the lives of many children. If this abandoned truth was to be erased from the history of psychoanalysis (it was certainly there at the beginning), traces of it would also have to be removed from the later theory. This was a task best left to the psychoanalysts who came after Freud. I believe they have succeeded: by and large most analysts would not agree with Freud's insights that in my view are implicit in the 1896 paper "The Aetiology of Hysteria" — that many (probably most) of their patients had violent and unhappy childhoods, not because of some defect in their character, but because of something terrible that had been done to them by their parents. If this etiological formula is true, and if it is further true that such events form the core of every serious neurosis, then it would be impossible to achieve a successful cure of a neurosis if this central event were ignored. I am inclined to accept the views of many recent authors, Florence Rush, Alice Miller, Judith Herman, and Louise Armstrong, among others, that the incidence of sexual violence in the early lives of children is much higher than generally acknowledged (Diana Russell believes it to be as high as one in every three women in the general population; it is undoubtedly higher among women who seek psychotherapy). But whether it is openly stated or merely accepted as a hidden theoretical premise, the analyst who sees such a patient is trained to believe that her memories are fantasies. As such, the analyst, no matter how benevolent otherwise, does violence to the inner life of his patient and is in covert collusion with what made her ill in the first place.

Genuine psychological discoveries—the unconscious, for example—cannot be properly used in such an atmosphere. No doubt much of the humiliation, hurt, and rage of the abused child would, in order for that child to survive, have to be repressed. If the analyst did not believe in the reality of events that would cause such emotions, he would have to ascribe the feelings to some inexplicable constitutional defect in the patient (a greater than usual need to be loved, for example). The entire analysis would be skewed. The irrational feelings that the patient develops for the analyst (the transference) would become inexplicable, since they would be rationally based on rage at the analyst for behaving like a parent who denied what he or she had done to the child. This is not a transference; it is a dim awareness of something that was done to the patient in childhood surfacing in the adult. Though rational and justified, such emotions would escape the comprehension of the analyst. In such an atmosphere, treatment could be "successful" only if the patient suppressed her (or his) own knowledge of her past, and began to believe, with the analyst, that she was in the throes of inexplicable emotions. To become healthy the patient would have to come to share the view of the analyst, in a word, to become more like him, or more like what the analyst would like her to become. This would involve denying the patient's very self. It spells the death of the patient's independence and freedom. The silence demanded of the child by the person who violated her (or him) is perpetuated and enforced by the very person to whom she has come for help. Guilt entrenches itself, the uncertainty of one's past deepens, and the sense of who one is is undermined.

Free and honest retrieval of painful memories cannot occur in the face of skepticism and fear of the truth. If the analyst is frightened of the real history of his own science, he will never be able to face the past of any of his patients. Freud's announcement of his new discoveries in the 1896 address on the etiology of hysteria met with no reasoned refutation or scientific discussion, only disgust and disavowal. The idea of sexual violence in the family was so emotionally charged that the only response it received was irrational distaste. Faced with his colleagues' hostility to his discoveries, Freud sacrificed his major insight. When Ferenczi, a generation later, was led by his patients to the same discovery, he met with a similar response, only this time Freud played the role that some forty years earlier had been Krafft-Ebing's. When, yet another forty years later, Robert Fliess urged upon the psychoanalytic community a re-examination of the theory of sexual trauma in childhood, he encountered the by now familiar response. In 1981 I attempted to call the attention of psychoanalysts to new evidence suggesting that the seduction theory deserved serious reconsideration. I too, like Freud, Ferenczi, and Robert Fliess, met with irrational antagonism and ostracism. I was challenged, not on the basis of my evidence, but because I had revealed this evidence. It seems clear that this recurring hostility was not based on any pre-existing animosity toward the individual proponent of the seduction theory, but has its source in an emotionally charged aversion to the truth of the theory itself.

The time has come to cease hiding from what is, after all,

one of the great issues of human history. For it is unforgivable that those entrusted with the lives of people who come to them in emotional pain, having suffered real wounds in childhood, should use their blind reliance on Freud's fearful abandonment of the seduction theory to continue the abuse their patients once suffered as children.

If it is not possible for the therapeutic community to address this serious issue in an honest and open-minded manner, then it is time for their patients to stop subjecting themselves to needless repetition of their deepest and earliest sorrow.

AFTERWORD

DID FREUD *REALLY* ABANDON THE SEDUCTION THEORY?

AMONG THE many criticisms that have been made of my book, the one that seems to have impressed the public the most is the often-repeated assertion that I have misled people into believing that Freud entirely rejected the seduction hypothesis in favor of fantasy. The criticism is that Freud did indeed give up the *theory* of seduction, but never ceased to believe that seduction played an important role in the origins of neurosis, though by no means an exclusive one. I have been accused of leaving out those passages in Freud's later writings in which he definitely asserts the existence of real seductions and speaks of their tragic consequences.

I would like to take this opportunity to clarify this matter, since we are not talking about opinions here, but facts, and they should not be impossible to ascertain. Let us, therefore, examine those passages in the twenty-four volumes of Freud that deal with sexual seductions and their role in neurosogenesis. I do not repeat the passages already cited in the book unless I explicitly state this. In the 1916 *Introductory Lectures on Psycho-Analysis (S.E.* 16, p. 370) Freud writes:

> Phantasies of being seduced are of particular interest, because so often they are not phantasies but real memories. Fortunately, however, they are nevertheless not real as often as seemed at first to be

shown by the findings of analysis. Seduction by an older child or by one of the same age is even more frequent than by an adult; and if in the case of girls who produce such an event in the story of their childhood their father figures fairly regularly as the seducer, there can be no doubt either of the imaginary nature of the accusation or of the motive that has led to it. A phantasy of being seduced when no seduction has occurred is usually employed by a child to screen the auto-erotic period of his sexual activity. He spares himself shame about masturbation by retrospectively phantasying a desired object into these earliest times. You must not suppose, however, that sexual abuse of a child by its nearest male relatives belongs entirely to the realm of phantasy. Most analysts will have treated cases in which such events were real and could be unimpeachably established; but even so they related to the later years of childhood and had been transposed into earlier times.

In this passage Freud certainly says that seductions occur. But note that he does not actually say "so often they are not phantasies," as Strachey translates, but in fact writes: *nur zu oft*, that is, "all too often." But then Freud goes on to lessen the impact of this admission by saying that the father can never be guilty and that if the girl accuses him, it is clearly only a fantasy. Now we know precisely the opposite: that the vast majority of sexual assaults on children happen to girls, and that they are often done by fathers or step-fathers. Freud, as I have shown in chapter two of my book, most likely knew the frequency with which fathers were guilty of this crime. He just didn't talk about it, except, as we shall see, in a single footnote. Moreover, Freud goes on to say that in the cases of boys, when such events do happen, they presumably only occur in the later years of childhood and not earlier. We know now that the average age is eight, and Freud, too, knew that many of these rapes happened in very early childhood (as his letters to Fliess prove beyond any doubt). But Freud's conclusion, stated in this essay and quoted in my book, is (to cite a passage I did not quote, from page 368): "Phantasies possess *psychical* as contrasted with *material* reality, and we gradually learn to understand that *in the world of the neuroses it is psychical reality which is the decisive kind* [emphasis in original]."

Then in 1924, in a footnote to the Katharina case, Freud acknowledged that the seducer was not the uncle, as he had stated in the printed text, but the father. I quote this passage in my book. It certainly does not show that Freud accorded the father any particular significance in the etiology of the neuroses, but only that he felt guilty for having suppressed this information. Again in 1924, in a footnote he added to the 1896 paper, "The Neuro-Psychoses of Defence," in which he had spoken at length of the reality of seduction, he writes (*S.E.* 3, p. 168):

> This section is dominated by an error which I have since repeatedly acknowledged and corrected. At that time I was not yet able to distinguish between my patients' phantasies about their childhood years and their real recollections. As a result, I attributed to the aetiological factor of seduction a significance and universality which it does not possess. When this error had been overcome, it became possible to obtain an insight into the spontaneous manifestations of the sexuality of children which I described in my *Three Essays on the Theory of Sexuality* (1905). Nevertheless, we need not reject everything written in the text above. Seduction retains a certain aetiological importance, and even to-day I think some of these psychological comments are to the point.

But if this passage indicates that Freud reassigned significance to the etiological importance of seduction, then we would have to find it in his later work. Does it in fact appear? Let us continue to examine the *only* passages on seduction in the later Freud. In fact, what Freud meant by this passage is clearly explained in his 1925 *Autobiographical Study* (*S.E.* 20, pp. 33–34), which contains his most carefully thought-out explanation for his early belief in the etiological significance of seduction. The passage is critical and deserves to be quoted in full:

> Before going further into the question of infantile sexuality I must

mention an error into which I fell for a while and which might well have had fatal consequences for the whole of my work. Under the influence of the technical procedure which I used at that time, the majority of my patients reproduced from their childhood scenes in which they were sexually seduced by some grown-up person. With female patients the part of seducer was almost always assigned to their father. I believed these stories, and consequently supposed that I had discovered the roots of the subsequent neurosis in these experiences of sexual seduction in childhood. My confidence was strengthened by a few cases in which relations of this kind with a father, uncle, or elder brother had continued up to an age at which memory was to be trusted. If the reader feels inclined to shake his head at my credulity, I cannot altogether blame him; though I may plead that this was at a time when I was intentionally keeping my critical faculty in abeyance so as to preserve an unprejudiced and receptive attitude towards the many novelties which were coming to my notice every day. When, however, I was at last obliged to recognize that these scenes of seduction had never taken place, and that they were only phantasies which my patients had made up or which I myself had perhaps forced on them, I was for some time completely at a loss . . . neurotic symptoms were not related directly to actual events but to wishful phantasies, and that as far as the neurosis was concerned psychical reality was of more importance than material reality. I do not believe even now that I forced the seduction-phantasies on my patients, that I 'suggested' them. I had in fact stumbled for the first time upon the *Oedipus complex,* which was later to assume such an overwhelming importance, but which I did not recognize as yet in its disguise of phantasy. Morever, seduction during childhood retained a certain share, though a humbler one, in the aetiology of neuroses. But the seducers turned out as a rule to have been older children.

Clearly, by his own admission, Freud is turning his interest away from real traumas, to the nature and significance of fantasy. Freud says explicitly, that from now on, for him, fantasy is *more* important than reality. And this statement is certainly borne out by his later writings. He does not, in any of his twenty-three volumes of collected writings, concentrate on reality after the 1896 papers. A few years later, in 1931, in his essay "Female Sexuality" (*S.E.* 21, p. 238) Freud writes what Strachey (p. 238, footnote 1) calls "the last phase of a long story":

> The women patients showing a strong attachment to their mother in which I have been able to study the pre-Oedipus phase have all told me that when their mother gave them enemas or rectal douches they used to offer the greatest resistance and react with fear and screams of rage. . . . In regard to the passive impulses of the phallic phase, it is noteworthy that girls regularly accuse their mother of seducing them. This is because they necessarily received their first, or at any rate their strongest, genital sensations when they were being cleaned and having their toilet attended to by their mother. . . . The fact that the mother thus unavoidably initiates the child into the phallic phase is, I think, the reason why, in fantasies of later years, the father so regularly appears as the sexual seducer. When the girl turns away from her mother, she also makes over to her father her introduction into sexual life.

Now it is clear what Freud meant by the real share of seduction — he regarded it as inevitable, and quite other than the kinds of criminal acts he originally described. Moreover, fathers recede ever further into the background. Freud either no longer believed, or was no longer prepared to say, that fathers often rape their daughters. The final mention of the theory of seduction occurs, appropriately enough, in the 1933 *New Introductory Lectures,* in the lecture on femininity (*S.E.* 22, p. 120):

> You will recall an interesting episode in the history of analytic research which caused me many distressing hours. In the period in which the main interest was directed to discovering infantile sexual traumas, almost all my women patients told me that they had been seduced by their father. I was driven to recognize in the end that these reports were untrue and so came to understand that hysterical symptoms are derived from phantasies and not from real occurrences. It was only later that I was able to recognize in this phantasy of being seduced by the father the expression of the typical Oedipus complex

in women. And now we find the phantasy of seduction once more in the pre-Oedipus prehistory of girls; but the seducer is regularly the mother. Here, however, the phantasy touches the ground of reality, for it was really the mother who by her activities over the child's bodily hygiene inevitably stimulated, and perhaps even roused for the first time, pleasurable sensations in her genitals.

This is Freud's last word on the theory of seduction.[1] Not only does he repeat here that the early reports were simply *untrue*; he also deprives his women patients even further of their real memories: for he has decided for them that when they do tell him what their mothers did to them, these memories should be translated into fantasies, and that nothing happened that was not entirely usual and normal. It is clear from this passage, written towards the end of his life, that Freud looked upon his earlier belief in the significance of seduction as an error, and that he was not prepared to accept as real memories from his women patients in which *either* men or women were accused of real sexual assault on children.

In the light of these passages, I do not believe that I distorted Freud's views, or led my readers to believe that Freud had renounced a theory he in fact continued to believe in, though to a modified extent. I think Freud's words are perfectly clear and unambiguous, but each reader can judge for him or herself whether I have misled anyone.

---

[1] There is some evidence that at the very end of his life (in 1938) Freud once again was inclined to assign significance to sexual traumas in the genesis of neuroses, but the passages are too sketchy to permit any definitive conclusion (see *S.E.* 23, pp. 75–76, and 187).

NOTES

German and French editions of this work, containing source material in the original languages, are being published by Rowohlt Verlag and Aubier Montaigne, respectively.

ABBREVIATIONS

G.W.   Sigmund Freud, *Gesammelte Werke* (Collected Works), edited by Anna Freud, with the collaboration of Marie Bonaparte, E. Bibring, W. Hoffer, E. Kris, and O. Isakower (18 vols.; London: Imago Publishing Co., 1940–1952).

Int. J. Psycho-Anal.   *International Journal of Psycho-Analysis*

Int. Z. Psychoanal.   *Internationale Zeitschrift für Psychoanalyse*

Jones   Ernest Jones, *Sigmund Freud: Life and Work* (3 vols.; New York: Basic Books, 1954–1957).

Origins   Sigmund Freud, *The Origins of Psychoanalysis: Letters to Wilhelm Fliess, Drafts and Notes: 1887–1902*, edited by Marie Bonaparte, Anna Freud, and Ernst Kris, authorized translation by Eric Mosbacher (letters) and James Strachey (drafts), introduction by Ernst Kris (New York: Basic Books, 1954).

S.E.   *The Standard Edition of the Complete Psychological Works of Sigmund Freud*, translated from the German under the general editorship of James Strachey, in collaboration with Anna Freud, assisted by Alix Strachey and Alan Tyson (24 vols.; London: Hogarth Press and the Institute of Psycho-Analysis, 1953–1974).

1. "The Aetiology of Hysteria"

1. "The Aetiology of Hysteria," *S.E.*, 3, pp. 191–221. For the German text, I have used *Gesammelte Werke* (Collected Works), edited by Anna Freud, with the collaboration of Marie Bonaparte,

E. Bibring, W. Hoffer, E. Kris, and O. Isakower (4th ed.; Frankfurt am Main: Fischer, 1972), I, pp. 425–459.

2. *S.E.*, 14, p. 21.

3. My translation of this passage (cf. *G.W.*, I, p. 452) differs somewhat from that given by Strachey, reproduced in Appendix B.

4. Max Schur, *Freud: Living and Dying* (New York: International Universities Press, 1972), p. 104.

5. *S.E.*, 3, p. 204. The German reads: *"höchst ungern erinnerte Realität,"* so the translation should read: "and remembered with the greatest reluctance."

6. *S.E.*, 3, p. 199.

7. On February 4, 1888, at the beginning of their correspondence, Freud wrote to Fliess:

> Honorable Christendom is very indecent. Yesterday there was a major scandal in the Medical Society. They wanted to force us to subscribe to a new weekly journal which is intended to represent the purified, exact, and Christian views of a few Hofräthe [high civil servants] who have long ago forgotten what work is like. Of course, they are succeeding; I feel very much like resigning. (*The Origins of Psychoanalysis*; first sentence omitted)

The journal in question was the *Wiener klinische Wochenschrift*, the first issue of which appeared on April 5, 1888. The vote in favor of subscribing was 93 to 29, with Freud, evidently, among those who rejected the proposal. In 1931 Freud was elected an honorary member of the very same society, and in fact never resigned. As far as I know, the April 21, 1896, meeting of the Society for Psychiatry and Neurology was reported in only one other journal, *Neurologisches Zentralblatt*, 15 (1896), pp. 709–710, but Freud's paper is not even mentioned there by title.

8. *Wiener klinische Rundschau*, 10 (1896), (22) pp. 379–381, (23) pp. 395–397, (24) pp. 413–415, (25) pp. 432–433, and (26) pp. 450–452 (May 31, June 7, 14, 21, and 28).

9. "An Autobiographical Study" (1925), *S.E.*, 20, p. 34 (*G.W.*, 14, p. 59).

10. *Ibid.* This is the strongest statement Freud was ever to make about the unreality of these events. By and large it has been followed by analysts ever since.

11. This was reported in a meeting of the Vienna Psycho-

analytic Society, January 24, 1912. The English version of the Society's proceedings, published in four volumes, is *Minutes of the Vienna Psychoanalytic Society*, edited by H. Nunberg and E. Federn, translated by Marianne Nunberg in collaboration with Harold Collines (New York: International Universities Press, 1962–1975). The account of this meeting is in vol. 4: *1912–1918*.

12. "On the History of the Psycho-Analytic Movement" (1914) (*S.E.*, 14, p. 13) and "An Autobiographical Study" (1925) (*S.E.*, 20, p. 13).

2. Freud at the Paris Morgue

1. Freud's obituary of Charcot was published on September 9, 1893, a few days after his death, in the *Wiener klinische Wochenschrift*, 43 (37), pp. 1513–1520, and is translated in *S.E.*, 3, pp. 11–23. Strachey (*S.E.*, 3, p. 9) says of Freud's work at the Salpêtrière: "This was the turning point in his career, for it was during this period that his interest shifted from neuropathology to psychopathology— from physical science to psychology. Whatever other and deeper factors were concerned in this change, the immediate determinant was undoubtedly the personality of Charcot." In the obituary (p. 17) Freud writes: "Charcot was positively fascinating. Each of his lectures was a little work of art in construction and composition; it was perfect in form and made such an impression that for the rest of the day one could not get the sound of what he had said out of one's ears or the thought of what he had demonstrated out of one's mind."

2. *Annales d'hygiène publique et de médecine légale*, 2nd ser., 13 (1860), pp. 361–398. All page references are to this first edition. The article was reprinted, more or less word for word, in Tardieu's book *Etude médico-légale sur les blessures* (A Forensic Study of Wounds) (Paris: J. B. Baillière, 1879), pp. 69–109.

3. *Dictionnaire encyclopédique des sciences médicales*, 3rd ser., 15 (1885), s.v. This article also contains a long list of publications. The *Catalogue général des livres imprimés de la Bibliothèque Nationale* (vol. 182) lists his major works; there are some 59 entries in the *National Union Catalogue*. There is a long article on Tardieu's

achievements in the *Grand Dictionnaire universel du 19 siècle* (Larousse), 14 (1875), p. 1472. *La Grande Encyclopédie*, 30, p. 933, says of him: "*Il a donné une grande impulsion aux études médicales, et a su traiter avec un tact parfait les affaires médico-légales les plus épineuses.*" There is an obituary by Paul Brouardel in *Annales d'hygiène publique et de médecine légale*, 3rd ser., 1 (1879), pp. 187–192. There is more about his teaching and publications in an article by L. Thoinot, "Histoire de la chaire de médecine légale de la faculté de Paris, 1795–1906," *Annales d'hygiène publique et de médecine légale*, 4th ser., 6 (1906), pp. 482–549. Chauffard, in an obituary published in *L'Union médicale*, 27 (1879), pp. 81–87, mentions that Tardieu had kept a notebook listing all the police reports he had made, and they numbered 5,239. His most famous books are the immense tome he wrote with Z. Roussin, *Etude médico-légale et clinique sur l'empoisonnement* (Paris: J. B. Baillière, 1867), and the three-volume *Dictionnaire d'hygiène publique et de salubrité* (Paris: J. B. Baillière, 1852–1854). Of interest to psychology is his *Etude médico-légale sur l'avortement, suivie d'observations et de recherches pour servir à l'histoire médico-légale des grossesses fausses et simulées* (Paris: J. B. Baillière, 1856), which went into three editions, and his later book, *Etude médico-légale sur l'infanticide* (Paris: J. B. Baillière, 1868), which, strangely enough, makes no use of the material from his 1860 article on the brutal treatment of children. His book on insanity, *Etude médico-légale sur la folie* (Paris: J. B. Baillière, 1872), is somewhat disappointing, though it does contain one fascinating case history (p. 172) of a beautiful young aristocratic Austrian woman, at the end of which Tardieu speaks of the "instinctive irresistible impulses that certain hysterical women fall prey to."

4. Both Tardieu's article on cruelty inflicted on children and his book on *attentats* were preceded by the work of Adolphe Toulmouche (1798–?), professor of medicine and pharmacy in Rennes and also a well-known archaeologist. In 1856 he published a long article in *Annales d'hygiène publique et de médecine légale* (2nd ser., 6, pp. 100–145) entitled "Des Attentats à la pudeur et du viol," which, together with another article in the same journal (22 [1864], pp. 333–383), entitled "Des Attentats à la pudeur: des tentatives de viol sur des enfants ou des filles à peine nubiles et sur des adultes, et des grossesses simulées ou réelles suivies ou non d'infanticides, particularités pratiques," was published in book form by J. B. Baillière in Paris in 1864. Toulmouche begins his 1856 article by stating:

Cases of attempted rape, of erotic acts against children or young girls, called in legal terms "assault on morals," being extremely frequent in large population centers and even in the country, it is important to be well aware of the nature of these criminal attempts. I will, therefore, devote the first part of this paper to their investigation and I will reveal what the experience of twenty-eight years of providing expert opinion to the courts has taught me in this respect.

Toulmouche is the first to point out (p. 102) that a sexual act can take place without leaving any trace, and that, especially on very young girls, seductive acts may be limited to rubbing and touching the genitals or may go as far as an attempt at intromission, but without success: "the legal physician should not conclude that attempted rape has not taken place, but only that the act of copulation was not entirely completed" (p. 104). Unlike Tardieu, however, Toulmouche rarely informs us who the perpetrator of the crime is, generally calling him simply *le prévenu* (the accused). In one case, though (p. 129), which caused a great public stir, a wealthy man was accused of raping his two-and-a-half-year-old daughter, and indeed Toulmouche was called upon by the court to examine the child and discovered that she was venereally infected. Tardieu, who by and large ignores other writers, even in later editions of his book, praises Toulmouche. In the 1860 article as well, he cites as his only predecessor an article by Toulmouche which appeared in *Annales d'hygiène publique et de médecine légale* (1st ser., 50 [1853], pp. 424–449), entitled "Considérations médico-légales sur deux cas assez rares d'aberration mentale." The second case (p. 437), which may indeed be the first ever reported of a sadistic assault on a young child, is that of a four-year-old girl who was whipped by her godfather, on November 23, 1838, from two o'clock in the afternoon until nightfall, and then more or less continuously over the next three days. Her godfather was "teaching her to count." She was asked to count the strokes of the whip as they fell on her, until "the sheets were covered in blood, the poor victim cried out miserably for a long time, then lost all strength, was completely motionless, and shortly thereafter died" (p. 438). Toulmouche notes that the medical expert did not examine the genitals of the young girl, and it is clear that he suspects that she was raped as well. On p. 441 he speaks of the effects the "terrible emotions and the continual pain and fear" had in causing "a profound depression of her entire sensibilities." For during the trial the defense argued that nobody ever died of pain (p. 443). Of particular interest is the discussion of the behavior of the godfather and his comments, which Toulmouche reproduces. He seemed to have no interest in the proceedings, looking impassive the entire time, mainly occupying himself by cutting licorice sticks into small pieces. Nevertheless, he often consulted his notes, and when his time to speak came, he "spoke at great length and in minute detail about the lies of the child." He only betrayed emotion when his lawyer spoke of the great affection his client had for the little girl, keeping a lock of her hair in a billfold next to his heart. The memory of his own affection caused tears to come to his eyes for the only time during his trial. Strictly speaking, then, Toulmouche can be credited with being the first to write about both these areas.

5. However, a doctoral thesis was published in France by Dominique Rabouille, *Les Jeunes Enfants victimes de sévices corporels*: Thèse pour obtenir le grade de docteur en médecine, Université de Nancy, Faculté de Médecine, no. 55 (Paris: Imprimerie R. Vancon, 1968), which mentions Tardieu. More important is the Rigler Lecture by Frederic N. Silverman, emeritus professor of pediatrics and radiology at Stanford University, "Unrecognized Trauma in Infants, the Battered Child Syndrome, and the Syndrome of Ambroise Tardieu," *Radiology*, 104 (1972), pp. 337–353. There Silverman writes (p. 350):

> The article [by Tardieu] appears to be the first in which the concept of the battered child, as presented by Kempe et al., 101 years later, was clearly stated, with demographic, social, psychiatric, and medical features identical to those in Kempe's and most subsequent studies.

He further states:

> With his recognition of "excuses habitually employed" by the abusers, and the discrepancy between the explanation offered and the lesions observed, Tardieu certainly takes his place ahead of those whose names have been linked with the syndrome. All of these, I am sure, would be pleased to yield their claims to identification with the syndrome to the prior claim which should justify the designation "The Syndrome of Ambroise Tardieu."

Neither Silverman nor Rabouille discusses any possible link with Freud and psychoanalysis.

6. E.g., Paul Brouardel's *L'Infanticide* (Paris: J. B. Baillière, 1897), which is primarily about abortion, does not cite Tardieu's article on child abuse, and in fact does not mention cruelty to children at all. Here he follows G. Tourde's article on infanticide in *Dictionnaire encyclopédique des sciences médicales* (1889), pp. 642–672, s.v.

7. The term *attentat aux moeurs* literally means "offense against morals" and comprises indecent exposure, attempted rape, and rape.

8. The book went through seven editions: 1857, 1858, 1859, 1862, 1867, 1873, and 1878. The first edition contained 176 pages; the last, 296 pages. There was a German translation of the third edition, *Die Vergehen gegen die Sittlichkeit in staatsärztlicher Beziehung*, translated by W. Thiele (Weimar: Voigt, 1860), which was widely cited in the German literature and clearly influenced Krafft-Ebing.

9. Nowhere in the literature of the time was I able to find mention of the psychological consequences of such violence on the later emotional life of the child, with one exception (apart from Freud's 1896 papers). That was Charles Samson Féré (1852–1907), in his *L'Instinct sexuel: évolution et dissolution* (Paris: Felix Alcan, 1899), a copy of which Freud owned. Féré mentions the work done on *attentats aux moeurs*, citing Tardieu, Brouardel, and Lacassagne. In chapter 12, "Education et hygiène sexuelles," Féré shows a great deal more understanding than other authors of his time in recognizing the long-term effects of early traumas, and the fact that they work below the surface of conscious memory. See in particular pp. 274, 291, and 296–297.

10. *Catalogue du Fond Lacassagne*, edited by Cl. Roux, Bibliothèque de la Ville de Lyon (Lyon: Imprimerie Nouvelle Lyonnaise, 1922). Manuscripts are listed as well. Curiously enough, not a single work by Freud is contained in the collection.

11. *Archives d'anthropologie criminelle et des sciences pénales*, 1 (1886), pp. 59–68. Lacassagne is also the author of a well-known textbook, *Précis de médecine légale*, written in collaboration with Etienne Martin (3rd ed.; Paris: Masson, 1921). The fifth chapter of that book is "Des Questions relatives à l'instinct sexuel et

aux fonctions de reproduction," and pp. 579–627 deal with *attentats aux moeurs*.

12. *Archives d'anthropologie criminelle et des sciences pénales*, 1 (1886), pp. 396–436.

13. Laboratoire de Médecine Légale de Lyon (Paris: Octave Doin, 1886). On the title page is the following quotation from Alfred Fournier:

> We will deal with sad things and with sad people, but public interest demands that both occupy our attention. This is a duty that the medical doctor must not shirk, for the very business of the physician is to be a witness to such shameful events.

In my opinion Bernard is citing this passage with a different interpretation than the one Fournier intended when he wrote it. For Fournier, the shameful events were the lies told by children; for Bernard, the shameful events are the deeds of adults, genuine traumas from the external world.

14. A more elaborate discussion of this problem is by L. Penard, "De l'Intervention du médecin-légiste dans les questions d'attentats aux moeurs," *Annales d'hygiène publique et de médecine légale*, 2nd ser., 14 (1860), pp. 130–205, 345–405. The only duty of the physician reporting to the courts, Penard says, is to bring the truth to light, and in order to do this "he must remain impartial, not allowing his convictions to be moved by any more or less pathetic incident he hears of, in a word, remaining completely impervious to the movements of passion" (p. 405).

15. E. Gley: "Les Aberrations de l'instinct sexuel," *Revue philosophique*, 17 (1884), p. 66. The article is a review of the literature on this subject, including the paper by Charcot and Magnan. On p. 91 he cites Tardieu, "who provided a justly famous portrait of men addicted to this vice." In effect, nearly half of Tardieu's book on *attentats aux moeurs* is devoted to homosexuality.

16. *S.E.*, 7, p. 143 n.

17. This article appeared in two parts, the first in *Archives de neurologie*, 7 (Jan.–Feb. 1882), pp. 53–60, and the second (with the full title, which was partially omitted in the first part) on pp. 296–322. Magnan was also a leading figure in the French tradition of the theory of degeneration and inherited dispositions. Freud had in his personal library a copy of Magnan and M. Legrain's *Les Dégénérés*

(Paris: Rueff, 1895), which he took with him to London, along with Magnan's psychiatric lectures.

18. *Annales médico-psychologiques*, 7th ser., 1 (1885), p. 455: "For the last eight years she has felt an irresistible need to sleep with one of her young nephews." There were, in fact, five nephews, and she felt the same compulsion to sleep with each of them until he reached the age of puberty, at which time she would switch her affection to the next younger one.

19. Published in *Progrès médical*, 2nd ser., 1 (1885), pp. 49–50, 65–68, 84–86. Also note Magnan's article, "Obsession et impulsion génitale," *Journal de médecine et de chirurgie pratique*, 54 (1883), pp. 21–25, which provides the curious story of a man who, from a very early age (five or six), was sexually aroused by the sight of a night bonnet, especially on the head of an older, and preferably ugly, woman. This sexual peculiarity stayed with him the rest of his life. Even in his marriage to a young and beautiful woman, he could only have an ejaculation by conjuring up the image of the night bonnet. In all these cases one sees the French authors approaching some understanding of the genesis of this form of perversion, namely an early sexual experience with a forbidden object, yet none of them actually is able to take this step, with the possible exception of Féré. Magnan, in this article (p. 24), even provides the hint:

> But his obsession goes back to his childhood; then, for a long time, he shared the bed of one of his relatives who was much older than he. He became aware that the mere sight of the night bonnet that his companion wore brought about some genital excitement. Later he often observed an old servant undress herself and put on a night bonnet. This similar sight produced the same effect, and later on the thought of an old and ugly face, but adorned with that bonnet, was enough to stimulate his sexual organ.

20. *Psychiatrische Vorlesungen von V. Magnan*, translated by P. J. Möbius (6 vols.; Leipzig: Georg Thieme, 1890–1894).

21. *Der Hypnotismus und die verwandten Zustände vom Standpunkte der gerichtlichen Medicin*, foreword by J. M. Charcot (Hamburg: A.-G. Richert, 1889), *Traité clinique et thérapeutique de l'hystérie, d'après l'enseignement de la Salpêtrière* (3 vols.; Paris: E. Plon, Nourrit, 1891–1895), and finally *Les Etats neurasthéniques*,

formes cliniques, traitement diagnostique (Paris: J. B. Baillière, 1898).

22. Published in *Bulletin de la société de médecine légale de France*, 9 (1887), pp. 380–399. On p. 67 of *Les Attentats aux moeurs* (1909; but note that the reference is to an event that took place in 1885), Brouardel cites from his student Gilles de la Tourette a case that Brouardel examined on December 29, 1885, in which he claimed that the woman was a hysteric and invented the rape. It is likely that Freud heard of this case when he attended Brouardel's classes over the next few months.

23. There is no study of Brouardel's life or work. Some biographical information is to be found in the *Dictionnaire de biographie française* (edited by Prevost and D'Amat), vol. 7 (1956). See also *La Grande Encyclopédie*, vol. 8, s.v. There is a long obituary by the successor to Brouardel's chair, Léon Thoinot, published in *Annales d'hygiène publique et de médecine légale* (which Brouardel founded), 4th ser., 6 (1906), pp. 193–245. According to Thoinot (p. 197) Brouardel gave his demonstrations at the morgue on Wednesdays, his assistants Descoust and Vibert on Mondays and Fridays. The subject was always a real one, e.g., infanticide, and not, as Thoinot emphasizes, "fictive." Like Charcot, Brouardel was interested in hypnotism, as we see from his article "Viol accompli pendant le sommeil hypnotique" (Rape Committed during Hypnotic Sleep), *Annales d'hygiène publique et de médecine légale*, 3rd ser., 1 (1879). A small book of his which brought him to the attention of the public was entitled *Le Secret médical* (Publications de Médecine Légale à la Faculté de Médecine de Paris) (Paris: J. B. Baillière, 1887). On p. 160 of that book he reports the case of "two brothers, seven and nine, infected with anal pustules, obvious signs of sexual assaults and of the transmission of syphilis." See also his "Signes attribués à la pédérastie," *Annales d'hygiène publique et de médecine légale*, 3rd ser., 4 (1880). Lacassagne published an obituary of Brouardel in his *Archives d'anthropologie criminelle*, 21 (1906), pp. 759–764. For a list of obituaries of Brouardel, see *Index Catalogue of the Library of the Surgeon General's Office*, 2nd ser., 3 (1922), s.v.

24. Quoted in Jaroslav Nemec, *Highlights in Medicolegal Relations*, DHEW Pub. no. 76–1109 (Washington: Superintendent of Documents, 1976).

25. Paul Brouardel, on p. 294 of his article "Institut Médico-

légal de l'Université de Paris," *Annales d'hygiène publique et de médecine légale*, 3rd ser., 50 (1903), pp. 289–297.

26. First printed in J. and R. Gicklhorn's *Sigmund Freuds akademische Laufbahn im Lichte der Dokumente* (Vienna: Urban und Schwarzenberg, 1960). Translated into English in *S.E.*, 1, pp. 3–15.

27. *Letters of Sigmund Freud, 1873–1939*, edited by Ernst L. Freud, translated by Tania and James Stern (New York: Basic Books, 1961). Cf. *La Gazette de France*, Thursday, January 22, 1886, under the heading *Faits Divers*, "*Le crime de la rue de Charenton.*"

28. The preface appeared in the 1913 German edition, and is translated into English in *S.E.*, 12, p. 335.

29. *S.E.*, 14, pp. 13–14.

30. P. Brouardel, *Les Attentats aux moeurs*, preface by Professor Thoinot (Paris: J. B. Baillière, 1909). Brouardel, who died in 1906, seems to have written the book in 1905. But clearly many of the lectures go back to a much earlier date.

31. Cf. what Brouardel writes on p. 95: "Don't forget that parents always have the tendency to ascribe every nervous illness to an emotional experience. This is a fact of common observation and physicians in the Salpêtrière know it well." It is worth noting that Brouardel's book is permeated by his interest in mental illness, which is not true of the other books in this area of legal medicine. For example, on p. 8 he says that these crimes are caused very often by "*troubles mentaux.*" Cf. p. 92 of the same book.

32. Léon Henri Thoinot (1858–1915) was Brouardel's successor to the chair of legal medicine. He too wrote a book with the familiar title *Attentats aux moeurs et perversions du sens génital: leçons professées à la Faculté de Médecine*, compiled by E. Dupré (Paris: Doin, 1898). After that, the tradition seems to have died out.

33. Another thesis in the same tradition, written under Lacassagne's direction in Lyon, though Brouardel's cases are cited, is a short book by Paul Duval, *Des Sévices et mauvais traitements infligés aux enfants* (Cruelty and Brutality Inflicted on Children) (Lyon: A. Storck; Paris: G. Masson, 1885). (It is published in the series *Documents de criminologie et de médecine légale*.) Cf. Paul Moreau de Tours (1844–1908), *Suicides et crimes étranges* (Paris: Société d'Editions Scientifiques, 1899), especially pp. 108–140: "Attentats contre les enfants."

34. See K. R. Eissler, "Bericht über die sich in den Vereinigten Staaten befindenden Bücher aus S. Freuds Bibliothek," *Jahrbuch der Psychoanalyse*, 11 (1979), pp. 10–50. The Hinterberger catalogue is reprinted in that article, and also in Nolan D. C. Lewis and Carney Landis, "Freud's Library," *Psychoanalytic Review*, 44 (1957), pp. 327–358. A catalogue of the books that Freud took with him to London, and which are now housed at Maresfield Gardens, was published in Harry Trosman and Roger Dennis Simmons, "The Freud Library," *Journal of the American Psychoanalytic Association*, 21 (1973), pp. 646–687. However, this list is by no means complete; for some reason, many of the most important books in Freud's library are not included—e.g., only one book by Fliess is mentioned —whereas I found four books by Fliess in Freud's house. On the top of each shelf, the books are filed in double rows, and the authors may not have realized this. See also E. Harms, "A Fragment of Freud's Library," *Psychoanalytic Quarterly*, 40 (1971), pp. 491–495, and Hans Lobner, "Some Additional Remarks on Freud's Library," *Sigmund Freud Haus Bulletin*, 1 (1975), pp. 18–29. A convenient compilation of the above sources has been arranged by Gerhard Fichtner, *Die Bibliothek Sigmund Freuds nach den vorhandenen Verzeichnissen* (Tübingen, 1980), and can be had from the Institut für Geschichte der Medizin, Goethestrasse 6, Tübingen 7400.

35. The librarian was kind enough to send me Xeroxed copies of the Bernard book (which was not obtainable elsewhere in the United States) and the Brouardel book. There are no notations of any kind in the books.

36. The lecture was delivered on October 26, 1880. The article was published in *Annales d'hygiène publique et de médecine légale*, 3rd ser., 4 (1880), pp. 498–519.

37. It was published in *Annales médico-psychologiques*, 6th ser., 9–10 (1883), pp. 53–67, 374–386.

38. *Annales d'hygiène publique et de médecine légale*, 3rd ser., 17 (1887), pp. 481–496.

39. *Annales d'hygiène publique et de médecine légale*, 3rd ser., 50 (1903), pp. 337–437. A number of earlier articles and books by Garnier reflect these same views, which were widely shared by European psychiatrists.

3. Freud, Fliess, and Emma Eckstein

1. Ronald Clark, in *Freud: The Man and the Cause* (New York: Random House, 1980), p. 149, writes that "Irma's real name was Emma." It is likely that he took this from Paul Roazen's *Freud and His Followers* (New York: Alfred A. Knopf, 1976), p. 249: "In the early 1890's Fliess had operated on the nose of one of Freud's patients, Irma (Emma Eckstein)." Roazen cites as his source an interview he had with Alfred Hirst. I saw the interview, and Hirst does not actually state that Irma is Emma; this is Roazen's surmise. Didier Anzieu, in *L'Auto-analyse de Freud* (2nd ed.; Paris Presses Universitaires de France, 1975), 1, p. 190, suggests that Irma is Anna Hammerschlag. This is also Marianne Krüll's opinion in *Freud und sein Vater* (Munich: C. H. Beck, 1979), p. 37. Anna Hammerschlag was the godmother of Anna Freud. Her husband (Lichtheim) died after they were married for one year. She saw Freud very briefly shortly thereafter, which would explain why her name is never mentioned in the letters to Fliess. Anna Freud confirmed to me that she was "Irma." Cf. Jones (1, p. 245).

2. Halle an der Saale: Carl Marhold, 1902.

3. In several unpublished letters (e.g., September 29, 1893), Freud mentions a *"Policlinic"* that he evidently hoped to establish with Fliess.

4. "Some Additional 'Day Residues' of the Specimen Dream of Psychoanalysis," in *Psychoanalysis: A General Psychology—Essays in Honor of Heinz Hartmann*, edited by R. M. Loewenstein, Lottie M. Newman, Max Schur, and A. J. Solnit (New York: International Universities Press, 1966), pp. 45–85. Many of the letters about Emma Eckstein that follow in the text were first published by Schur in this important article. Unless so indicated, passages were first published by Schur.

It should be clear from what follows that Schur and I have reached very different conclusions about the significance of the material that Schur first revealed (the letters had been omitted from the published edition of the Freud/Fliess letters). For Schur, the Emma Eckstein incident reflected primarily on Freud's personal attachment to Fliess. (Cf. his book, pp. 79–80.) He thought that the incident shed new light on the dream theory, by widening the concept of the "day residue" (the event during the day preceding a dream which supplies the manifest content of the dream). While Schur believed that Emma Eckstein was the first patient who offered Freud a clue to his emerging "insight" that fantasies, not reality, lay at the heart of neurosis, thereby encouraging him to abandon the seduction hypothesis, he did not speculate, and probably did not believe, that Freud made this decision for reasons having to do with the operation itself.

5. The complete letters of Freud to Fliess, which I have edited and translated, will be published by Harvard University Press.

6. Ernst Freud and Max Schur had planned to edit the complete edition of Freud's letters to Fliess, and, for this purpose, Schur had in his possession some of the original manuscripts and part of the transcript. The text was not complete (p. 84 n.): "I plan at a later date to study once again the originals of this correspondence because some of the letters still have to be transcribed." Schur considered "the link between the Emma episode and the Irma dream" to be self-evident, since

here was a patient being treated by Freud for hysteria who *did* have an organic, largely "iatrogenic" illness; who had narrowly escaped death because a physician really had committed an error; whose pathology was located in the nasal cavity; whose case had confronted Freud with a number of emergencies requiring him urgently to call in several consultants, all of whom had been helpless and confused; Emma's lesions had a foetid odor (propylamyl); Freud had had to look repeatedly into her nose and mouth.

Schur certainly did not see the sentence from the letter of December 12, 1897, about Emma Eckstein seeing patients of her own, for he writes, with reference to Freud's letter of January 24, 1897: "This is the last reference to the case of Emma I was able to find in Freud's correspondence with Fliess." Mrs. Schur informs me that she is almost certain that Schur had never discussed Emma Eckstein with Freud, and she was not aware that he knew anything about her beyond what appears in the letters themselves.

7. Robert Gersuny (1844–1924) was the first director of the Rudolfinerhaus, a hospital in Vienna which was opened in 1882.

8. In the letter of January 24, 1895, Freud had suggested to Fliess that Gersuny collaborate on some aspect of the operation.

9. I. Rosanes (1857–1922) was an old friend of Freud's, mentioned in the letters to Eduard Silberstein, a schoolmate of Freud's. He was director of the Stephaniespital in Vienna. A short time after this, Freud treated his wife.

10. Possibly a reference to Therese Schlesinger, Emma Eckstein's sister.

11. The widow of Max Schur kindly allowed me to see the notebooks Schur used in researching his article on the operation. In notebook A, p. 131, Schur writes: ". . . Fliess had inadvertently left a half-meter strip of iodoform gauze (!!!) in the cavity (which had obviously been created by the removal of the turbinal bone and the opening of a sinus) (!!!)." The same sentence, without the exclamation marks, is found in Schur's 1972 book (p. 80).

12. A copy of this paper is in the Isakower Archives of the Library of Congress.

13. Karl Gussenbauer (1842–1903) was Billroth's (1829–1894) successor in the Chirurgische Klinik in Vienna. See Erna Lesky, *Die Wiener Medizinische Schule im 19. Jahrhundert* (Graz-Köln: H. Böhlaus, 1965), pp. 447 ff.

14. Dr. Helen E. Kapit, a relative of Dr. Elias, has permitted me to quote from the interview which Dr. Elias gave to the Sigmund Freud Archives in 1951. The interview, which was recorded, is a particularly valuable source of information on Emma Eckstein. The German reads: *Damit hat sie ein verunstaltetes Gesicht bekommen, der Knochen ist weggemeisselt worden und es ist die eine Seite eingefallen gewesen.*

15. The extent of Freud's involvement with Fliess, many years after they last saw each other, is demonstrated in the following statement by Freud in a letter (October 6, 1910) to his closest colleague of later years, Sándor Ferenczi, cited by Jones (2, p. 93): "My dreams at that time were concerned, as I hinted to you, entirely with the Fliess affair, which in the nature of things would be hard to arouse your sympathy." It is remarkable that in 1910, nine years after Freud and Fliess had seen each other for the last time, Freud's dreams were "entirely" concerned with the Fliess affair. Freud, in an unpublished letter to Ferenczi of October 17, 1910, writes:

> You probably imagine that I have secrets quite other than those
> I have reserved for myself, or you believe that [my secret] is

connected with a special sorrow, whereas I feel myself capable of handling everything and am pleased with the resultant greater independence that comes from having overcome my homosexuality.

On December 16, 1910, in an unpublished letter to Ferenczi, Freud returns to Fliess once again: "I have now overcome Fliess, about whom you were so curious."

16. Jones, I, p. 316. When Anna Freud read this passage in Jones she wrote him, remarking rather drily: "When the friendship was conceived my father was not yet 31 which is still far from middle age, and he did not have six children but only one." This letter is dated January 28, 1952. It is in the Jones Archives of the London Institute of Psycho-Analysis.

17. This was Jones's "official" version; in private he could express himself even more forcefully. He wrote to James Strachey (in a letter preserved in the Strachey Archives of the London Institute of Psycho-Analysis) on January 11, 1954: "I don't quite agree with what you say about Freud gradually reconciling himself to bisexuality. I think myself he was over-reconciled to it, if you see what I mean. He never really emancipated himself from Fliess and was avowedly struggling with that question in 1910 in Sicily. A lot of which then got passed on to Adler, Stekel, Jung and most of all to Ferenczi." Strachey had written to Jones on October 24, 1951, concerning the Fliess letters (unpublished letter from the Strachey Archives): "I was very much interested by your account of the suppressed passages in the Fliess letters. It's really a complete instance of *folie à deux*, with Freud in the unexpected role of hysterical partner to a paranoiac. I do hope that if they ever come out in English the censorship may be lifted a bit. Unless Anna proposes to burn the originals, they're bound to come out in the end, and surely it's better that they should while people are alive who can correct their effect."

18. Freud wrote to Ida Fliess, Wilhelm's widow, on December 17, 1928, in response to her request for Fliess's letters (the letter, unpublished, is preserved in the Library of the Hebrew University, in Jerusalem, having been donated to the library by Fliess's daughter, Pauline Jacobsen):

Esteemed Madame:

I hasten to answer your letter although I cannot, at present, communicate anything decisive with respect to fulfilling your request. My memory tells me that I destroyed the greater part of our correspondence at some point after 1904. But this leaves open the possibility that a select number of letters were preserved and could turn up after a careful search of the room that I have lived in for the last 37 years. I beg you, therefore, to allow me time over Christmas. Whatever I find will be at your disposal, without conditions. If I do not find anything, you will have to assume that nothing escaped the destruction. Naturally I would be happy to learn that my letters to your husband, for so many years my close friend, have found a fate that will assure their protection against any future use. I remain,

Sincerely yours,
Freud

This letter strikes me as important because it raises the possibility that Freud did not destroy all the letters he received from Fliess; hence these letters may yet surface. However, a careful search of Maresfield Gardens turned up only one letter from Fliess to Freud, written in 1904.

19. Cf. *Origins*, p. 73 ("Draft C").

20. This paper was printed in the *Verhandlungen des Congresses für innere Medizin*, 12th Congress, 1893 (Wiesbaden: J. F. Bergmann). Fliess's paper is on pp. 384–394. There was also a French version (*Autoreferat*), "Les Réflexes d'origine nasale," published in *Archives d'otologie et de rhinologie* (Archives de Laryngologie), 6 (1893), pp. 266–269.

21. Leipzig and Vienna: Franz Deuticke. Fliess's paper was a summary of the information contained in this book.

22. Leipzig and Vienna: Franz Deuticke. Freud kept most of Fliess's books, and took them with him to London, but for some reason they were not included in the list of his books published by Trosman and Simmons ("The Freud Library," *Journal of the American Psychoanalytic Association*, 21 [1973], pp. 646–687). This book is marked with many marginal checks by Freud.

23. As noted, by "actual neuroses" (sometimes called the simple neuroses), Freud meant neurasthenia and anxiety neurosis (*S.E.*, 3, p. 279) as opposed to the psychoneuroses (hysteria and obsessional neurosis), also called neuro-psychoses. Cf. *S.E.*, 1, p. 179; and *S.E.*, 3, p. 39, and Strachey's note in *S.E.*, 11, p. 224. Freud believed the "actual neuroses" had a purely physical and contemporary

causation—i.e., some irregularity in the sexual sphere (coitus interruptus, masturbation, the use of condoms).

24. The German word that Freud uses here is *Versuchung*, which means, literally, a "temptation," as if Freud were implying that the fourteen-year-old girl *wanted* the assault on the part of her father.

25. See the excellent study by Albrecht Hirschmüller, *Physiologie und Psychoanalyse im Leben und Werk Josef Breuers* (Bern: Hans Huber, 1978).

26. It is clear that Freud is referring to a patient. Possibly he compared her to Marion Delorme, the heroine in Victor Hugo's 1829 play by that name.

27. Jones (1, p. 279) was the first to note that Breuer, in his sections of *Studies on Hysteria*, was willing to grant significance to sexuality. But in his 1915 account of Breuer's collaboration (*S.E.*, 14, p. 12) Freud himself wrote:

> When I later began more and more resolutely to put forward the significance of sexuality in the etiology of neuroses, he [Breuer] was the first to show the reaction of distaste and repudiation which was later to become so familiar to me, but which at that time I had not yet learnt to recognize as my inevitable fate.

But Breuer said (*S.E.*, 2, p. 246): "The great majority of severe neuroses in women have their origin in the marriage bed," which would seem to contradict Freud unless Breuer was referring to the "actual" neuroses, and not the psychoneuroses. That is, he was prepared to accept a purely physiological explanation of neuroses, but did not grant sexuality any psychological role—at least not sexuality as Freud was beginning to see it then, namely childhood seductions. Jones (1, p. 280) writes: "I would make the purely personal guess that Breuer's acceptance referred rather to the later ages, and what he balked at was Freud's views concerning the incestuous seduction of children; but I have no authority for this suggestion."

28. Richard von Krafft-Ebing, *Psychopathia Sexualis, mit besonderer Berücksichtigung der conträren Sexualempfindung: Eine klinisch-forensische Studie* (9th ed.; Stuttgart: Ferdinand Enke, 1894).

29. In a discussion of these passages with Anna Freud, she said there was no doubt as to when her father might have made the markings; it was always his habit to read and mark a book as soon

as he purchased it. These marginalia, therefore, would go back to 1894.

30. On p. 413 Freud marked a passage which reads: "Psychically unexplored are cases such as the one in which a woman laid her five-and-a-half-year-old son on top of her and carried out perverse sexual acts with him."

31. We cannot be certain when Freud purchased the book by Tardieu, but it is possible that he bought it during his Paris stay. Marking the passage in Krafft-Ebing, therefore, could be a way of noting to himself that Krafft-Ebing was already familiar with this kind of material. It must have been all the more puzzling for Freud to encounter Krafft-Ebing's total skepticism on the evening of April 21, 1896, when he presented his paper "The Aetiology of Hysteria," since he would have expected, from reading these and other citations in the *Psychopathia Sexualis*, that Krafft-Ebing would not be unprepared for Freud's revelations. For Freud had simply added the psychological dimension to material already discovered by the French authors, and acknowledged to be true by Krafft-Ebing. Nor was Krafft-Ebing alone: all the major German writers on this topic had acknowledged the work of Tardieu, including Eduard von Hofmann, professor of legal medicine at the University of Vienna, who mentions Tardieu's book in an obituary on the French professor, as I note below (chapter 4, note 29).

32. Freud's review, which was signed, appeared in the *Wiener klinische Rundschau*, 9 (1895), pp. 140–142. The book by G. J. Möbius was entitled *Die Migräne* and appeared in vol. 12 of *Specielle Pathologie und Therapie*, edited by H. Nothnagel (Vienna: Alfred Hölder, 1894).

33. Cf. *S.E.*, 3, p. 167 n.: "*The traumas of childhood operate in a deferred fashion as though they were fresh experiences; but they do so unconsciously*" (emphasis in original).

34. Freud writes in "Heredity and the Aetiology of the Neuroses" (1896) (*S.E.*, 3, p. 152): "The event of which the subject has retained an unconscious memory is *a precocious experience of sexual relations with actual excitement of the genitals, resulting from sexual abuse committed by another person*; and *the period of life* at which this fatal event takes place is *earliest youth—* the years up to the age of eight to ten, before the child has reached sexual maturity" (emphasis in original). In "Further Remarks on the Neuro-Psychoses of Defence" (1896) (*S.E.*, 3, p. 163), Freud

repeats that "*these sexual traumas must have occurred in early childhood (before puberty), and their content must consist of an actual irritation of the genitals (of processes resembling copulation)*" (emphasis in original). Freud says later in that essay (p. 165): "I cannot say for certain what the upper age-limit is below which sexual injury plays a part in the aetiology of hysteria; but I doubt whether sexual passivity can bring on repression later than between the eighth and tenth years, unless it is enabled to do so by previous experiences." Cf. below, in the same article (p. 166), and later in the volume (*S.E.*, 3, p. 212). Did Freud consider Emma Eckstein's later repression to have been caused by an even earlier sexual seduction than the one at eight (which certainly did not involve "processes resembling copulation")?

35. "Scene" is used to mean a real event in "The Aetiology of Hysteria," *S.E.*, 3, p. 204 (*G.W.*, 1, 440, 455).

36. *Revue neurologique*, 4 (6), pp. 161–169. "Heredity and the Aetiology of the Neuroses," *S.E.*, 3, pp. 143–156.

37. *Neurologisches Zentralblatt*, 15 (10), pp. 434–448. *S.E.*, 3, pp. 159–185.

38. See, notably, the introduction by Kris to *Origins*, and Martin Gardner, "Freud's Friend Wilhelm Fliess and His Theory of Male and Female Life Cycles," *Scientific American*, 215 (1966), pp. 108–112. The most concerted attempt to place Fliess's views in the historical and scientific context in which they arose is by Frank Sulloway in his book *Freud: Biologist of the Mind* (New York: Basic Books, 1979). See my review article, *Journal of the American Psychoanalytic Association*, 31, no. 3 (1983), pp. 739–747.

39. *Zur Periodenlehre: Gesammelte Aufsätze* (Jena: Eugen Diederichs, 1925), p. 15. Fliess's views do not seem to have changed much over the years. Precisely when he developed his theories is difficult to say, but it is clear from Freud's references in the letters, especially in 1897, that Fliess had already developed the entire system before his friendship with Freud and that Freud, for some time, accepted it.

40. From Aristotle's *De partibus animalium*, 1, 5: *Introite, nam et hic dii sunt!* Freud uses the same quotation in a reference to Charcot and hysteria (*S.E.*, 20, p. 13). For a discussion of the quotation in Freud, and in Lessing (who also uses it), see Walter Schönau, *Sigmund Freuds Prosa* (Stuttgart: J. B. Metzler, 1968), pp. 58–61.

41. Wilhelm Fliess, *Vom Leben und vom Tod: Biologische Vorträge* (Jena: Eugen Diederichs, 1919), p. 59.

42. This passage is from Marie Bonaparte's unpublished notebook, which I found in Freud's desk in Maresfield Gardens.

43. *Zur Periodenlehre*, p. 112. Fliess, in his book *Der Ablauf des Lebens: Grundlegung zur exakten Biologie* (Leipzig and Vienna: Franz Deuticke, 1906), several times tells the story of the death of his sister.

44. Schur, "Some Additional 'Day Residues' of the Specimen Dream of Psychoanalysis," p. 83.

45. It is not clear whether Freud is reporting a dream or a fantasy. When he writes that "the *labia minora* . . . is still shorter today," we do not know whether he is merely reporting Emma's statement or whether he accepts it as true. If the latter is the case, then Freud tacitly accepts that some real trauma took place (even if not necessarily the one "remembered" by Emma).

4. *Freud's Renunciation of the Theory of Seduction*

1. Jones (2, p. 5) has amplified the story even further:

Freud at first accepted his patients' stories of their parents' sexual overtures towards them when they were children, but came to realize that the stories were simply fantasies derived from his patients' own childhood.

Cf. Jones (2, p. 478):

Less astonishing perhaps and certainly more fateful for good, was the credulous acceptance of his patients' stories of paternal seduction which he narrated in his earlier publications on psycho-pathology. When I commented to my friend James Strachey on Freud's strain of credulity he very sagely remarked: "It was lucky for us that he had it." Most investigators would have simply disbelieved the patients' stories on the ground of their inherent improbability—at least on such a large scale—and have dismissed the matter as one more example of the untrustworthiness of hysterics.

As noted above, Freud himself in 1925 (*S.E.*, 20, p. 34) wrote: "If the reader feels inclined to shake his head at my credulity I cannot altogether blame him."

2. Portions of the letter were included by Strachey in vol. 1 of the *S.E.* (pp. 259–260), with an improved translation. For commentaries, see, in particular, Max Schur, *Freud: Living and Dying* (New York: International Universities Press, 1972). See also: Didier Anzieu, *L'Auto-analyse de Freud* (2nd ed.; Paris: Presses Universitaires de France, 1975); A. Schusdek, "Freud's 'Seduction Theory': A Reconstruction," *Journal of the History of the Behavioral Sciences*, 2 (1966), pp. 159–166; M. B. Macmillan, "Freud's Expectations and the Childhood Seduction Theory," *Australian Journal of Psychology*, 29 (1977), pp. 223–236; Marianne Krüll, *Freud und sein Vater*; Arthur Efron, "Freud's Self-Analysis and the Nature of Psychoanalytic Criticism," *International Review of Psycho-Analysis*, 4 (1977), pp. 253–280; Frank Sulloway, *Freud: Biologist of the Mind* (New York: Basic Books, 1979).

3. The editors of the German text misread the manuscript. The German text, as printed in *Anfänge* (*Origins*), reads: "*Die fortgesetzten Enttäuschungen bei den Versuchen, meine Analyse zum wirklichen Abschluss zu bringen . . .*" which Strachey correctly translates as: ". . . continual disappointments in my attempts at bringing my analysis to a real conclusion . . ." But *meine* is an error in the transcription of the original manuscript. The manuscript reads *eine Analyse*, "a single analysis."

4. Schur (*Freud: Living and Dying*, p. 191) writes: "The meaning of this Jewish joke is obvious: 'You were once a proud bride, but you got into trouble, the wedding is off—take off your bridal gown.' " Another interpretation, which I believe to be correct, was suggested to me by Anna Freud, namely, that Freud believed himself, with his theory of the neuroses, privileged and happy as a bride. Those days were now over, and he had to return to his earlier ordinary status. He had made no discovery. *Kalle* is a slang word that can also mean prostitute. See *Jüdisches Lexicon*, 1930 ed., vol. 4, under *Vulgärausdrücke*.

5. There has been a great deal of speculation about the significance of Freud's letter to Fliess of October 3, 1897 (published in *Origins*), centering on Freud's comments about his nursemaid. Freud often indicated to Fliess that he regarded himself as mildly hysterical. In this letter, which deals with his self-analysis through

dreams, Freud writes: "I can only indicate that the old man plays no active part in my case . . . that in my case the 'prime originator' [*Urheberin*] was an ugly, elderly but clever woman who told me a great deal about God Almighty and hell and who instilled in me a high opinion of my own capacities." Later in the letter Freud writes: "She was my teacher in sexual matters and complained because I was clumsy and unable to do anything. . . . Moreover, she washed me in reddish water in which she had previously washed herself. (The interpretation is not difficult; I find nothing like this in the chain of my memories; so I regard it as a genuine ancient discovery.)" In fact, interpretation of this detail (the recovery of a memory through a dream) has proved more elusive than Freud thought. It seems to me that Freud is hinting at a sexual seduction by the nursemaid, but this is not entirely clear. It is interesting that this letter should follow by only a few weeks the letter (of September 21) in which Freud says that he has given up the seduction hypothesis.

According to Josef Sajner ("Sigmund Freuds Beziehungen zu seinem Geburtsort Freiberg [Příbor] und zu Mähren," *Clio Medica*, 3 [1968], pp. 167–180), the woman's name was Monika Zajíc. (Cf. Krüll, *Freud und sein Vater*, p. 144.) Professor Sajner informed me, in a personal communication, that he has not been able to find out any particulars about this woman. When Freud says she was elderly it is not clear whether he is speaking from the point of view of the child or of the adult. Anna Freud told me she thinks she may have been in her forties. (Cf. Renée Gicklhorn: "The Freiberg Period of the Freud Family," *Journal of the History of Medicine*, 24 [1969], pp. 37–43.)

6. In a letter to Fliess of April 28, 1897 (published in *Origins*), Freud writes: "The complete interpretation occurred to me only after a lucky chance this morning brought a fresh confirmation of paternal etiology," where "paternal etiology" clearly refers to seduction.

7. Cf. K. R. Eissler, *Goethe: A Psychoanalytic Study* (Detroit: Wayne State University Press, 1963), 2, p. 756.

8. Leopold Löwenfeld, *Die psychischen Zwangserscheinungen* (Wiesbaden: J. F. Bergmann, 1904). The preface is dated 1903. Freud had the book in his library in London. Löwenfeld was one of the few psychiatrists who had attempted to take Freud's views on seduction seriously. This is evident from a number of his publications. In his *Lehrbuch der gesammten Psychotherapie* (Wiesbaden:

J. F. Bergmann, 1897, p. 166) he makes it clear that he was impressed by the method of Freud and Breuer as revealed in *Studies on Hysteria*, and attempted some form of psychoanalysis in his own clinical practice (cf. *Die psychischen Zwangserscheinungen*, p. 298: ". . . I used in these attempts the same analytic method described by Freud in *Studies on Hysteria*"). See also his book *Die moderne Behandlung der Nervenschwäche (Neurasthenie) der Hysterie und verwandter Leiden* (Wiesbaden: J. F. Bergmann, 1904), p. 147: "It seems evident from the above that the use of this method will, for the time being, probably be restricted to its discoverer." After Löwenfeld published Freud's essay in his *Die psychischen Zwangserscheinungen*, he writes a chapter comparing Freud's method with hypnotherapy, and ends (p. 553) by saying: "For the time being, physicians in any event have no choice but to fall back on the use of other psychotherapeutic methods." It is clear from a passage on p. 474 of *Die psychischen Zwangserscheinungen* that Löwenfeld could not take in what Freud meant by a sexual trauma, for he distinguishes there a sexual etiology from an emotional etiology. It did not occur to him (any more than it did to any other of Freud's colleagues or the French authors on rape) that a "sexual seduction" is also an emotional assault. Cf. his conclusions on etiology on p. 477 of the book.

9. *S.E.*, 7, pp. 125–245. It was published under the title *Drei Abhandlungen zur Sexualtheorie* (Leipzig and Vienna: Franz Deuticke, 1905).

10. The Dora case was written during Freud's transitional period, right after 1900, though he waited five years to publish it ("Fragment of an Analysis of a Case of Hysteria," *S.E.*, 7, pp. 3–122). The first draft was completed in January 1901, but it was not published until 1905.

11. Strachey gives a 1913 date for the Ellis book, but this is merely the date of the edition that Strachey used (the second edition). In *G.W.* Freud gives 1903, which is the date of the first edition. I consulted a first edition of *Drei Abhandlungen*, and 1903 is also the date given there. (Ellis did not publish any other book in 1903.)

12. Freud says, according to Strachey's translation: ". . . similar narratives were what led me to make the modifications in my aetiological hypotheses . . ." But Freud did not really use the word "narrative." The German text reads "*Erkundigungen der*

gleichen Art." This means, literally, "inquiries of a similar nature." It is not entirely clear what Freud means; possibly that he began to make inquiries of his own. But since he does not reveal to us the nature of these inquiries, or the results, we cannot evaluate their relative worth in leading him to abandon his theory.

13. *S.E.*, 7, p. 191.

14. Havelock Ellis, *Studies in the Psychology of Sex*, vol. 3: *Analysis of the Sexual Impulse; Love and Pain; The Sexual Impulse in Women* (Philadelphia: F. A. Davis, 1903).

15. Although Ellis does not mention the fact in the appendix itself, the appendix had already appeared in print as an article entitled "The Development of the Sexual Instinct" in *Alienist and Neurologist*, 32, no. 3 (July 1901), pp. 500–521. It consists of the introduction that appears in the 1903 edition of the book, word for word, plus eight case histories, more or less identical to the ones in *Studies*. There are, however, some, albeit minor, changes. For example, p. 503: "She then provoked genital excitation," is, on p. 252 of the book, reproduced as "She then succeeded in causing erection." Ellis does not, then, quote verbatim, although the very first history is prefaced with the words: "I reproduce this history, written in the third person, as it reached my hands." The 1913 edition of the book contains the case history as it appears in 1903, but in this edition there are 64 pages as opposed to the 35 pages in the first edition. Ellis sent Freud a copy of the seven volumes of the *Studies*, but it is not clear from the catalogue (Trosman and Simmons, no. 38) which edition it is. If I remember correctly, from seeing the set in Maresfield Gardens, it was a later edition, not the first (cited by Freud in *Three Essays*). Freud did have in his private library Ellis's "The Analysis of the Sexual Impulse," which appeared in *Alienist and Neurologist*, 21 (1900), pp. 247–262. In the article itself is a footnote: "This article is an abstract of a chapter which will appear in volume 3 of the author's *Studies in the Psychology of Sex*." But in fact there are no case histories in this article, so it could not be the source of Freud's comment.

16. *Havelock Ellis: A Biography* (New York: Alfred A. Knopf, 1980), p. 219.

17. 2 vols., foreword by Albert Eulenburg, Dresden: H. R. Dohrn. Sulloway mentions in *Freud: Biologist of the Mind*, p. 316, that he saw this copy of Bloch's book in Freud's London library, as well as another copy in the New York library, which may have

belonged to Freud or to Friedrich Krauss. Iwan Bloch (1872–1922), who wrote his first books on the Marquis de Sade under the pseudonym Eugene Dühren, was a Berlin dermatologist who wrote on syphilis and on sexuality from an anthropological point of view. His influence on the scientific study of sexuality has been discussed by Sulloway, *op. cit.*, and by Annemarie Wettley and W. Leibbrand in *Von der "Psychopathia sexualis" zur Sexualwissenschaft* (Stuttgart: Ferdinand Enke, 1959; see especially p. 137 n.).

18. In view of Freud's reluctance to admit that in cases he had investigated the father was often the person to be blamed for sexual assaults (as we see from the Katharina case in *Studies on Hysteria* and from the letter to Fliess of September 21, 1897), it would be interesting to follow his thinking about the role of servants in this respect. For here was a class of people who could be accused with complete safety. Freud marked several passages in his personal reading in which servants were accused, including those in Krafft-Ebing's book and in the Bloch book. There is still another source. Freud owned Albert Moll's *Untersuchungen über die Libido sexualis* (Berlin: H. Kornfeld, 1895). On p. 195 of his copy the following passage is marked: "Tardieu draws particular attention to female servants who exchange sexual touchings with children who are confided to them." Sulloway (*op. cit.*, pp. 313–314) feels that Moll was influential in Freud's abandonment of the seduction theory. He comments:

> Finally, Moll's *Libido Sexualis* was notable for one other important insight that was not lost upon Freud at this time. As a clinician, Moll faced a problem similar to that confronting Freud in the mid-1890's: How does one know whether autobiographical confessions of childhood sexual activity are really true? Indeed, they are often not so, Moll contended, citing a variety of psychological reasons: distortions of memory, the patient's desire to rationalize a perversion as innate, subsequent repression of normal heterosexual memories, and so forth. Not only did Moll discuss this point in some detail in the *Libido Sexualis* (315–316), but he also compared it with the problem of weighing the often outrageous complaints and accusations of hysterical patients, and he cautioned moderation in believing hysterics and perverts alike. To be sure, there was nothing terribly new in Moll's recommendations; but this timely reminder, in a passage

scored by Freud in the margin of his personal copy of Moll's book, could hardly have come at a more appropriate time in Freud's wavering support for the seduction theory. In *The Sexual Life of the Child* (1909), Moll later warned against the danger of accepting too readily the accusations of sexual misconduct that little girls often lodge against men, and called it *"one of the gravest scandals of our present penal system"* that such charges were so frequently believed by judges. The problem was particularly marked, he also emphasized, with *child hysterics* (1912a trans.: 204, 228; Moll's italics).

See, too, Sulloway, pp. 299–305, for details about Moll and his possible influence on Freud, and the appendix D: "The Dating of Freud's Reading of Albert Moll's *Untersuchungen über die Libido sexualis*" (pp. 516–518). It is possible that Emma Eckstein's interest in the wretched sexual treatment of servants (see Appendix A) was awakened by her awareness of Freud's attempt to blame them for abuse of children. It was, of course, completely safe to blame servants for seductions; nobody would object.

19. The English translation of Bloch's 1902 book is entitled *Anthropological Studies in the Strange Sexual Practices of All Races in All Ages, Ancient and Modern, Oriental and Occidental, Primitive and Civilized*, translated by Keene Wallis (New York: Privately printed by the Anthropological Press, 1933). Note p. 174, for some of the cases that follow are the same as those published in the *Studies*, but one (no. 3), at least, is not mentioned there.

20. Freud had another book by Iwan Bloch in his personal library: *Das Sexualleben unserer Zeit in seinen Beziehungen zur modernen Kultur* (Berlin: Louis Marchus, 1907) (I have used the 1909 edition). The date precludes any direct influence on Freud's developing views, but Freud may well have been aware of Bloch's views from the many articles that he published between 1900 and 1907. The same views, moreover, are contained in the earlier books, as we saw. Bloch's book had a considerable influence in Europe for some time. On p. 273, Bloch says:

Finally, an important point should not be forgotten: the *untrust-worthiness* of children's statements, which the pediatrician Adolf Baginsky ("Die Impressionabilität des Kindes unter dem Einfluss des Milieus," in *Medizinische Reform*, edited by Rudolf Lennhoff, 1906, nos. 43 and 44, esp. pp. 533–534) has recently dealt with in an excellent work. This remarkably wise man, who knows the soul of the child so well, explains:

"Children's declarations before the law are, for the truly experienced knower of children, downright *null* and *hollow*, absolutely worthless and without significance; all the more insignificant and all the more hollow the more often the child repeats the declaration and the more determined he is to stick to his statements."

One can appreciate the resistance Freud would have encountered had he stood by his earlier views when one reads such a comment, for Bloch was considered (and is still so considered) to be the leader of the liberal reform movement concerning the laws dealing with sexual perversions. In a chapter in that book on the sexual seduction of children, Bloch writes (p. 731):

In conclusion, another point must be made with respect to sexual crimes involving children, which has legal significance, namely the fact that frequently there is no question of the "seduction" of children, but rather the instigation derives in the first place from the children themselves. . . . The so frequent [sexual] crimes of priests and teachers against young girls in their care often appear in a different light if one subjects the denunciations of children to an exacting interrogation, including a physical examination. This often reveals a deeply rooted promiscuity which goes back a long way and brings to light the fact that long before this sexual crime, sexual intercourse had taken place with other men, and that willingly.

Here then was an authority who contradicted all the major points of Freud's 1896 papers: seductions did not as a rule occur; *if* they occurred, they were harmless; in any event, the people who perpetrated these acts (for in *Das Sexualleben* Bloch acknowledges crimes against children) were, for the most part, servants (thereby perpetuating the dissimulation that Freud had resorted to in *Studies on Hysteria* when he disguised the identity of Katharina's father); and finally, Bloch supported the current of thought to which Freud had been subjected in Paris, represented by Fournier and others, namely that children invent these tales.

21. 5th ed.; Wiesbaden: J. F. Bergmann, 1904. A copy of this book is in Freud's library in London.

22. Freud says quite openly in the concluding section of the essays that he has replaced seduction (what he calls "accidental influences") with constitutional factors: ". . . accidental influences have been replaced by constitutional factors and 'defense' in the purely psychological sense has been replaced by organic 'sexual repression' " (p. 278). In other words, Freud has shifted from a psychology which depends on personal memories to phylogenetic explanations. The concept of "organic sexual repression," which refers to the "organic defense . . . achieved with man's erect gait against his earlier animal existence [i.e., the free play of sexuality]," is explained in a footnote to *Civilization and Its Discontents* (*S.E.*, 21, pp. 105–106, 99). (Cf. the end of *Three Essays*, p. 242.) Freud's comments imply that with early sexual tragedies (which are only of significance for those whose sexual constitution "predisposes" them to react strongly) any psychological defense becomes irrelevant, since this response will in any event be governed by a biological repression of the original act. Such a view is inimical to any psychology of the emotions, but is one that would undoubtedly appeal to Fliess, and possibly derives from Fliess's influence. (Cf. Sulloway, *op. cit.*, p. 177.) On August 7, 1901, Freud wrote to Fliess that he intended to write a book called *Bisexuality in Man*, and asked Fliess to write the book with him. This was already after their break, and Fliess refused. What emerged from Freud's plan was *Three Essays* and it is not surprising, therefore, that there are traces of Fliess in the book, and attempts to adopt his point of view even when this would preclude a psychological perspective. Bisexuality was regarded, not as a psychological problem, but as an organic one. In one of the last papers that Freud wrote, "Analysis Terminable and Interminable" (1937), he mentions and dismisses Fliess's view that repression derives from bisexuality (*S.E.*, 23, p. 251), but then a page later he writes:

> We often have the impression that with the wish for a penis and the masculine protest we have penetrated through all the psychological strata and have reached bedrock, and that thus our activities are at an end. This is probably true, since, for the psychical field, the biological field does in fact play the part of the underlying bedrock.

23. The article ("Das Erleiden sexueller Traumen als Form infantiler Sexualbetätigung") was published in the *Centralblatt für Nervenheilkunde und Psychiatrie*, 18 (1907), pp. 854–865. It was

Abraham's first psychoanalytic publication. The English translation
is from *Selected Papers of Karl Abraham*, with an Introductory
Memoir by Ernest Jones, translated by Douglas Bryan and Alix
Strachey (London: Hogarth Press, 1973), pp. 47–63. The German
text is reprinted in Karl Abraham, *Psychoanalytische Studien*, vol.
2, 167–181, edited by Johannes Cremerius (Frankfurt am Main: S. Fischer,
1971).

    24. The German (p. 171) reads: "*Erst als er seinen Zweck
nahezu oder ganz erreicht hat, gelingt es dem Kinde, sich zu befreien.*"
Does Abraham mean the child did not know whether the man had
"attained his purpose"?

    25. *S.E.*, 20, p. 273.

    26. Vol. 8 (1895–1896), pp. 159–161. The relevant sentence
reads: "I am afraid that many hysterics will be encouraged to give
free rein to their fantasy and invent stories."

    27. Vol. 7 (1896), pp. 451–452.

    28. See *Vierteljahrsschrift für gerichtliche Medicin und
öffentliches Sanitätswesen*, 3rd ser., vol. 8 (1894): *Festschrift für
Prof. Eduard von Hofmann*, edited by A. Haberda, where a list of his writings is given.

    29. *Wiener medizinische Wochenschrift*, 29 (1879), pp.
89–92.

    30. "Angebliche Notzucht mit nachfolgender Blenorrhoe und
hystero-epileptischen Anfällen. Fraglicher Geisteszustand," no. 1,
pp. 9–10; no. 2, pp. 31–32.

    31. Berlin: August Hirschwald. The subtitle reads: *Nach
eigenen Erfahrungen* (Based on My Own Experiences).

    32. Krafft-Ebing wrote an article, "Über Unzucht mit
Kindern und Pädophilia erotica" (On Sexual Abuse of Children and
Pedophilia Erotica), published in *Friedrichs Blätter für gerichtliche
Medicin*, in 1895. It was reprinted, with additions, in his *Arbeiten aus
dem Gesammtgebiet der Psychiatrie und Neuropathologie* (Leipzig:
Johann Ambrosius Barth, 1898), 3, pp. 91–127. This is a volume that
Freud owned (Hinterberger, no. 302). The article, which is sub-
stantially similar to the chapter published in *Psychopathia Sexualis*,
is more elaborate, and treats the literature in greater detail. Krafft-
Ebing cites Tardieu, Brouardel, Bernard, Casper, and Hofmann.
Freud owned works by the first three, and undoubtedly knew the
work of the other two. Krafft-Ebing shows sympathy (e.g., p. 113)
for the accused, but not for the children. It is interesting that in

many of his own cases the adult admitted having committed these acts (e.g., p. 112), thereby ruling out the possibility that they were fantasies on the part of the child.

33. Wiesbaden: J. F. Bergmann, 1894. In the margin of p. 18, where Löwenfeld speaks of a *"neuropathische Prädisposition,"* Freud asks: *"Woher?"*—in other words, where would such a thing come from? Again, on p. 19, where Löwenfeld speaks of an abnormal constitution and inherited tendencies in hysteria, Freud has the same question in the margin. At the top of p. 20 Freud pencils in: *"Neurasth = Degeneration, warum?"*—that is, why should neurasthenia be equated with degeneration (i.e., constitution)?

34. Elenore Fliess, Robert Fliess's wife, wrote a short biography, *Robert Fliess: The Making of a Psychoanalyst* (written in 1974; it was privately published, printed by Roffey & Clark, 12 High Street, Croydon, England). Robert Fliess received his analytic training in Berlin. He was best known to American analysts through his books *The Psychoanalytic Reader: An Anthology of Essential Papers with Critical Introductions* (New York: International Universities Press, 1948) and *The Revival of Interest in the Dream: A Critical Study of Post-Freudian Psychoanalytic Contributions* (New York: International Universities Press, 1952). His next two books were also well received: *Erogeneity and Libido: Addenda to the Theory of the Psychosexual Development of the Human*—Psychoanalytic Series, vol. 1 (New York: International Universities Press, 1956) and *Ego and Body Ego: Contributions to Their Psychoanalytic Psychology*—Psychoanalytic Series, vol. 2 (New York: Schulte Pub. Co., 1962; International Universities Press, 1970). But with his last volume, *Symbol, Dream, and Psychosis with Notes on Technique*, he fell afoul of the psychoanalytic establishment, though in my opinion it is his most profound work and one of the most brilliant works in psychoanalysis (Psychoanalytic Series, vol. 3 [New York: International Universities Press, 1973]).

35. Personal communication from Mrs. Robert Fliess.

5. *The Strange Case of Ferenczi's Last Paper*

1. The original title was "Die Leidenschaften der Erwachsenen und deren Einfluss auf Character- und Sexualentwicklung der Kinder"

(The [Sexual] Passions of Adults and Their Influence on the Character Development and Sexual Development of Children). It was published in the *Int. Z. Psychoanal.*, 19 (1933), pp. 5–15, and in *Bausteine* (see note 3 below), 3, pp. 511–525, as "Sprachverwirrung zwischen den Erwachsenen und dem Kind (Die Sprache der Zärtlichkeit und der Leidenschaft)" (Confusion of Tongues between Adults and the Child—The Language of Tenderness and of Passion).

2. I first read the diary (which was written in German) in the Library of Congress, but could not secure permission from the Sigmund Freud Archives to quote from it. Dr. Judith Dupont generously sent me a copy, and has allowed me to cite from it in this chapter. Dr. Dupont is preparing a French translation of the entire diary, and I understand that Michael Balint, before he died, had prepared an English translation which will be published in England.

3. The English translation of Ferenczi's paper by Michael Balint is not entirely accurate; in some cases he adds words Ferenczi did not use, in others he omits words that Ferenczi did use. I have therefore made my own translation in collaboration with Marianne Loring. For the German text I have used vol. 3 of *Bausteine zur Psychoanalyse*, by Dr. S. Ferenczi (*Arbeiten aus den Jahren 1908–1933*), edited by Vilma Kovács (Bern: Hans Huber, 1939). The passages quoted come from pp. 517 and 522. There is an excellent and reliable French translation by Judith Dupont in vol. 4 of her edition of Ferenczi's collected works, *Dr. Sándor Ferenczi: Oeuvres complètes*, vol. 4: *1927–1933, Psychoanalyse*, 4, translated by Coq-Héron (a translation group composed of Judith Dupont, Suzanne Hommel, Françoise Samson, Pierre Sabourin, Bernard This) (Paris: Payot, 1982).

4. "Identification with the aggressor" (*Identifizierung mit dem Aggressor*) is usually attributed to Anna Freud's 1936 book, *The Ego and the Mechanisms of Defence*. In fact, the term occurs for the first time in Ferenczi's article. Cf. p. 11 of the original German article published in *Int. Z. Psychoanal.*, where Ferenczi writes of an *ängstliche Identifizierung und Introjektion* (identification and introjection based on fear). In the diary, too, Ferenczi uses the term and the concept repeatedly.

5. Cf. John E. Gedo, "The Wise Baby Reconsidered," in *Freud: The Fusion of Science and Humanism—The Intellectual History of Psychoanalysis*, edited by John E. Gedo and George H.

Pollock (New York: International Universities Press, 1976), pp. 357–378.

6. "Korrespondenzblatt der Internationalen Psychoanalytischen Vereinigung," edited by Anna Freud, *Int. Z. Psychoanal.*, 18 (1932), pp. 239–299.

7. From a review by A. Bromley of Ferenczi's *Final Contributions to the Problems and Methods of Psycho-Analysis*, edited by Michael Balint, translated by Eric Mosbacher et al. (London: Hogarth Press and the Institute of Psycho-Analysis, 1955). The review appeared in the *Psychoanalytic Quarterly*, 26 (1957), pp. 112–113.

8. Joan Riviere (1883-1962) translated many of Freud's and Ferenczi's papers into English. She was an analyst herself and was in analysis with Jones.

9. S. Ferenczi, "Confusion of Tongues between Adults and the Child: The Language of Tenderness and the Language of Passion," *Int. J. Psycho-Analy.*, 30 (1949), pp. 225–230.

10. The best-known works (though none is very informative) are those by Michael Balint: "Sándor Ferenczi's Technical Experiments," in *Psychoanalytic Techniques*, edited by Benjamin B. Wolman (New York: Basic Books, 1967), pp. 147–167. *The Basic Fault: Therapeutic Aspects of Regression* (London: Tavistock, 1968), chapter 23: "The Disagreement between Freud and Ferenczi and Its Repercussions." "Dr. Sándor Ferenczi as Psychoanalyst" (1933), reprinted in *Problems of Human Pleasure and Behaviour* (New York: Liveright, 1956), pp. 235–242. See also Clara Thompson, "The Therapeutic Technique of Sándor Ferenczi: A Comment," *Int. J. Psycho-Anal.*, 24 (1943), pp. 64–66; Béla Grunberger, "De la 'technique active à la confusion de langues,'" *Revue française de psychoanalyse*, 38 (1974), pp. 521–546; Ilse Barande, *Sándor Ferenczi* (Paris: Payot, 1972); Janine Chasseguet-Smirgel, "A propos de la technique active de Ferenczi," in *Pour une psychoanalyse de l'art et de la créativité* (Paris: Payot, 1967). Edward Glover's treatment of active technique in his book *The Technique of Psycho-Analysis* (New York: International Universities Press, 1955, pp. 165–184) is useful.

11. Jones, 2, pp. 91–93.

12. The letters between Freud and Ferenczi were transcribed by Michael Balint and Ernst Freud, for an edition planned many years ago, though never published. This transcript, which is not free

of errors, exists in several copies, including one at the Library of Congress. I saw the copy in Maresfield Gardens.

13. Curiously enough, the actual text of the letter does not say this. The German reads: *"Ich bin auch jener PsA Übermensch den wir konstruiert haben, habe auch die Gegenübertragung nicht überwunden."* There is no negative (*nicht*) in the text, even if the sense seems to demand it. I saw only the transcript, the same one that Jones saw. The original letters are in the possession of Mrs. Enid Balint and are not available.

14. This is what the sense demands, and later letters from Freud to Ferenczi show that this is how it was understood (see note 15, chapter 3). But the actual German reads: *"N.B. Glauben Sie ja nicht, dass ich bei Ihnen irgendwelche grossartigen Geheimnisse vermute?"* which translates, literally, as: "You must not believe that I intuit that you have some magnificent secret." But in that case, the question mark is out of order. Perhaps the manuscript has been incorrectly read.

15. "Beitrag zur Diskussion über Onanie," *Bausteine*, 3, p. 37. Ferenczi's original discussion appeared in vol. 2 of *Diskussionen des Wiener psychoanalytischen Vereins: Die Onanie. Vierzehn Beiträge zu einer Diskussion der Wiener Psychoanalytischen Vereinigung* (Wiesbaden: J. F. Bergmann, 1912). The meetings began in November 1911 and the proceedings can be found in *Minutes of the Vienna Psychoanalytic Society*, edited by Herman Nunberg and Ernst Federn, translated by M. Nunberg (4 vols.; New York: International Universities Press, 1962–1975); the volumes cover the years 1906–1918.

16. *James Jackson Putnam and Psychoanalysis*, edited by Nathan G. Hale, Jr., translation of German texts by Judith Bernays Heller (Cambridge: Harvard University Press, 1971), p. 312. The reference is to a book by Jeno Kollaritz (*sic*) (1870–1940), *Charakter und Nervosität* (Berlin: Springer, 1912).

17. In 1923, Otto Rank and Sándor Ferenczi published a joint work, *Entwicklungsziele der Psychoanalyse: Zur Wechselbeziehung von Theorie und Praxis* (Leipzig, Vienna, and Zurich: Int. Psychoanal. Verlag), translated as *The Developmental Aims of Psycho-Analysis* (New York: Dover, 1956), which brought into the open the controversy over Ferenczi's technique. (See Jones, 3, p. 58, for a trenchant critique.) Four previously unpublished Freud/Ferenczi letters which discuss questions of analytic technique were recently

published in an article by Ilse Simitis, "Sigmund Freud/Sándor Ferenczi: Sechs Briefe zur Wechselbeziehung von psychoanalytischer Theorie und Technik," in *Zur Psychoanalyse der Objektbeziehungen,* edited by Gemma Jappe and Carl Nedelmann, *Problemata Fromann-Holzboog,* 88 (1981), pp. 139–174. On January 11, 1930 (p. 143), Freud told Ferenczi that he was "fed up" (he used the English words) with the therapeutic aspects of psychoanalysis, in contrast to Ferenczi's *furor sanandi,* his desire to heal at all costs.

18. *Int. J. Psycho-Anal.,* 8 (1927), pp. 417–421.

19. Letter to the author, December 20, 1979.

20. "Ferenczi's Contributions to Psychoanalysis," *Psychiatry,* 7 (1944), pp. 245–252.

21. Jones, 3, p. 197. The German translation of Jones's book gives the original German (when available) of letters that Jones had translated into English. *Das Leben und Werk von Sigmund Freud,* translated by Gertrud Meili-Dworetzki with the assistance of Katherine Jones (Bern: Hans Huber, 1978; original German translation, 1962). Freud's letter is dated December 13, 1931. Jones's translation of the first sentence misses the ironic tone: ". . . *die Differenz zwischen uns sich auf ein Kleinstes, ein Detail der Technik, zuspitzt . . .*" (Our differences come to a head over a very minor thing, a detail of technique.) Jones has omitted the words *ein Kleinstes* (a very minor thing), which is used sarcastically here, for kissing patients is hardly a minor detail of technique. Freud, in his original letter, did not write "God the Father" as Jones has translated, but used the English "godfather," i.e., that Ferenczi was godfather to these ideas.

22. "*Sexuelle Spielerei.*" The recently published letters from Ferenczi to Groddeck reveal that, in 1904 or 1905, Ferenczi began an affair with a married woman, Gizella Pálos, whose family he had known for many years. She had a daughter, Elma, who was in analysis with Ferenczi. Ferenczi fell in love with his patient, the daughter of his future wife, and wished to marry her. The unpublished letters from Ferenczi to Freud show that Freud urged him against acting on his inclinations, and, in fact, on March 1, 1919, Ferenczi married Gizella, who was eight years older than he. (Her former husband, who had not wanted the divorce, died of a heart attack the same day.) They had no children. The emotional complication of the two affairs seems not to have unduly bothered Freud. But Ferenczi felt (as revealed in his letters to Groddeck) that Freud had destroyed his chances for

sexual happiness and was angry with him. He told Groddeck (December 25, 1921): "I want . . . not an analytic interpretation, but something real, a young woman, a child." In "Analysis Terminable and Interminable," written in 1937, Freud said that Ferenczi's analysis "had a completely successful result. He married the woman he loved . . ." (*S.E.*, 23, p. 221). For the letters to Groddeck, available only in French, see *Sándor Ferenczi/Georg Groddeck: Correspondance (1921–1933)*, translation, notes, and commentaries by Coq-Héron (a translation group composed of Judith Dupont, Suzanne Hommel, Françoise Samson, Pierre Sabourin, Bernard This) (Paris: Payot, 1982). The introduction by Judith Dupont is excellent.

23. Wilhelm Stekel (1868–1940), one of Freud's earliest followers, was noted for a tendency to invent case histories. He resigned from the Psychoanalytic Society in 1912, to Freud's evident relief.

24. Letter to the author from Dr. Judith Dupont of April 28, 1983.

25. The German paper appeared in *Int. Z. Psychoanal.*, 17 (1931), pp. 161–175; English translation in *Int. J. Psycho-Anal.*, 12 (1931), pp. 468–482. Reprinted in *Final Contributions*, cited above, pp. 126–142; the passage cited is on p. 133.

26. *Int. Z. Psychoanal.*, 16 (1930), pp. 149–164; English translation in *Int. J. Psycho-Anal.*, 11 (1930), pp. 428–443. Reprinted in *Final Contributions*, pp. 108–125; the passage cited is on p. 121. Along with "Confusion of Tongues" these papers, in which Ferenczi speaks of real traumas, are comparable to Freud's three 1896 papers: "Heredity and the Aetiology of the Neuroses" (*S.E.*, 3, pp. 142–156), "Further Remarks on the Neuro-psychoses of Defence" (*S.E.*, 3, pp. 159–185), and "The Aetiology of Hysteria" (*S.E.*, 3, pp. 191–221).

27. "Gedanken über das Trauma" appeared in *Int. Z. Psychoanal.*, 20 (1934), pp. 5–12. It comes from the Ferenczi literary estate (*Nachlass*), but is not identical to what appears in *Bausteine*, the most complete collection of Ferenczi's writings in German. Most of the passages can be found somewhere in *Bausteine*, but there are also whole paragraphs which cannot be found in print anywhere. There are also discrepancies between the two texts, and it is impossible to tell which is the more authentic. At the beginning of vol. 3 of *Bausteine* (which contains the *Nachlass* material), Vilma Kovács says that "discretion demanded leaving out material from the

Nachlass." The French translation, cited above, by Judith Dupont et al., is much better than anything that now exists in English and also more reliable. Judith Dupont (*op. cit.*, p. 266) notes that these "notes and fragments" are the less intimate part of the diary.

28. August 29, 1932: "*Jones ist auch kein ungetrübtes Vergnügen für die Zukunft.*"

29. Cf. Jones, 3, p. 184.

30. Freud knew the thrust of Ferenczi's paper. An unpublished letter from Ferenczi to Freud written on May 31, 1931, contains a summary of two "preliminary communications" that Ferenczi proposed giving at the Congress:

> Does the dream have a second function? Supported by experiences that took place in deep relaxation in the course of analysis, during which traumatic experiences tend to be repeated, as well as by the analysis of dreams in general, one comes to suspect that the states of sleeping and dreaming are always attempting to empty the psychical system of traumatic day- and life-residues by means of living through them again [in the form of dreams] and thereby reveal something of the nature of traumatic-neurotic dream processes.

Freud's response was that the "so-called second function of the dream is also its first function," and he refers to *Beyond the Pleasure Principle*. Ferenczi answered on June 14, 1931:

> Dear Professor:
> Naturally I know only too well that the function of the dream that I emphasize is the same that you have described and explained (in *Beyond the Pleasure Principle*) as being characteristic of the dreams of the person who has been traumatized. My experiences, however, force me to emphasize this point of view more than you did in *The Interpretation of Dreams*. In other words: I would like to generalize the point of view that in sleep and dreams traumas are mastered.

31. On September 27, 1932, Ferenczi wrote to Freud to complain of Brill's presence at their meeting. Freud's answer (October 2, 1932), which is unpublished, is substantially what Jones used in his account of the meeting:

> It was never intended that Brill should play the role of arbiter. Nor did he ever begin to play such a role. Remember, he wasn't

even there when you came in. You said, without a word of greeting: "I will read to you my Congress paper out loud."

32. Dr. Lampl-de Groot wrote to me on December 20, 1979:

I still have a vivid picture of him, when my husband and I approached him during the boat trip on the *Rhejn* off Wiesbaden. He was lonely and looked forlorn and distressed. As Hans Lampl and I myself had always liked him as one of the finest and most sensitive of the "older" generation of analysts, we talked to him and tried to cheer him up a little bit. . . . I feel, the cuddling and kissing of his patients was a real traumatic seduction for them. That, at least, was the case with the American woman who came to me after Ferenczi's death. She was completely confused and prone to the severest anxieties one can imagine. . . .

One of the tragedies of sexually seduced children is their later need, in some cases (especially where they have not been able to acknowledge their experiences), to repeat these experiences in a setting where they are no longer the victim but the perpetrator of the seduction. The same is true of physical beatings. It is a tragic compulsion to repeat past sorrows by acting them out against someone else. Ferenczi's sexualized behavior toward some of his patients was no doubt an example of this. I do not understand why Ferenczi did not see that any form of disguised sexuality with a patient who had been misused in this same manner during her childhood was bound to be hurtful.

33. In every other case I have been able to trace the origin of Jones's statements. But I have not succeeded in finding a source for his claims that Ferenczi had homicidal outbursts. It should be noted that Jones had been analyzed by Ferenczi. Relations between the two men were not good. The correspondence between Jones and Ferenczi at the Colchester Archives is enlightening: On December 13, 1926, Ferenczi wrote to Jones (in English): "Who of us is quite free from character difficulties?" He defends himself against Jones's accusation that his works are "fantastic" with these words (in a German letter of January 6, 1930):

I don't always read your works with unmixed pleasure either. If mine are wild and fantastic, yours often give the impression of a kind of logical-sadistic violence, especially since the works, which, by the way, are equally fantastic, on child analysis have appeared. These works of your English group have not charmed me in the least.

In the same letter, Ferenczi writes:

> Perhaps we should draw the lesson, from this event, that psycho-analysts in particular, more than has been the case until now, should not allow scientific and scientific-technique differences of opinion to degenerate into personal attacks. . . . It would be useless to deny that what is really a question of scientific technique, the problem of lay analysis in America, as well as certain differences of opinion with regard to the analysis of children, has given occasion to the rise of a certain angry mood between us, old friends. As a lone worker I have used the last years, somewhat withdrawn, to attempt to go deeper into theory and technique. Perhaps by the next Congress I will be able to speak about some of these things.

34. 1933, p. 464. Cf. Michael Balint's letter to the editor, *Int. J. Psycho-Anal.*, 39 (1938), p. 68, "Sándor Ferenczi's Last Years." Jones responded:

> The varying value of Ferenczi's last writings remain, as Dr. Balint rightly remarks, controversial. I merely recorded my acquiescence in the opinions expressed so firmly by Freud, Eitingon, and everyone I knew in 1933. . . .

Cf. Imre Hermann, "Die Objektivität in Jones' Diagnose über Ferenczis Krankheit," *Psyche*, 7 (1953), p. 116, who takes a stand in favor of Ferenczi's last opinions. This is also true of the obituary by Michael Balint (a former analysand of Ferenczi's), which was based on a paper read on the occasion of the fifteenth anniversary of Ferenczi's death, at the British Psycho-Analytic Society, on May 5, 1948, and published in *Int. J. Psycho-Anal.*, 30 (1949). However, Balint seems to have taken his remarks from the German article by Max Eitingon published in *Imago*, 19 (1933), pp. 289–295, quoted below.

35. *Imago*, 19 (1933), p. 292. Ernst Simmel gave an elaborate obituary at a special meeting of the Berlin Psychoanalytic Society, "Gedenkrede für Sándor Ferenczi," published in *Imago*, 19. He mentions all of Ferenczi's important papers except the 1932 paper. See, too, the obituary by Paul Federn in *Int. Z. Psychoanal.*, 19

(1933), pp. 305–321, also published in English in *Int. J. Psycho-Anal*. According to S. Lorand (obituary published in the *Psychoanalytic Review*, 22 [1933], p. 360): "In another year, he would have seen the special jubilee number of the *Internationale Zeitschrift für Psychoanalyse* which was planned for his 60th birthday." However, the 1934 issue of the *Zeitschrift* was *not* dedicated to Ferenczi, though it began with an unpublished article by him.

36. *Int. Z. Psychoanal.*, 19 (1933), pp. 301–304. *S.E.*, 22, pp. 226–229.

37. This book, published in 1924 (though written in 1918), contains the trace of many ideas passed on by Freud in the course of their conversations, which may have played some role in Freud's admiration of the work. The German text is reproduced in *Schriften zur Psychoanalyse*, vol. 2, edited by M. Balint (Frankfurt am Main: Conditio Humana, 1972). The book appeared in English in 1938 as *Thalassa: A Theory of Genitality* (Albany, N.Y.: The Psychoanalytic Quarterly, Inc.). Note the footnote to p. 77 in the German text and cf. *S.E.*, 4, p. 116.

38. The German text of this revealing letter has not been published, but the French translation, by Judith Dupont et al., appears in *Sándor Ferenczi/Georg Groddeck: Correspondance (1921–1933)*, p. 55.

39. New York: Basic Books, 1959, p. 200.

40. Ferenczi evidently believed that Freud was not prepared to accept the reality of traumatic events in early childhood because of a personal reluctance to examine his own childhood. Thus in his diary (August 4, 1932) Ferenczi writes: "In his behavior Freud plays the role of the castrating god. He does not want to know anything at all about the traumatic aspects [*Momente*] of his own castration in childhood, and deems himself to be the only one who need not be analyzed." Toward the end of this diary (Aug. 7, 1932), Ferenczi makes a comment that will strike a responsive chord in many analytic patients today:

> Mrs. F. felt, rightly so, attracted by the essence of psychoanalysis, trauma and reconstruction, but is repelled by the way analysts make use of these concepts [in treatment]. On the other hand, Professor K., who is not an analyst, is helpful to her because he supportively [*vertrauensvoll*] allows the patient's own intelligence to flourish.

APPENDIX A

FREUD AND EMMA ECKSTEIN

EMMA Eckstein's relationship to Freud and to psychoanalysis has been shrouded in mystery. Only vague hints as to her connection with Freud have emerged from the standard sources. Jones (2, p. 469) writes that Freud

> found the psychology of women more enigmatic than that of men. . . . Freud was interested in another type of woman, of a more intellectual and perhaps masculine cast. Such women several times played a part in his life, accessory to his men friends though of a finer caliber, but they had no erotic attraction for him. Minna Bernays, then in chronological order: Emma Eckstein, Loe Kann, Lou Andreas-Salomé, Joan Riviere, Marie Bonaparte.

It is not clear from whom Jones heard this, whether from Freud himself, or, more likely, from his daughter Mathilde. (The letters between Jones and Mathilde are in the Jones Archives in the Institute for Psycho-Analysis in London. I could not find any reference to Emma Eckstein there.)

Emma Eckstein was born in Vienna on January 28, 1865, the child of Albert (born in 1825) and Amalia (born Wehle, in 1836) Eckstein, and died on July 30, 1924, of apoplexia cerebri. Emma Eckstein had five sisters and two brothers. Her eldest sister, Käthe Hirsch, was the mother of Albert Hirst and Dr. A. Elias, both of whom granted interviews to K. R. Eissler in the 1950's about their Aunt Emma. (These interviews are now at the Library of Congress, in sealed archives.) One of Emma's brothers, Friedrich Eckstein, was referred to by Freud in *Civilization and Its Discontents* (*S.E.*, 21, p. 72), according to Anna Freud:

Another friend of mine, whose insatiable craving for knowledge has led him to make the most unusual experiments and has ended by giving him encyclopaedic knowledge, has assured me that through the practices of Yoga, by withdrawing from the world, by fixing the attention on bodily functions and by peculiar methods of breathing, one can in fact evoke new sensations and coenesthesias in oneself, which he regards as regressions to primordial states of mind which have long ago been overlaid.

Friedrich Eckstein, called "the philosopher of the Ringstrasse," was a Sanskritist, a vegetarian, a close friend of Hugo Wolf, Brückner, and other musicians, and wrote articles about psychoanalysis. His autobiography, which Freud took with him to London, *Alte unnennbare Tage! Erinnerungen aus 70 Lehr- und Wanderjahren* (Ineffable Days of Old: Memories of Seventy Years of Travel and Study) (Vienna, Leipzig, Zurich: Herbert Reichner Verlag, 1936), mentions Freud several times (pp. 20–24). There is some information given about the father, Albert Eckstein, an inventor, who had a parchment factory, but otherwise he says little about the family. Emma Eckstein is not mentioned by name. The other brother, Gustav Eckstein (1875–1916), a Social Democrat, was an associate of Karl Kautsky, the leader of the Socialist Party in Austria. Gustav died of tuberculosis at an early age. He is mentioned on p. 214 of the *Oesterreichische Biographische Lexicon* (1815–1950). Karl Kautsky's son, an obstetrician, was a friend of Emma Eckstein. According to Mrs. Ella Heinz, a friend of his, whom I interviewed in Berkeley (1981), he spoke of an ill-fated gynecological operation that Freud encouraged, which eventually led to Emma E's death. (See below, p. 245.) I have not been able to confirm this from any other source, and Mrs. Heinz's memory of what Dr. Kautsky told her about this was rather vague. Emma Eckstein's sister Therese Schlesinger was one of the first women members of parliament. Her biography is found in Alfred Magaziner, *Die Wegbereiter: Aus der Geschichte der Arbeiterbewegung* (Vienna: Volksbuchverlag [1975], pp. 216–219).

We do not know much about Emma Eckstein's early life.

Until 1905, she wrote articles (discussed below); after that, she seems to have withdrawn from the world and lived in a room, surrounded by books, never leaving her couch, apparently confined to it by a puzzling ailment which those around her considered hysterical in origin but which she felt was organic.

A single mysterious line from an unpublished passage in a letter to Fliess (December 12, 1897) indicates that Emma Eckstein, at Freud's request, saw patients. The passage itself is about the seduction theory. The first line begins:

> *Die Eckstein hat ihre Patientin so behandelt, dass sie . . .*
> [Eckstein treated her patient in such a way that . . .]

From the rest of the passage (see above, p. 114), it is clear that the treatment she used was nothing other than psychoanalysis. It is, unfortunately, the only such passage in the letters—nothing further is said about Emma's seeing patients. Fliess seems to have known about it, since Freud does not feel it necessary to explain to him why Emma would be seeing patients. Under what circumstances, for how long, and with what results, are all questions that cannot be answered.

In the Library of Congress there is a series of fourteen unpublished letters, given to the library by Emma Eckstein's nephew, Albert Hirst, that Freud wrote to Emma Eckstein between 1895 and 1910. One of these is simply a visiting card, which reads, on the envelope:

Fräulein Emma Eckstein
V Siebenbrunnengasse 15

On the other side is written:

Dr. Sigm. Freud
Dozent für Nervenkrankheiten a. d. Universität
                   Wien,
ord. 3–5 h.   IX., Berggasse 19
Dies ist Fräulein Stella Pfeffer, 19 J. Ihr
Pflegekind usw.

The card is not dated. But since Freud uses the title *Dozent*, this was before he received the title of *Ausserordentlicher* (Associate) Professor; i.e., before 1902. The text reads:

> This is [to introduce] Miss Stella Pfeffer, 19 years old, your foster child, etc.

No doubt the "etc." referred to the fact that Freud had already discussed the "case" with Emma Eckstein before sending her. It appears to be a referral of a patient.

Emma Eckstein had written about the sexual enlightenment of children as early as 1899, in an article published in the socialist *Die neue Zeit* entitled "Eine wichtige Erziehungsfrage" (An Important Question in Education) (*Die neue Zeit, Revue des geistigen und öffentlichen Lebens,* 18 [1899–1900], pp. 666–669). She writes there that

> a child knows shame only slightly, or not at all, knows no sexual feelings of any kind, and so can only guess that there are other reasons, besides the desire to have children, that would fuel the desire to have sexual intercourse.

She ends the essay (which is only two pages long) by saying that she would tell a child that adults "mate when they like each other, in fact, love each other [*die sich lieb haben*] so much that each of them wishes that their child will look like their partner." There is a dim echo of this thought, and even similar wording, in the minutes from a meeting of the Vienna Psychoanalytic Society, on May 12, 1909, where Freud says of children: "Enlightenment should above all make it clear to them that this is a matter of acts of tenderness, that their parents love each other very much" (". . . *dass sich die Eltern dabei sehr lieb haben*"). At a meeting on January 4, 1911, Paul Federn, whose family was close to the Eckstein family, mentions Emma's article, calling it the first work on this subject written under the influence of psychoanalysis (*Protokolle der Wiener psychoanalytischen Vereinigung,* 3, p. 107). Dr. Wolfgang Huber kindly drew my attention to a book review signed "E.E." (in the table of contents her full name is given) which appeared in

Die neue Zeit, 21, no. 24 (1902–1903), p. 768, of a book by
E. Stiehle: *Eine Mutterpflicht. Beitrag zur sexuellen Pädagogik*
(A Mother's Duty. Contribution to Sexual Pedagogy) (Leipzig:
Hermann Seemann, n.d.). Emma is very indignant, and eloquent,
about mothers who instill in their daughters the social shame
that comes from having a child out of wedlock. She quotes a
dialogue between mother and daughter which, she says, is as
bad as depositing the bogeyman in the child's memory for life,
causing her to fear her own instincts. She calls this "complete
idiocy." It is the most liberal piece that Emma Eckstein wrote.

Emma Eckstein's major work was a short (38 pages) book,
entitled *Die Sexualfrage in der Erziehung des Kindes* (The Question of Sexuality in Child-Rearing) (Leipzig: Curt Wigand,
1904). A friendly but critical review by Bernhard Steiner appeared in *Mutterschutz*, 10 (1905–1906), pp. 448–450. Freud
was apparently involved in its creation (see below). Half of the
citations come from books that were in Freud's library (and we
know from his letters to Emma Eckstein, written between 1895
and 1910, that she was borrowing books from his library; e.g., in
letters of 1902): Möbius, *On the Natural Feeble-Mindedness
of Women;* Rohleder on masturbation; Havelock Ellis on the
sexual instincts; Multatuli; and Carpenter on "Love's Coming-
of-Age." Most of her book is devoted to the subject of masturbation in childhood. It is surprising to learn that Emma Eckstein
shares the views of most contemporary physicians. She begins
by saying that it is the duty of mothers to develop "insight into
the great danger of precociously awakened sexual feelings and
the extraordinarily common and dangerous practice, even among
children, of masturbation" (p. 7). She continues (p. 9):

> Masturbation is an insidious enemy for the child. Unnoticed and
> unsuspected, it slinks into the nursery and works away there,
> assiduously and with no hindrance, at its goal of destroying the
> youth and strength, both physical and mental, of its victims. These
> victims were exposed to it because the appointed guardians of the
> child did not repress the danger, or had not even learned to see
> the danger.

She describes (p. 12) with approval the use of special night clothing to prevent masturbation, but notes that "once the sexual feelings have been awakened," there is no end to the ways the child will find to provide himself with sexual stimulation. She then takes up a position against the view she herself held earlier (in the 1899 article quoted above), and says that women "must overcome the disinclination to allow the possibility of sexual feelings in children" (p. 12). She refers to Rohleder's book on masturbation (p. 13) (Hermann Rohleder, *Die Masturbation* [2nd ed; Berlin: H. Kornfeld, 1902]; Freud owned a copy of this book, now in Maresfield Gardens). She agrees with Rohleder in complaining "that universities do not offer courses on how to treat masturbation effectively." For there is no question, as the leading figures in psychiatry tell us, that "masturbation practiced in early childhood can have dire consequences for the mental development of the individual" (p. 14). She bemoans the fact that mechanical and forceful measures (e.g., bandages) are necessary in earliest childhood, but "nevertheless it would be misplaced sentimentality to stand aloof from these temporary restrictions and inconveniences and thus provide room for the evil [to grow]" (p. 15). She is not in favor of punishing the child, but wishes to ally herself with a healthy part of him that must learn to recognize this "bad habit as a hateful one," and to strengthen the cleavage in the child that separates his will from his ability (p. 18). The way to do this is to gain the confidence of the child, and try to invade his secret practice—learn the times and the method and create an atmosphere such that the "little sinner will dare to ruefully say: Mother, against my will, I did it again" (p. 19). For the child must be encouraged to experience "disdain for his own feelings." One cannot help but feel the autobiographical thrust of this section:

> Few are so lucky that they emerge from this battle the victor through their energetic will and the practice, begun early on, of self-control. Most people torture themselves in mental agony, which they keep a closely guarded secret and which grows even stronger until it poisons their life (p. 19).

She continues:

> It is not seldom that a single individual considers his craving for masturbation and the pleasure he takes in it to be completely unique to him, and thinks of himself therefore as more evil and more animal-like than others would ever guess. He considers it completely impossible to communicate his suffering and sorrow to even his most trusted friend. The mere fact that an older, more experienced person provides him with enlightenment as to the character as well as the frequency of this practice is often sufficient to help him and free him [from his misery] (p. 19).

It is hard to avoid seeing here a thinly veiled reference to her treatment with Freud. Albert Hirst, interviewed in 1952 by K. R. Eissler for the Sigmund Freud Archives (I saw a copy of this interview in the Jones Archives in London), mentioned that he had a terrible feeling of shame over masturbation, and that Freud helped him considerably (during a period of analysis in 1910) by explaining to him that masturbation was practically universal and not likely to do him any harm. This is in marked contrast to Freud's earlier views. Appalling as the views described in Emma E's pamphlet are, they were still, just as were those of Freud, in advance of most of the views on masturbation of the time. The attempt, even though often self-righteous and pretentious, was nonetheless to seek out some of the psychological sources and consequences of masturbation. For example, she writes that masturbation is a replacement for love from another person (*op. cit.*, p. 17: she calls it *"Entschädigung für entzogene Liebe,"* a compensation for lost love)—an obvious point now, but not at the time. However, it is not difficult to see in this essay another tendency, an attempt to distance herself from any thoughts about sexual seduction. She seems eager to lay the blame for a precociously awakened genital sexuality on something she feels is a particularly dangerous seed-bed of sexual vice in the case of little girls: fantasies. "Daydreams," she writes (p. 21), are "parasitic plants," which take over more and more of the life of the young girl. They are not, she explains, content to live at night, in dreams, but invade the day as well. And what are these daydreams? "The range of ideas in daydreams is a very limited one. They are primarily imaginings about sexuality," and they are, moreover, "of a highly fantastic kind." Could this possibly be a reference to the shame she felt at having had ideas of being seduced as a child? No doubt, by this time, she was well aware that Freud felt she had never, in fact, been seduced, but was a severe masturbator, given over to inventing stories "of a highly fantastic kind." At the end of her book, Emma Eckstein speaks of a fear that many young women had that "by dancing, by topical [medical] treatment such as massages and the like, or through a kiss, they could become pregnant" (p. 30). She hints that she herself "treated" such cases:

> Here I wish to stress as well: I am not aware of a single case that can be thought of as the result of a constitutional predisposition to illness or lack of intelligence. When I for the first time succeeded with much difficulty in eliciting such a secret from a well-read, gifted 18-year-old girl who had been educated accordingly, when for the first time I came to see the emotional anguish of such a helpless being, I believed, deeply shaken, I was faced with the specific product of a diseased imagination. Once my attention had been drawn to it, though, experience taught me that this fantasy was not at all unusual, but is the exceedingly painful result of a lack of knowledge.

She then proceeds to the device of an invented letter:

> I believe the best way to express my views and ideas in regard to this subject is by means of the following letter which is conceived [*gedacht*] as part of a correspondence between a mother and her child and is to provide the desired enlightenment from afar.

Why would Emma choose to include a letter that could be mistaken for a real one to an imaginary son (who could also be mistaken for a real son)? The theme of an unmarried mother (vaguely hinted at by the fact that the mother is writing to her son from far away—almost as if they were not to meet again) was very important to Emma Eckstein. She has a short article in *Dokumente der Frauen*, "Das Dienstmädchen als Mutter" (Servant as Mother), published in 1899 (*Dokumente der Frauen*,

2, no. 14 [1899–1900], edited by August Fickert, Marie Lang, and Rosa Mayreder, pp. 594–598). The article is about "unmarried girls who come at a very tender age from the country to the city" (p. 595), where they take up service in a wealthy household, convinced they are "under the protection of the family." But in reality their protectors too often turn into their seducers: "The inexperienced girls are only too easily made the victims of the men of the household." Emma then points out:

> Our laws, which protect all our property, do not recognize the honor of somebody who serves, and these poor young girls are without rights and without protection even in the eyes of the law. A telling proof of this is paragraph No. 504 of our Laws of Tort: A guest in the house who dishonors a minor daughter, or a minor relative of the male or female head of the house who belongs to the household, is liable, for this transgression, to be punished with incarceration from 1 to 3 months according to the relationship to the family. Paragraph 505 says that the same punishment is to be meted out to a woman servant in the family who commits a sexual felony on a minor son or a minor relative who is living in the house. So we see: according to [Austrian] law, a woman serving in a household can well be punished as a seducer, but cannot, by the same law, be herself protected from seduction.

Emma Eckstein is pointing out that Austrian laws against seduction are class-oriented and protect the rights of the wealthy, adding to the financial power over their servants a legal one.

In 1907 Freud wrote an open letter to Dr. M. Fürst, the editor of *Soziale Medicin und Hygiene,* which was published in the magazine (2, no. 6 [June 1907], pp. 360–367) ("The Sexual Enlightenment of Children," *S.E.,* 9, pp. 130–139), in which he says:

> It seems that the large majority of authors, both men and women, who have written about the sexual enlightenment of youth have concluded in favor of it. But the clumsiness of most of their proposals as to when and how this enlightenment is to take place tempts one to think that they have not found it easy to arrive at this conclusion. So far as my knowledge of the literature goes, a single outstanding exception is provided by the charming letter of

explanation which a certain Frau Emma Eckstein quotes as having been written by her to her son when he was about ten years old.

Actually, Strachey has mistranslated the last sentence: *"Ganz vereinzelt steht nach meiner Literaturkenntnis jener reizende Aufklärungsbrief da, den eine Frau Emma Eckstein an ihren etwa zehnjährigen Sohn zu schreiben vorgibt."* What Freud actually says is that Emma Eckstein *pretends* (*vorgibt*) to write a letter to her son. It is not clear from the German whether just the letter is "pretend" or the "son" as well. Freud's reference to a ten-year-old is puzzling. Nowhere in her book does Emma Eckstein suggest that the fictive child she is writing to is ten years old. Nor does Emma Eckstein make it clear that she has invented the child she is writing to. The word she uses, *gedacht*, could mean either "planned" or "imagined."

This same essay by Freud contains a very moving letter which appears to have been included for its charm:

> The following little document shows how tormenting this curiosity can become in older children. It is a letter written by a motherless girl of eleven and a half who had been speculating on the problem with her younger sister.

> "Dear Aunt Mali,
> "Will you please be so kind as to tell me how you got Christel and Paul. You must know because you are married. We were arguing about it yesterday evening and we want to know the truth. We have nobody else to ask. When are you coming to Salzburg? You know, Aunt Mali, we simply can't understand how the stork brings babies. Trudel thought the stork brings them in a shirt. Then we want to know as well if the stork gets them out of the pond and why one never sees babies in ponds. And will you please tell me, too, how one knows beforehand when one is going to have one. Write and tell me everything about it.
> "With thousands of greetings and kisses from us all,
> > "Your inquisitive niece,
> > Lili"

I do not believe that this touching letter brought the two sisters the enlightenment they wanted. Later on the writer of it fell ill from unanswered questions—of obsessional brooding.

Freud clearly knows a great deal about the letter and the person who wrote it, and the person who did not answer it. As if impelled by some inner need that he does not communicate, Freud adds a footnote in 1924: "After some years, however, her obsessional brooding gave way to a dementia praecox."

It is not beyond the realm of possibility that Emma Eckstein had an illegitimate child, and that her letter is in fact based on reality. If the child was ten at the time this book was written in 1904, then she would have given birth in 1894, during her analysis. Being in analysis, she would have told Freud, and possibly nobody else. I must stress that none of the six people I spoke to who knew Emma Eckstein had ever heard any such rumor. Nor do I believe this is anything more than speculation. But it is one more piece of evidence that the mystery surrounding Emma Eckstein has by no means been resolved.

One more, perhaps minor but nevertheless intriguing revelation comes from an unpublished letter that Freud wrote to Emma Eckstein on April 17, 1904:

> Dear Emma:
> At last I can give you the answer I owe you—I have been speaking so much that I did not get around to writing. So, as far as the thesis [or sentence] is concerned, you can make whatever use of it you wish. As soon as your work has seen the light of day, I will write, in accordance with your ideas, a review, add to it the censure [*Tadel?*] you and I both wish, and then offer the whole thing to the *Neue Freie Presse*. Anyway, it will take some time before it is printed. I will not demand that it appear in the Sunday issue. I know that such wishes do not allow themselves to be fulfilled, and in any event it is entirely immaterial [on what day the review appears].

This comes from the collection of fourteen (unpublished) letters to Emma Eckstein in the Library of Congress. It could well be that because Freud never did manage to publish the review, the open letter to Dr. Fürst appeared in place of the promised review.

From a later letter of February 11, 1905, from Freud to Emma Eckstein, we learn that the *Neue Freie Presse* rejected the review, and Freud intended to rewrite it and send it elsewhere:

Dear Emma:

So that you don't do away with yourself, which would be a grave loss for me, I am enclosing the response of the *Neue Freie Presse* to the letter [we] discussed. I answered: [I] am perfectly prepared to rewrite it, but this time I must request assurance that it will appear next Sunday. As of now there has been *no* answer. And now I believe we are finally free of the *Neue Freie Presse* and can write the article for another newspaper and I hope get it published. And this time it should be better.

Cordial greetings
Your
Dr. Freud

Whether he ever did so, or whether he repaid this "debt" to a patient with the reference to her in the 1907 article, is not known. My attempts to find the review have been unsuccessful.

At the end of his life, in 1937, Freud published "Analysis Terminable and Interminable" (*S.E.*, 23). It would seem that to the end of his days he was preoccupied with Emma Eckstein. For, if I am not mistaken, that work contains a hidden reference to her case. Freud writes (p. 222):

I now pass on to my second example, which raises the same problem [as Ferenczi's analysis]. An unmarried woman, no longer young, had been cut off from life since puberty by an inability to walk, owing to severe pains in the legs. Her condition was obviously of a hysterical nature, and it had defied many kinds of treatment. An analysis lasting three-quarters of a year removed the trouble and restored to the patient, an excellent and worthy person, her right to a share in life. In the years following her recovery she was consistently unfortunate. There were disasters in her family, and financial losses, and, as she grew older, she saw every hope of happiness in love and marriage vanish. But the one-time invalid stood up to all this valiantly and was a support to her family in difficult times. I cannot remember whether it was twelve or fourteen years after the end of her analysis that, owing to profuse haemorrhages, she was obliged to undergo a gynecological examination. A myoma was found, which made a complete hysterectomy advisable. From the time of this operation, the woman became ill once more. She fell in love with her surgeon, wallowed in masochistic phantasies about the fearful changes in her inside—phantasies with which she concealed her romance—and proved inaccessible to a further attempt at analysis. She remained abnormal to the end of her life. The successful analytic treatment took place so long ago that we cannot expect too much from it; it was in the earliest years of my work as an analyst. No doubt the patient's second illness may have sprung from the same source as her first one which had been successfully overcome: it may have been a different manifestation of the same repressed impulses, which the analysis had only incompletely resolved. But I am inclined to think that, were it not for the new trauma, there would have been no fresh outbreaks of neurosis.

Certain facts speak in favor of identifying this patient as Emma Eckstein. First of all, the dates: when Freud speaks of the analysis having taken place "in the earliest years of my work as an analyst," we must assume this to be between 1894 and 1898. Emma Eckstein's analysis certainly fell within this period. The letters to Fliess about her cover a period of about three quarters of a year, precisely the time Freud mentions as having been given over to her analysis. The gynecological operation took place twelve to fourteen years later, i.e., between 1908 and 1912. Do we have anything from that period that would indicate that Freud was in contact with Emma Eckstein? Yes. In the Library of Congress, among the papers that Emma Eckstein left her nephew, Albert Hirst, is a medical prescription, dated May 24, 1910. It is for boric acid for the vagina. It is made out to Miss Emma Eckstein (Emma Eckstein never married), and it is signed by Sigmund Freud. Freud says that this was one of his earliest cases. Albert Hirst, her nephew, in an interview with K. R. Eissler, on March 16, 1952 (from the Jones Archives in London), writes: "This Aunt Emma, Freud's first patient, while her whole life was marred by a hysteria, still had unusual qualities." Freud says that she was "an excellent and worthy person." Freud writes that the analysis of this patient was a success. Hirst also wrote an autobiography, *Analysed and Reeducated by Freud Himself,*

Emma Eckstein in the
last year of her life

which was never published. (Albert Hirst's niece, Dr. Hanna E. Kapit, in New York, kindly sent me a copy of this autobiography.) He begins the chapter entitled "Aunt Emma" with these words:

> One of Freud's earliest successes as an analyst, perhaps his earliest, was the cure of the neurosis of my aunt Emma.

In the interview with Eissler he said:

> I think it was of importance to him [Freud] in his practice that he had this great success, this well-known girl, this girl of a well-known family. Now she was a very beautiful woman and after he had this great success, she for several years led a perfectly normal life.

Freud says "she was a support to her family." Hirst in the interview says: "She also, after the marriage of her two older sisters, ran my grandmother's household. That was quite a task— 6 members, and always open house." Freud tells us that this patient suffered a relapse. Hirst, in his chapter on Emma Eckstein, writes: "Then Emma suffered a relapse. I have a notion that she was all her life in love with a certain Vienna architect, and that her relapse came after he got married, or after she became convinced in some other way that her love was hopeless." Freud says that there were disasters in the family and financial losses, and Hirst (interview) says that she "ran a rather complicated household which had to be run in a certain way on very little money, with most incredible efficiency." As for the symptom of not being able to walk, Hirst (autobiography) writes that "she spent all her days on her couch, never left her room, not even for meals, could not walk." (This is also mentioned in a letter to Fliess.) Freud writes that "she proved inaccessible to a further attempt at analysis," and Hirst (interview) says: "There was a time when, I remember, I don't think it was during the time that I was in analysis, but it may have been. Anyhow, Freud would come to her and try to continue the analysis. There was a conflict between him and her." Freud ends by saying that "she remained abnormal to the end of her life." Hirst (autobiography) writes: "Emma . . . soon returned to her couch on which she had lived so long. She survived, as a hopeless invalid, for another ten years."

A LETTER TO EMMA ECKSTEIN

November 30, 1905
Dear Emma:

It won't do you any good if you deprive me of my title. It cannot change much between us, and I change my sentiments with as much difficulty as I do my opinions. Let me therefore repeat that it is only a nasty accident if I cannot resume your treatment. As though it had waited for you, the onslaught started after you stayed away so that within one week I had to accept 4 [patients] and decline 2. You are only too familiar with the sad necessity of having to make a living; and the touchiness you betray, though at a distance—that I should have treated you without expecting money from you—is something that is so little like you that I am convinced this will be the first thing you will take back.

But it naturally has as much to do with the other. That you could be so misled, could so misunderstand the freedom to say anything in the treatment, and attribute to me the intention of offending [you] when I relied on my unshakable trust in your friendship and your love of truth in order to permit you to obtain insight into a delicate but nevertheless usual and expectable transference—that, it is true, did not shake my opinion of you, but it did again instill in me respect for the elemental femaleness with which I constantly have to struggle. I am not surprised then that you also do not comprehend other sentences in my letter which cannot be misunderstood. I cannot possibly have meant anything but that it is impossible for me to let the discontinuation of treatment (the interruption, I hope) be explained with the pretext that I regard your pains as organic. That you would have to say something else instead which is closer to the truth, to explain [the break], for example, that we had a quarrel; that you could not accept something that I asserted and the like; that you wanted some time in which to think things over or something similar.

May I at the end draw your attention to a small contradiction which is in fact at the bottom of your being angry. At one time I am supposed to have offended you by denying you the qualities that would attract a man; the other time I must have offended you by explaining to you how it happened that in our relationship love did not appear. Can both injuries really be comprehended from the same standpoint? I hope you will soon tell me: No (which, after all, you like to say) and therefore I remain with

cordial greetings
your
Dr. Freud

The 1952 interview with Emma's nephew, Albert Hirst, is instructive. He tells Dr. Eissler:

There was a Viennese woman physician, the daughter of a rather well-known physician—a Dr. Dora Teleky. Now she was a friend of the family and I thought she was a very good-looking woman, incidentally, and I admired her. She one day was visiting Emma, while Freud was analyzing Emma in the second stage, and discovered a—oh, some ulcer or something, anyhow some pus collection on her abdomen, and pretended to operate it and that was supposed to be the answer for the trouble, and Emma immediately had a great recovery and could get up. and here was the proof that this thing was physical. And that must have happened while I was in analysis because I remember how indignant Freud was about Dr. Teleky for this interference, and he immediately stopped the analysis and said "Well, that's the end of Emma. That dooms her from now on, nobody can cure her neurosis."

Hirst tells the same story, slightly differently, in his unpublished autobiography:

The second event: Dr. Dora T., a friend of the family, a woman physician, came to see Emma as a friendly visitor. She claimed suddenly to have discovered an abscess near Emma's navel and drained it. Dora claimed that she had found the source of Emma's illness and had cured it. She thus confirmed Emma in her rejection of Freud's diagnosis of a recurrence of her old neurosis. When I told that to Freud the next day he was furious. He took Dora's "diagnosis" as a fake. That to him was a matter of course. He called it a highly unprofessional interference with a patient under another doctor's care. He immediately withdrew from the case, saying: "That is Emma's end. Now she will never get well." He was right. Emma was up and about for a short time, but soon returned to her couch on which she had lived so long. She survived, as a hopeless invalid, for another ten years. It may be unjust to him, but I had the impression, or let me say, the suspicion, justified by nothing I can adduce, that Freud was not unhappy to be rid of a burdensome charity case.

There is a striking contrast between Freud's behavior at the time of Emma's operation by Dora Teleky—of which he thoroughly disapproved—and that at the earlier operation by Fliess, which he not only approved of but helped to arrange. The irony is that the operation by Fliess was, in its very nature, unnecessary and unprofessional, whereas Dora Teleky's operation, based on a "claim" (to use Hirst's word) that Emma had an abdominal abscess, is at least within ordinary medical practice. Freud, many years earlier, should have been angry at himself and his friend Fliess for recommending a dangerous and unnecessary operation. Is his "fury" at the latest operation anything other than a projection of his repressed anger onto Dora Teleky and Emma Eckstein, precisely because he was still unable to acknowledge what he and Fliess had done to Emma Eckstein?

APPENDIX B

THE AETIOLOGY OF HYSTERIA[1]
[TRANSLATED BY JAMES STRACHEY]

I

GENTLEMEN,—When we set out to form an opinion about the causation of a pathological state such as hysteria, we begin by adopting the method of anamnestic investigation: we question the patient or those about him in order to find out to what harmful influences they themselves attribute his having fallen ill and developed these neurotic symptoms. What we discover in this way is, of course, falsified by all the factors which commonly hide the knowledge of his own state from a patient—by his lack of scientific understanding of aetiological influences, by the fallacy of *post hoc, propter hoc,* by his reluctance to think about or mention certain noxae and traumas. Thus in making an anamnestic investigation of this sort, we keep to the principle of not adopting the patients' belief without a thorough critical examination, of not allowing them to lay down our scientific opinion for us on the aetiology of the neurosis. Although we do, on the one hand, acknowledge the truth of certain constantly repeated assertions, such as that the hysterical state is a long-persisting after-effect of an emotion experienced in the past, we have, on the other hand, introduced into the aetiology of hysteria a factor which the patient himself never brings forward and

[1] Read before the Society for Psychiatry and Neurology, Vienna, April 21, 1896. [JMM]

whose validity he only reluctantly admits—namely, the hereditary disposition derived from his progenitors. As you know, in the view of the influential school of Charcot heredity alone deserves to be recognized as the true cause of hysteria, while all other noxae of the most various nature and intensity only play the part of incidental causes, of *"agents provocateurs."*

You will readily admit that it would be a good thing to have a second method of arriving at the aetiology of hysteria, one in which we should feel less dependent on the assertions of the patients themselves. A dermatologist, for instance, is able to recognize a sore as luetic from the character of its margins, of the crust on it and of its shape, without being misled by the protestations of his patient, who denies any source of infection for it; and a forensic physician can arrive at the cause of an injury, even if he has to do without any information from the injured person. In hysteria, too, there exists a similar possibility of penetrating from the symptoms to a knowledge of their causes. But in order to explain the relationship between the method which we have to employ for this purpose and the older method of anamnestic enquiry, I should like to bring before you an analogy taken from an advance that has in fact been made in another field of work.

Imagine that an explorer arrives in a little-known region where his interest is aroused by an expanse of ruins, with remains of walls, fragments of columns, and tablets with half-effaced and unreadable inscriptions. He may content himself with inspecting what lies exposed to view, with questioning the inhabitants— perhaps semi-barbaric people—who live in the vicinity, about what tradition tells them of the history and meaning of these archaeological remains, and with noting down what they tell him—and he may then proceed on his journey. But he may act differently. He may have brought picks, shovels and spades with him, and he may set the inhabitants to work with these imple-ments. Together with them he may start upon the ruins, clear away the rubbish, and, beginning from the visible remains, un-cover what is buried. If his work is crowned with success, the discoveries are self-explanatory: the ruined walls are part of the ramparts of a palace or a treasure-house; the fragments of columns can be filled out into a temple; the numerous inscriptions, which, by good luck, may be bilingual, reveal an alphabet and a language, and, when they have been deciphered and translated, yield undreamed-of information about the events of the remote past, to commemorate which the monuments were built. *Saxa loquuntur!*

If we try, in an approximately similar way, to induce the symptoms of a hysteria to make themselves heard as witnesses to the history of the origin of the illness, we must take our start from Josef Breuer's momentous discovery: *the symptoms of hysteria* (apart from the stigmata) *are determined by certain experiences of the patient's which have operated in a traumatic fashion and which are being reproduced in his psychical life in the form of mnemic symbols.* What we have to do is to apply Breuer's method—or one which is essentially the same—so as to lead the patient's attention back from his symptom to the scene in which and through which the symptom arose; and, having thus located the scene, we remove the symptom by bringing about, during the reproduction of the traumatic scene, a subsequent correction of the psychical course of events which took place at the time.

It is no part of my intention to-day to discuss the difficult technique of this therapeutic procedure or the psychological discoveries which have been obtained by its means. I have been obliged to start from this point only because the analyses conducted on Breuer's lines seem at the same time to open up the path to the causes of hysteria. If we subject a fairly large number of symptoms in a great number of subjects to such an analysis, we shall, of course, arrive at a knowledge of a correspondingly large number of traumatically operative scenes. It was in these experiences that the efficient causes of hysteria came into action. Hence we may hope to discover from the study of these traumatic scenes what the influences are which produce hysterical symptoms and in what way they do so.

This expectation proves true; and it cannot fail to, since Breuer's theses, when put to the test in a considerable number of cases, have turned out to be correct. But the path from the symptoms of hysteria to its aetiology is more laborious and leads through other connections than one would have imagined.

For let us be clear on this point. Tracing a hysterical symptom back to a traumatic scene assists our understanding only if the scene satisfies two conditions; if it possesses the relevant *suitability to serve as a determinant* and if it recognizably possesses the necessary *traumatic force*. Instead of a verbal explanation, here is an example. Let us suppose that the symptom under consideration is hysterical vomiting; in that case we shall feel that we have been able to understand its causation (except for a certain residue) if the analysis traces the symptom back to an experience which *justifiably produced a high amount of disgust*— for instance, the sight of a decomposing dead body. But if, instead of this, the analysis shows us that the vomiting arose from a great fright, e.g. from a railway accident, we shall feel dissatisfied and will have to ask ourselves how it is that the fright has led to the particular symptom of vomiting. The derivation lacks *suitability as a determinant*. We shall have another instance of an insufficient explanation if the vomiting is supposed to have arisen from, let us say, eating a fruit which had partly gone bad. Here, it is true, the vomiting *is* determined by disgust, but we cannot understand how, in this instance, the disgust could have become so powerful as to be perpetuated in a hysterical symptom; the experience lacks *traumatic force*.

Let us now consider how far the traumatic scenes of hysteria which are uncovered by analysis fulfil, in a fairly large number of symptoms and cases, the two requirements which I have named. Here we meet with our first great disappointment. It is true, indeed, that the traumatic scene in which the symptom originated does in fact occasionally possess both the qualities— suitability as a determinant and traumatic force—which we require for an understanding of the symptom. But far more frequently, incomparably more frequently, we find one of the three other possibilities realized, which are so unfavourable to an understanding. Either the scene to which we are led by analysis and in which the symptom first appeared seems to us unsuited for determining the symptom, in that its content bears no relation to the nature of the symptom; or the allegedly traumatic experience, though it *does* have a relation to the symptom, proves to be an impression which is normally innocuous and incapable as a rule of producing any effect; or, lastly, the "traumatic scene" leaves us in the lurch in both respects, appearing at once innocuous and unrelated to the character of the hysterical symptom.

(Here I may remark in passing that Breuer's view of the origin of hysterical symptoms is not shaken by the discovery of traumatic scenes which correspond to experiences that are insignificant in themselves. For Breuer assumed—following Charcot—that even an innocuous experience can be heightened into a trauma and can develop determining force if it happens to the subject when he is in a special psychical condition—in what is described as a *hypnoid state*. I find, however, that there are often no grounds whatever for presupposing the presence of such hypnoid states. What remains decisive is that the theory of hypnoid states contributes nothing to the solution of the other difficulties, namely that the traumatic scenes so often lack suitability as determinants.)

Moreover, Gentlemen, this first disappointment we meet with in following Breuer's method is immediately succeeded by another, and one that must be especially painful to us as physicians. When our procedure leads, as in the cases described above, to findings which are insufficient as an explanation both in respect to their suitability as determinants and to their traumatic effectiveness, we also fail to secure any therapeutic gain; the patient retains his symptoms unaltered, in spite of the initial result yielded by the analysis. You can understand how great the temptation is at this point to proceed no further with what is in any case a laborious piece of work.

But perhaps all we need is a new idea in order to help us out of our dilemma and lead to valuable results. The idea is this. As we know from Breuer, hysterical symptoms can be resolved if, starting from them, we are able to find the path back to the memory of a traumatic experience. If the memory which we have uncovered does not answer our expectations, it may be that we ought to pursue the same path a little further; perhaps behind the first traumatic scene there may be concealed the memory of a second, which satisfies our requirements better and whose reproduction has a greater therapeutic effect; so that the scene that was first discovered only has the significance of a connecting link in the chain of associations. And perhaps this situation may repeat itself; inoperative scenes may be interpolated more than once, as necessary transitions in the process of reproduction, until we finally make our way from the hysterical symptom to the scene which is really operative traumatically and which is satisfactory in every respect, both therapeutically and analytically. Well, Gentlemen, this supposition is correct. If the first-discovered scene is unsatisfactory, we tell our patient that this experience explains nothing, but that behind it there must be hidden a more significant, earlier, experience; and we direct his attention by the same technique to the associative thread which connects the two memories—the one that has been discovered and the one that has still to be discovered. A continuation of the analysis then leads in every instance to the reproduction of new scenes of the character we expect. For example, let us take once again the case of hysterical vomiting which I selected before, and in which the analysis first led back to a fright from a railway accident—a scene which lacked suitability as a determinant. Further analysis showed that this accident had aroused in the patient the memory of another, earlier accident, which, it is true, he had not himself experienced but which had been the occasion of his having a ghastly and revolting sight of a dead body. It is as though the combined operation of the two scenes made the fulfilment of our postulates possible, the one experience supplying, through fright, the traumatic force and the other, from its content, the determining effect. The other case, in which the vomiting was traced back to eating an apple which had partly gone bad, was amplified by the analysis somewhat in the following way. The bad apple reminded the patient of an earlier experience: while he was picking up windfalls in an orchard he had accidentally come upon a dead animal in a revolting state.

I shall not return any further to these examples, for I have to confess that they are not derived from any case in my experience but are invéntions of mine. Most probably, too, they are bad inventions. I even regard such solutions of hysterical symptoms as impossible. But I was obliged to make up fictitious examples for several reasons, one of which I can state at once. The real examples are all incomparably more complicated: to relate a single one of them in detail would occupy the whole period of this lecture. The chain of associations always has more than two links; and the traumatic scenes do not form a simple row, like a string of pearls, but ramify and are interconnected like genealogical trees, so that in any new experience two or more earlier ones come into operation as memories. In short, giving an account of the resolution of a single symptom would in fact amount to the task of relating an entire case history.

But we must not fail to lay special emphasis on one conclusion to which analytic work along these chains of memory has unexpectedly led. We have learned that *no hysterical symptom can arise from a real experience alone, but that in every case the memory of earlier experiences awakened in association to it plays a part in causing the symptom.* If—as I believe—this proposition holds good *without exception*, it furthermore shows us the basis on which a psychological theory of hysteria must be built.

You might suppose that the rare instances in which analysis is able to trace the symptom back direct to a traumatic scene that is thoroughly suitable as a determinant and possesses traumatic force, and is able, by thus tracing it back, at the same time to remove it (in the way described in Breuer's case history of Anna O.)—you might suppose that such instances must, after all, constitute powerful objections to the general validity of the proposition I have just put forward. It certainly looks so. But I must assure you that I have the best grounds for assuming that even in such instances there exists a chain of operative memories which stretches far back behind the first traumatic scene, *even though* the reproduction of the latter alone may have the result of removing the symptom.

It seems to me really astonishing that hysterical symptoms can only arise with the co-operation of memories, especially when we reflect that, according to the unanimous accounts of the patients themselves, these memories did not come into their consciousness at the moment when the symptom first made its appearance. Here is much food for thought; but these problems must not distract us at this point from our discussion of the aetiology of hysteria. We must rather ask ourselves: where shall we get to if we follow the chains of associated memories which the analysis has uncovered? How far do they extend? Do they come anywhere to a natural end? Do they perhaps lead to experiences which are in some way alike, either in their content or the time of life at which they occur, so that we may discern in these universally similar factors the aetiology of hysteria of which we are in search?

The knowledge I have so far gained already enables me to answer these questions. If we take a case which presents several symptoms, we arrive by means of the analysis, starting from each symptom, at a series of experiences the memories of which are linked together in association. To begin with, the chains of memories lead backwards separately from one another; but, as I have said, they ramify. From a single scene two or more memories are reached at the same time, and from these again side-chains proceed whose individual links may once more be associatively connected with links belonging to the main chain. Indeed, a comparison with the genealogical tree of a family whose members have also intermarried, is not at all a bad one. Other complications in the linkage of the chains arise from the circumstance that a single scene may be called up several times in the same chain, so that it has multiple relationships to a later scene, and exhibits both a direct connection with it and a connection established through intermediate links. In short, the concatenation is far from being a simple one; and the fact that the scenes are uncovered in a reversed chronological order (a fact which justifies our comparison of the work with the excavation of a stratified ruined site) certainly contributes nothing to a more rapid understanding of what has taken place.

If the analysis is carried further, new complications arise. The associative chains belonging to the different symptoms begin to enter into relation with one another; the genealogical trees become intertwined. Thus a particular symptom in, for instance, the chain of memories relating to the symptom of vomiting, calls up not only the earlier links in its own chain but also a memory from another chain, relating to another symptom, such as a headache. This experience accordingly belongs to both series, and in this way it constitutes a *nodal point*. Several such nodal points are to be found in every analysis. Their correlate in the clinical picture may perhaps be that from a certain time onwards both symptoms have appeared together, symbiotically, without in fact having any internal dependence on each other. Going still further back, we come upon nodal points of a different kind. Here the separate associative chains converge. We find experiences from which two more symptoms have proceeded; one chain has attached itself to one detail of the scene, the second chain to another detail.

But the most important finding that is arrived at if an analysis is thus consistently pursued is this. Whatever case and whatever symptom we take as our point of departure, *in the end we infallibly come to the field of sexual experience*. So here for the first time we seem to have discovered an aetiological precondition for hysterical symptoms.

From previous experience I can foresee that it is precisely against this assertion or against its universal validity that your contradiction, Gentlemen, will be directed. Perhaps it would be better to say, your *inclination* to contradict; for none of you, no doubt, have as yet any investigations at your disposal which, based upon the same procedure, might have yielded a different result. As regards the controversial matter itself, I will only remark that the singling out of the sexual factor in the aetiology of hysteria springs at least from no preconceived opinion on my part. The two investigators as whose pupil I began my studies of hysteria, Charcot and Breuer, were far from having any such presupposition; in fact they had a personal disinclination to it which I originally shared. Only the most laborious and detailed investigations have converted me, and that slowly enough, to the view I hold to-day. If you submit my assertion that the aetiology of hysteria lies in sexual life to the strictest examination, you will find that it is supported by the fact that in some eighteen cases of hysteria I have been able to discover this connection in every single symptom, and, where the circumstances allowed, to confirm it by therapeutic success. No doubt you may raise the objection that the nineteenth or the twentieth analysis will perhaps show that hysterical symptoms are derived from other sources as well, and thus reduce the universal validity of the sexual aetiology to one of eighty per cent. By all means let us wait and see; but, since these eighteen cases are at the same time *all* the cases on which I have been able to carry out the work of analysis and since they were not picked out by anyone for my convenience, you will find it understandable that I do not share such an expectation but am prepared to let my belief run ahead of the evidential force of the observations I have so far made. Besides, I am influenced by another motive as well, which for the moment is of merely subjective value. In the sole attempt to explain the physiological and psychical mechanism of hysteria which I have been able to make in order to correlate my observations, I have come to regard the participation of sexual motive forces as an indispensable premiss.

Eventually, then, after the chains of memories have converged, we come to the field of sexuality and to a small number of experiences which occur for the most part at the same period of life—namely, at puberty. It is in these experiences, it seems, that we are to look for the aetiology of hysteria, and through them that we are to learn to understand the origin of hysterical symptoms. But here we meet with a fresh disappointment and a very serious one. It is true that these experiences, which have been discovered with so much trouble and extracted out of all the mnemic material, and which seemed to be the ultimate traumatic experiences, have in common the two characteristics of being sexual and of occurring at puberty; but in every other respect they are very different from each other both in *kind* and in *importance*. In some cases, no doubt, we are concerned with experiences which must be regarded as severe traumas—an

attempted rape, perhaps,[2] which reveals to the immature girl
at a blow all the brutality of sexual desire, or the involuntary
witnessing of sexual acts between parents, which at one and the
same time uncovers unsuspected ugliness and wounds childish
and moral sensibilities alike, and so on. But in other cases the
experiences are astonishingly trivial. In one of my women patients it turned out that her neurosis was based on the experience
of a boy of her acquaintance stroking her hand tenderly and, at
another time, pressing his knee against her dress as they sat
side by side at table, while his expression let her see that he was
doing something forbidden. For another young lady, simply
hearing a riddle which suggested an obscene answer had been
enough to provoke the first anxiety attack and with it to start
the illness. Such findings are clearly not favourable to an understanding of the causation of hysterical symptoms. If serious and
trifling events alike, and if not only experiences affecting the
subject's own body but visual impressions too and information
received through ears are to be recognized as the ultimate traumas
of hysteria, then we may be tempted to hazard the explanation
that hysterics are peculiarly constituted creatures—probably on
account of some hereditary disposition or degenerative atrophy—
in whom a shrinking from sexuality, which normally plays
some part at puberty, is raised to a pathological pitch and is
permanently retained; that they are, as it were, people who are
psychically inadequate to meeting the demands of sexuality. This
view, of course, leaves hysteria in men out of account. But even
without blatant objections such as that, we should scarcely be
tempted to be satisfied with this solution. We are only too
distinctly conscious of an intellectual sense of something half-
understood, unclear and insufficient.

Luckily for our explanation, some of these sexual experiences
at puberty exhibit a further inadequacy, which is calculated to
stimulate us into continuing our analytic work. For it sometimes happens that they, too, lack suitability as determinants—

[2] The word "perhaps" is not in the original German text. [JMM]

although this is much more rarely so than with the traumatic scenes belonging to later life. Thus, for instance, let us take the two women patients whom I have just spoken of as cases in which the experiences at puberty were actually innocent ones. As a result of those experiences the patients had become subject to peculiar painful sensations in the genitals which had established themselves as the main symptoms of the neurosis. I was unable to find indications that they had been determined either by the scenes at puberty or by later scenes; but they were certainly not normal organic sensations nor signs of sexual excitement. It seemed an obvious thing, then, to say to ourselves that we must look for the determinants of these symptoms in yet other experiences, in experiences which went still further back—and that we must, for the second time, follow the saving notion which had earlier led us from the first traumatic scenes to the chains of memories behind them. In doing so, to be sure, we arrive at the period of earliest childhood, a period before the development of sexual life; and this would seem to involve the abandonment of a sexual aetiology. But have we not a right to assume that even the age of childhood is not wanting in slight sexual excitations, that later sexual development may perhaps be decisively influenced by childhood experiences? Injuries sustained by an organ which is as yet immature, or by a function which is in process of developing, often cause more severe and lasting effects than they could do in maturer years. Perhaps the abnormal reaction to sexual impressions which surprises us in hysterical subjects at the age of puberty is quite generally based on sexual experiences of this sort in childhood, in which case those experiences must be of a similar nature to one another, and must be of an important kind. If this is so, the prospect is opened up that what has hitherto had to be laid at the door of a still unexplained hereditary predisposition may be accounted for as having been acquired at an early age.[3] And since infantile

---

[3] What Freud is saying is that the hereditary predisposition is, after all (*doch*), not intelligible (*nicht verständlich*). Strachey seems to have read *noch* for *doch*. [JMM]

experiences with a sexual content could after all only exert a psychical effect through their *memory-traces*, would not this view be a welcome amplification of the finding of psycho-analysis which tells us that *hysterical symptoms can only arise with the co-operation of memories*?

II

You will no doubt have guessed, Gentlemen, that I should not have carried this last line of thought so far if I had not wanted to prepare you for the idea that it is this line alone which, after so many delays, will lead us to our goal. For now we are really at the end of our wearisome and laborious analytic work, and here we find the fulfilment of all the claims and expectations upon which we have so far insisted. If we have the perseverance to press on with analysis into early childhood, as far back as a·human memory is capable of reaching, we invariably bring the patient to reproduce experiences which, on account both of their peculiar features and of their relations to the symptoms of his later illness, must be regarded as the aetiology of his neurosis for which we have been looking. These *infantile* experiences are once more *sexual* in content, but they are of a far more uniform kind than the scenes at puberty that had been discovered earlier. It is now no longer a question of sexual topics having been aroused by some sense impression or other, but of sexual experiences affecting the subject's own body —of *sexual intercourse* (in the wider sense). You will admit that the *importance* of such scenes needs no further proof; to this may now be added that, in every instance, you will be able to discover in the details of the scenes the *determining* factors which you may have found lacking in the other scenes—the scenes which occurred later and were reproduced earlier.

I therefore put forward the thesis that at the bottom of every case of hysteria there are *one or more occurrences of premature sexual experience*, occurrences which belong to the earliest years of childhood but which can be reproduced through the work of psycho-analysis in spite of the intervening decades. I believe that this is an important finding, the discovery of a *caput Nili* in neuropathology; but I hardly know what to take as a starting-point for a continuation of my discussion of this subject. Shall I put before you the actual material I have obtained from my analyses? Or shall I rather try first to meet the mass of objections and doubts which, as I am surely correct in supposing, have now taken possession of your attention? I shall choose the latter course; perhaps we shall then be able to go over the facts more calmly.

(*a*) No one who is altogether opposed to a psychological view of hysteria, who is unwilling to give up the hope that some day it will be possible to trace back its symptoms to "finer anatomical changes" and who has rejected the view that the material founda-tions of hysterical changes are bound to be of the same kind as those of our normal mental processes—no one who adopts this attitude will, of course, put any faith in the result of our analyses; however, the difference in principle between his prem-isses and ours absolves us from the obligation of convincing him on individual points.

But other people, too, although they may be less averse to psychological theories of hysteria, will be tempted, when con-sidering our analytic findings, to ask what degree of certainty the application of psycho-analysis offers. Is it not very possible either that the physician forces such scenes upon his docile patients, alleging that they are memories, or else that the pa-tients tell the physician things which they have deliberately invented or have imagined and that he accepts those things as true? Well, my answer to this is that the general doubt about the reliability of the psycho-analytic method can be appraised and removed only when a complete presentation of its technique and results is available. Doubts about the genuineness of the infantile sexual scenes can, however, be deprived of their force here and now by more than one argument. In the first place, the behaviour of patients while they are reproducing these infantile experiences is in every respect incompatible with the assumption that the scenes are anything else than a reality which is being felt with distress and reproduced with the greatest reluctance. Before they come for analysis the patients know nothing about these scenes. They are indignant as a rule if we warn them that such scenes are going to emerge. Only the strongest compulsion of the treatment can induce them to embark on a reproduction of them. While they are recalling these infantile experiences to consciousness, they suffer under the most violent sensations, of which they are ashamed and which they try to conceal; and, even after they have gone through them once more in such a convincing manner, they still attempt to withhold belief from them, by emphasizing the fact that, unlike what happens in the case of other forgotten material, they have no feeling of remembering the scenes.

This latter piece of behaviour seems to provide conclusive proof. Why should patients assure me so emphatically of their unbelief, if what they want to discredit is something which—from whatever motive—they themselves have invented?

It is less easy to refute the idea that the doctor forces reminiscences of this sort on the patient, that he influences him by suggestion to imagine and reproduce them. Nevertheless it appears to me equally untenable. I have never yet succeeded in forcing on a patient a scene I was expecting to find, in such a way that he seemed to be living through it with all the appropriate feelings. Perhaps others may be more successful in this.

There are, however, a whole number of other things that vouch for the reality of infantile sexual scenes. In the first place there is the uniformity which they exhibit in certain details, which is a necessary consequence if the preconditions of these experiences are always of the same kind, but which would otherwise lead us to believe that there were secret understandings between the various patients. In the second place, patients sometimes describe as harmless events whose significance they obviously do not understand, since they would be bound otherwise to be horrified by them. Or again, they mention details without laying any stress on them, which only someone of experience in life can understand and appreciate as subtle traits of reality.

Events of this sort strengthen our impression that the patients must really have experienced what they reproduce under the compulsion of analysis as scenes from their childhood. But another and stronger proof of this is furnished by the relationship of the infantile scenes to the content of the whole of the rest of the case history. It is exactly like putting together a child's picture-puzzle: after many attempts, we become absolutely certain in the end which piece belongs in the empty gap; for only that one piece fills out the picture and at the same time allows its irregular edges to be fitted into the edges of the other pieces in such a manner as to leave no free space and to entail no overlapping. In the same way, the contents of the infantile scenes turn out to be indispensable supplements to the associative and logical framework of the neurosis, whose insertion makes its course of development for the first time evident, or even, as we might often say, self-evident.

Without wishing to lay special stress on the point, I will add that in a number of cases therapeutic evidence of the genuineness of the infantile scenes can also be brought forward. There are cases in which a complete or partial cure can be obtained without our having to go as deep as the infantile experiences. And there are others in which no success at all is obtained until the analysis has come to its natural end with the uncovering of the earliest traumas. In the former cases we are not, I believe, secure against relapses; and my expectation is that a complete psycho-analysis implies a radical cure of the hysteria. We must not, however, be led into forestalling the lessons of observation.

There would be one other proof, and a really unassailable one, of the genuineness of childhood sexual experiences—namely, if the statements of someone who is being analysed were to be confirmed by someone else, whether under treatment or not. These two people will have had to have taken part in the same experience in their childhood—perhaps to have stood in some sexual relationship to each other. Such relations between children are, as you will hear in a moment, by no means rare. Moreover, it quite often happens that both of those concerned subsequently fall ill of neuroses; yet I regard it as a fortunate accident that, out of eighteen cases, I have been able to obtain an objective confirmation of this sort in two. In one instance, it was the brother (who had remained well) who of his own accord confirmed—not, it is true, his earliest sexual experiences with his sister (who was the patient)—but at least scenes of that kind from later childhood, and the fact that there had been sexual relations dating further back. In the other instance, it happened that two women whom I was treating had as children had sexual relations with the same man, in the course of which certain scenes had taken place *à trois*. A particular symptom, which was derived from these childhood events, had developed in both women, as evidence of what they had experienced in common.

(*b*) Sexual experiences in childhood consisting in stimulation of the genitals, coitus-like acts, and so on, must therefore be recognized, in the last analysis, as being the traumas which lead to a hysterical reaction to events at puberty and to the development of hysterical symptoms. This statement is certain to be met from different directions by two mutually contradictory objections. Some people will say that sexual abuses of this kind, whether practised upon children or between them, happen too seldom for it to be possible to regard them as the determinant of such a common neurosis as hysteria. Others will perhaps argue that, on the contrary, such experiences are very frequent— much too frequent for us to be able to attribute an aetiological significance to the fact of their occurrence. They will further maintain that it is easy, by making a few enquiries, to find people who remember scenes of sexual seduction and sexual abuse in their childhood years, and yet who have never been hysterical. Finally we shall be told, as a weighty argument, that in the lower strata of the population hysteria is certainly no more common than in the highest ones, whereas everything goes to show that the injunction for the sexual safeguarding of childhood is far more frequently transgressed in the case of the children of the proletariat.

Let us begin our defence with the easier part of the task. It seems to me certain that our children are far more often exposed to sexual assaults than the few precautions taken by parents in this connection would lead us to expect. When I first made enquiries about what was known on the subject, I learnt from colleagues that there are several publications by paediatricians which stigmatize the frequency of sexual practices by nurses and nursery maids, carried out even on infants in arms; and in the last few weeks I have come across a discussion of "Coitus in Childhood" by Dr. Stekel (1895) in Vienna. I have not had time to collect other published evidence; but even if it were only scanty, it is to be expected that increased attention to the subject will very soon confirm the great frequency of sexual experiences and sexual activity in childhood.

Lastly, the findings of my analysis are in a position to speak for themselves. In all eighteen cases (cases of pure hysteria and of hysteria combined with obsessions, and comprising six men and twelve women) I have, as I have said, come to learn of sexual experiences of this kind in childhood. I can divide my cases into three groups, according to the origin of the sexual stimulation. In the first group it is a question of assaults—of single, or at any rate isolated, instances of abuse, mostly practised on female children, by adults who were strangers, and who, incidentally, knew how to avoid inflicting gross, mechanical injury. In these assaults there was no question of the child's consent, and the first effect of the experience was preponderantly one of fright. The second group consists of the much more numerous cases in which some adult looking after the child—a nursery maid or governess or tutor, or, unhappily all too often, a close relative—has initiated the child into sexual intercourse and has maintained a regular love relationship with it—a love relationship, moreover, with its mental[4] side developed—which has often lasted for years. The third group, finally, contains child-relationships proper—sexual relations between two children of different sexes, mostly a brother and sister, which are often prolonged beyond puberty and which have the

[4] Freud uses the word *seelisch*, which is better translated here as "emotional." [JMM]

most far-reaching consequences for the pair. In most of my cases I found that two or more of these aetiologies were in operation together; in a few instances the accumulation of sexual experiences coming from different quarters was truly amazing. You will easily understand this peculiar feature of my observations, however, when you consider that the patients I was treating were all cases of severe neurotic illness which threatened to make life impossible.

Where there had been a relation between two children I was sometimes able to prove that the boy—who, here too, played the part of the aggressor—had previously been seduced by an adult of the female sex, and that afterwards, under the pressure of his prematurely awakened libido and compelled by his memory, he tried to repeat with the little girl exactly the same practices that he had learned from the adult woman, without making any modification of his own in the character of the sexual activity.

In view of this, I am inclined to suppose that children cannot find their way to acts of sexual aggression unless they have been seduced previously. The foundation for a neurosis would accordingly always be laid in childhood by adults, and the children themselves would transfer to one another the disposition to fall ill of hysteria later. I will ask you to consider a moment longer the special frequency with which sexual relations in childhood occur precisely between brothers and sisters and cousins, as a result of their opportunities for being together so often; supposing, then, ten or fifteen years later several members of the younger generation of the family are found to be ill, might not this appearance of a family neurosis naturally lead to the false supposition that a hereditary disposition is present where there is only a *pseudo-heredity* and where in fact what has taken place is a handing-on, an infection in childhood?

Now let us turn to the other objection, which is based precisely on an acknowledgement of the frequency of infantile sexual experiences and on the observed fact that many people who remember scenes of that kind have *not* become hysterics. Our first reply is that the excessive frequency of an aetiological factor cannot possibly be used as an objection to its aetiological significance. Is not the tubercle bacillus ubiquitous and is it not inhaled by far more people than are found to fall ill of tuberculosis? And is its aetiological significance impaired by the fact that other factors must obviously be at work too before the tuberculosis, which is its specific effect, can be evoked? In order to establish the bacillus as the specific aetiology it is enough to show that tuberculosis cannot possibly occur without its playing a part. The same doubtless applies to our problem. It does not matter if many people experience infantile sexual scenes without becoming hysterics, provided only that all the people who become hysterics have experienced scenes of that kind. The area of occurrence of an aetiological factor may be freely allowed to be wider than that of its effect, but it must not be narrower. Not everyone who touches or comes near a smallpox patient develops smallpox; nevertheless infection from a smallpox patient is almost the only known aetiology of the disease.

It is true that if infantile sexual activity were an almost universal occurrence the demonstration of its presence in every case would carry no weight. But, to begin with, to assert such a thing would certainly be a gross exaggeration; and secondly, the aetiological pretensions of the infantile scenes rest not only on the regularity of their appearance in the anamneses of hysterics, but, above all, on the evidence of there being associative and logical ties between those scenes and the hysterical symptoms—evidence which, if you were given the complete history of a case, would be as clear as daylight to you.

What can the other factors be which the "specific aetiology" of hysteria still needs in order actually to produce the neurosis? That, Gentlemen, is a theme in itself, which I do not propose to enter upon. To-day I need only indicate the point of contact at which the two parts of the topic—the specific and the auxiliary aetiology—fit into one another. No doubt a considerable quantity of factors will have to be taken into account. There will be the subject's inherited and personal constitution, the inherent importance of the infantile sexual experiences, and, above all, their number: a brief relationship with a strange boy, who afterwards becomes indifferent, will leave a less powerful effect on a girl than intimate sexual relations of several years' standing with her own brother. In the aetiology of the neuroses quantitative preconditions are as important as qualitative ones: there are threshold-values which have to be crossed before the illness can become manifest. Moreover, I do not myself regard this aetiological series as complete; nor does it solve the riddle of why hysteria is not more common among the lower classes. (You will remember, by the way, what a surprisingly large incidence of hysteria was reported by Charcot among working-class *men*.) I may also remind you that a few years ago I myself pointed out a factor, hitherto little considered, to which I attribute the leading role in provoking hysteria after puberty. I then put forward the view that the outbreak of hysteria may almost invariably be traced to a *psychical conflict* arising through an incompatible idea setting in action a *defence* on the part of the ego and calling up a demand for repression. What the circumstances are in which a defensive endeavour of this kind has the pathological effect of actually thrusting the memory which is distressing to the ego into the unconscious and of creating a hysterical symptom in its place I was not able to say at that time. But to-day I can repair the omission. *The defence achieves its purpose of thrusting the incompatible idea out of consciousness if there are infantile sexual scenes present in the (hitherto normal) subject in the form of unconscious memories, and if the idea that is to be repressed can be brought into logical or associative connection with an infantile experience of that kind.*

Since the ego's efforts at defence depend upon the subject's total moral and intellectual development, the fact that hysteria is so much rarer in the lower classes than its specific aetiology would warrant is no longer entirely incomprehensible.

Let us return once again, Gentlemen, to the last group of objections, the answering of which has led us such a long way. We have heard and have acknowledged that there are numerous people who have a very clear recollection of infantile sexual experiences and who nevertheless do not suffer from hysteria. This objection has no weight; but it provides an occasion for making a valuable comment. According to our understanding of the neurosis, people of this kind *ought* not to be hysterical at all, or at any rate, not hysterical as a result of the scenes which they consciously remember. With our patients, those memories are never conscious; but we cure them of their hysteria by transforming their unconscious memories of the infantile scenes into conscious ones. There was nothing that we could have done or needed to do about the fact that they have had such experiences. From this you will perceive that the matter is not merely one of the existence of the sexual experiences, but that a psychological precondition enters in as well. The scenes must be present as *unconscious memories*; only so long as, and in so far as, they are unconscious are they able to create and maintain hysterical symptoms. But what decides whether those experiences produce conscious or unconscious memories—whether that is conditioned by the content of the experiences, or by the time at which they occur, or by later influences—that is a fresh problem, which we shall prudently avoid. Let me merely remind you that, as its first conclusion, analysis has arrived at the proposition that *hysterical symptoms are derivatives of memories which are operating unconsciously.*

(*c*) Our view then is that infantile sexual experiences are the fundamental precondition for hysteria, are, as it were, the *disposition* for it and that it is they which create the hysterical symptoms, but that they do not do so immediately, but remain without effect to begin with and only exercise a pathogenic action later, when they have been aroused after puberty in the form of unconscious memories. If we maintain this view, we shall have to come to terms with the numerous observations which show that a hysterical illness may already make its appearance in childhood and before puberty. This difficulty, however, is cleared up as soon as we examine more closely the data gathered from analyses concerning the chronology of the infantile experiences. We then learn that in our severe cases the formation of hysterical symptoms begins—not in exceptional instances, but, rather, as a regular thing—at the age of eight, and that the sexual experiences which show no immediate effect invariably date further back, into the third or fourth, or even the second year of life. Since in no single instance does the chain of effective experiences break off at the age of eight, I must assume that this time of life, the period of growth in which the second dentition takes place, forms a boundary line for hysteria, after which the illness cannot be caused. From then on, a person who has not had sexual experiences earlier can no longer become disposed to hysteria; and a person who *has* had experiences earlier, is already able to develop hysterical symptoms. Isolated instances of the occurrence of hysteria on the other side of this boundary line (that is, *before* the age of eight) may be interpreted as a phenomenon of precocious maturity. The existence of this boundary line is very probably connected with developmental processes in the sexual system. Precocity of somatic sexual development may often be observed, and it is even possible that it can be promoted by too early sexual stimulation.

In this way we obtain an indication that a certain *infantile* state of the psychical functions, as well as of the sexual system, is required in order that a sexual experience occurring during this period shall later on, in the form of a memory, produce a pathogenic effect. I do not venture as yet, however, to make any more precise statement on the nature of this psychical infantilism or on its chronological limits.

(*d*) Another objection might arise from exception being taken to the supposition that the *memory* of infantile sexual experiences produces such an enormous pathogenic effect, while the actual experience itself has none. And it is true that we are not accustomed to the notion of powers emanating from a mnemic image which were absent from the real impression. You will moreover notice the consistency with which the proposition that symptoms can only proceed from memories is carried through in hysteria. None of the later scenes, in which the symptoms arise, are the effective ones; and the experiences which *are* effective have at first no result. But here we are faced with a problem which we may very justifiably keep separate from our theme. It is true that we feel impelled to make a synthesis, when we survey the number of striking conditions that we have come to know: the fact that in order to form a hysterical symptom a defensive effort against a distressing idea must be present, that this idea must exhibit a logical or associative connection with an un-conscious memory through a few or many intermediate links, which themselves, too, remain unconscious at the moment, that this unconscious memory must have a sexual content, that its content must be an experience which occurred during a certain infantile period of life. It is true that we cannot help asking ourselves how it comes about that this memory of an experience that was innocuous at the time it happened, should posthumously produce the abnormal effect of leading a psychical process like defence to a pathological result, while it itself remains un-conscious.

But we shall have to tell ourselves that this is a purely psycho-logical problem, whose solution may perhaps necessitate certain hypotheses about normal psychical processes and about the part played in them by consciousness, but that this problem may be allowed to remain unsolved for the time being, without detracting from the value of the insight we have so far gained into the aetiology of hysterical phenomena.

III

Gentlemen, the problem, the approaches to which I have just formulated, concerns the *mechanism* of the formation of hysteri-cal symptoms. We find ourselves obliged, however, to describe the *causation* of those symptoms without taking that mechanism into account, and this involves an inevitable loss of completeness and clarity in our discussion. Let us go back to the part played by the infantile sexual scenes. I am afraid that I may have misled you into over-estimating their power to form symptoms. Let me, therefore, once more stress the fact that every case of hysteria exhibits symptoms which are determined, not by infantile but by later, often by recent, experiences. Other symptoms, it is true, go back to the very earliest experiences and belong, so to speak, to the most ancient nobility. Among these latter are above all to be found the numerous and diverse sensations and paraesthesias of the genital organs and other parts of the body, these sensations and paraesthesias being phenomena which simply correspond to the sensory content of the infantile scenes, reproduced in a hallucinatory fashion, often painfully intensified.

Another set of exceedingly common hysterical phenomena— painful need to urinate, the sensation accompanying defaeca-tion, intestinal disturbances, choking and vomiting, indigestion and disgust at food—were also shown in my analyses (and with surprising regularity) to be derivatives of the same childhood experiences and were explained without difficulty by certain invariable peculiarities of those experiences. For the idea of these infantile sexual scenes is very repellent to the feelings of a sexually normal individual; they include all the abuses known to debauched and impotent persons, among whom the buccal cavity and the rectum are misused for sexual purposes. For physicians, astonishment at this soon gives way to a complete understanding. People who have no hesitation in satisfying their sexual desires upon children cannot be expected to jib at finer shades in the methods of obtaining that satisfaction;[5] and the sexual impotence which is inherent in children inevitably forces them into the same substitutive actions as those to which adults descend if they become impotent. All the singular conditions under which the ill-matched pair conduct their love-relations— on the one hand the adult, who cannot escape his share in the mutual dependence necessarily entailed by a sexual relationship,

[5] "One cannot expect people who have no hesitation in satisfying their sexual desires upon children to take exception to nuances in the methods of obtaining that satisfaction." [JMM]

and who is yet armed with complete authority and the right to punish, and can exchange the one role for the other to the uninhibited satisfaction of his moods, and on the other hand the child, who in his helplessness is at the mercy of this arbitrary will, who is prematurely aroused to every kind of sensibility and exposed to every sort of disappointment, and whose performance of the sexual activities assigned to him is often interrupted by his imperfect control of his natural needs—all these grotesque and yet tragic incongruities reveal themselves as stamped upon the later development of the individual and of his neurosis, in countless permanent effects which deserve to be traced in the greatest detail. Where the relation is between two children, the character of the sexual scenes is none the less of the same repulsive sort, since every such relationship between children postulates a previous seduction of one of them by an adult. The psychical consequences of these child-relations are quite extraordinarily far-reaching; the two individuals remain linked by an invisible bond throughout the whole of their lives.

Sometimes it is the accidental circumstances of these infantile sexual scenes which in later years acquire a determining power over the symptoms of the neurosis. Thus, in one of my cases the circumstance that the child was required[6] to stimulate the genitals of a grown-up woman with his foot was enough to fixate his neurotic attention for years on to his legs and to their function, and finally to produce a hysterical paraplegia. In another case, a woman patient suffering from anxiety attacks which tended to come on at certain hours of the day could not be calmed unless a particular one of her many sisters stayed by her side all the time. Why this was so would have remained a riddle if analysis had not shown that the man who had committed the assaults on her used to enquire at every visit whether this sister, who he was afraid might interrupt him, was at home.

It may happen that the determining power of the infantile

---

[6] The German word that Strachey translates as "required" is *abgerichtet*, which is generally used of an animal who is trained to do something its owner wishes. [JMM]

scenes is so much concealed that, in a superficial analysis, it is bound to be overlooked. In such instances we imagine that we have found the explanation of some particular symptom in the content of one of the later scenes—until, in the course of our work, we come upon the same content in one of the *infantile* scenes, so that in the end we are obliged to recognize that, after all, the later scene only owes its power of determining symptoms to its agreement with the earlier one. I do not wish because of this to represent the later scene as being unimportant; if it was my task to put before you the rules that govern the formation of hysterical symptoms, I should have to include as one of them that the idea which is selected for the production of a symptom is one which has been called up by a combination of several factors and which has been aroused from various directions simultaneously. I have elsewhere tried to express this in the formula: *hysterical symptoms are over-determined.*

One thing more, Gentlemen. It is true that earlier I put the relation between recent and infantile aetiology aside as a separate theme. Nevertheless, I cannot leave the subject without overstepping this resolution at least with one remark. You will agree with me that there is *one* fact above all which leads us astray in the psychological understanding of hysterical phenomena, and which seems to warn us against measuring psychical acts in hysterics and in normal people with the same yardstick. That fact is the discrepancy between psychically exciting stimuli and psychical reactions which we come upon in hysterical subjects. We try to account for it by assuming the presence in them of a general abnormal sensitivity to stimuli, and we often endeavour to explain it on a physiological basis, as if in such patients certain organs of the brain which serve to transmit stimuli were in a peculiar chemical state (like the spinal centres of a frog, perhaps, which has been injected with strychnine) or as if these cerebral organs had withdrawn from the influence or higher inhibiting centres (as in animals being experimented on under vivisection). Occasionally one or other of these concepts may be perfectly valid as an explanation of hysterical phenomena; I do not dispute this. But the main part of the phenomenon—of the abnormal, exaggerated, hysterical reaction to psychical stimuli—admits of another explanation, an explanation which is supported by countless examples from the analyses of patients. And this is as follows: *The reaction of hysterics is only apparently exaggerated; it is bound to appear exaggerated to us because we only know a small part of the motives from which it arises.*

In reality, this reaction is proportionate to the exciting stimulus; thus it is normal and psychologically understandable. We see this at once when the analysis has added to the manifest motives, of which the patient is conscious, those other motives, which have been operative without his knowing about them, so that he could not tell us of them.

I could spend hours demonstrating the validity of this important assertion for the whole range of psychical activity in hysteria, but I must confine myself here to a few examples. You will remember the mental "sensitiveness" which is so frequent among hysterical patients and which leads them to react to the least sign of being depreciated as though they had received a deadly insult. What would you think, now, if you were to observe this high degree of readiness to feel hurt on the slightest occasion, if you came across it between two normal people, a husband and wife, perhaps? You would certainly infer that the conjugal scene you had witnessed was not solely the result of this latest trifling occasion, but that inflammable material had been piling up for a long time and that the whole heap of it had been set alight by the final provocation.

I would ask you to carry this line of thought over on to hysterical patients. It is not the latest slight—which, in itself, is minimal—that produces the fit of crying, the outburst of despair or the attempt at suicide, in disregard of the axiom that an effect must be proportionate to its cause; the small slight of the present moment has aroused and set working the memories of very many, more intense, earlier slights, behind all of which there lies in addition the memory of a serious slight in childhood which has never been overcome. Or again, let us take the instance of a young girl who blames herself most frightfully for having allowed a boy to stroke her hand in secret, and who from that time on has been overtaken by a neurosis. You can, of course, answer the puzzle by pronouncing her an abnormal, eccentrically disposed and over-sensitive person; but you will think differently when analysis shows you that the touching of her hand reminded her of another, similar touching, which had happened very early in her childhood and which formed part of a less innocent whole, so that her self-reproaches were actually reproaches about that old occasion. Finally, the problem of the hysterogenic points is of the same kind. If you touch a particular spot, you do something you did not intend: you awaken a memory which may start off a convulsive attack, and since you know nothing of this psychical intermediate link you refer the attack directly to the operation of your touch. The patients are in the same state of ignorance and therefore fall into similar errors. They constantly establish "false connections" between the most recent cause, which they are conscious of, and the effect, which depends on so many intermediate links. If, however, the physician has been able to bring together the conscious and unconscious motives for the purpose of explaining a hysterical reaction, he is almost always obliged to recognize that the seemingly exaggerated reaction is appropriate and is abnormal only in its form.

You may, however, rightly object to this justification of the hysterical reaction to psychical stimuli and say that nevertheless the reaction is not a normal one. For why do healthy people behave differently? Why do not all *their* excitations of long ago come into operation once more when a new, present-day, excitation takes place? One has an impression, indeed, that with hysterical patients it is as if all their old experiences—to which they have already reacted so often and, moreover, so violently— had retained their effective power; as if such people were incapable of disposing of their psychical stimuli. Quite true, Gentlemen, something of the sort must really be assumed. You must not forget that in hysterical people when there is a present-day precipitating cause, the old experiences come into operation in the form of *unconscious memories*. It looks as though the difficulty of disposing of a present impression, the impossibility of transforming it into a powerless memory, is attached precisely to the character of the psychical unconscious. You see that the remainder of the problem lies once more in the field of psychology—and, what is more, a psychology of a kind for which philosophers have done little to prepare the way for us.

To this psychology, which has yet to be created to meet our needs—to this future *psychology of the neuroses*—I must also refer you when, in conclusion, I tell you something which will at first make you afraid that it may disturb our dawning comprehension of the aetiology of hysteria. For I must affirm that the aetiological role of infantile sexual experience is not confined to hysteria but holds good equally for the remarkable neurosis of obsessions, and perhaps also, indeed, for the various forms of chronic paranoia and other functional psychoses. I express myself on this with less definiteness, because I have as yet analysed far fewer cases of obsessional neurosis than of hysteria; and as regards paranoia, I have at my disposal only a single full analysis and a few fragmentary ones. But what I discovered in these cases seemed to be reliable and filled me with confident expectations for other cases. You will perhaps remember that already, at an earlier date, I recommended that hysteria and obsessions should be grouped together under the name of *"neuroses of defence,"* even before I had come to know of their common infantile aetiology. I must now add that—although this need not be expected to happen in general—every one of my cases of obsessions revealed a substratum of hysterical symptoms, mostly sensations and pains, which went back precisely to the earliest childhood experiences. What, then, determines whether the infantile sexual scenes which have remained unconscious will later on, when the other pathogenic factors are super-added, give rise to hysterical or to obsessional neurosis or even to paranoia? This increase in our knowledge seems, as you see, to prejudice the aetiological value of these scenes, since it removes the specificity of the aetiological relation.

I am not yet in a position, Gentlemen, to give a reliable

answer to this question. The number of cases I have analysed is not large enough nor have the determining factors in them been sufficiently various. So far, I have observed that obsessions can be regularly shown by analysis to be disguised and transformed *self-reproaches about acts of sexual aggression in childhood*, and are therefore more often met with in men than in women, and that men develop obsessions more often than hysteria. From this I might conclude that the character of the infantile scenes— whether they were experienced with pleasure or only passively —has a determining influence on the choice of the later neurosis; but I do not want to underestimate the significance of the age at which these childhood actions occur, and other factors as well. Only a discussion of further analyses can throw light on these points. But when it becomes clear which are the decisive factors in the choice between the possible forms of the neuro-psychoses of defence, the question of what the mechanism is in virtue of which that particular form takes shape will once again be a purely psychological problem.

I have now come to the end of what I have to say to-day. Prepared as I am to meet with contradiction and disbelief, I should like to say one thing more in support of my position. Whatever you may think about the conclusions I have come to, I must ask you not to regard them as the fruit of idle specula-tion. They are based on a laborious individual examination of patients which has in most cases taken up a hundred or more hours of work. What is even more important to me than the value you put on my results is the attention you give to the procedure I have employed. This procedure is new and difficult to handle, but it is nevertheless irreplaceable for scientific and therapeutic purposes. You will realize, I am sure, that one cannot properly deny the findings which follow from this modi-fication of Breuer's procedure so long as one puts it aside and uses only the customary method of questioning patients. To do so would be like trying to refute the findings of histological technique by relying upon macroscopic examination. The new method of research gives wide access to a new element in the psychical field of events, namely, to processes of thought which have remained unconscious—which, to use Breuer's expression, are "inadmissible to consciousness." Thus it inspires us with the hope of a new and better understanding of all functional psychical disturbances. I cannot believe that psychiatry will long hold back from making use of this new pathway to knowledge.

APPENDIX C

CONFUSION OF TONGUES BETWEEN ADULTS AND THE CHILD[1]

(The Language of Tenderness and the Language of [Sexual] Passion)[2]

[A NEW TRANSLATION BY
JEFFREY M. MASSON AND MARIANNE LORING]

IT would be a mistake to attempt to force the vast theme of the external origin of the formation of character and of neuroses into a Congress paper.

I will, therefore, confine myself to a short extract from what I could say on this topic. It is perhaps appropriate for me to begin by communicating to you how I came to the problem suggested by the title of my paper. In the address I gave before the Vienna Psychoanalytic Society on the occasion of Professor Freud's seventy-fifth birthday, I reported on a regression in technique, partly one in the theory of the neuroses as well, which certain failures or incomplete results [in my analyses] forced upon me. I am referring to [my] recent stronger emphasis on traumatic factors, which have been undeservedly neglected of

---

[1] Read before the International Psycho-Analytic Congress, Wiesbaden, September 1932.

[2] The original title of the paper as announced was "The [Sexual] Passions of Adults and Their Influence on the Character Development and Sexual Development of Children."

late, in the pathogenesis of the neuroses. Insufficiently deep exploration of the exogenous factor carries with it the danger that one resorts to premature explanations in terms of disposition and constitution.

The impressive manifestations, as I like to call them, the near-hallucinatory repetitions of the traumatic experiences which began to accumulate in my practice justified my hope that as a result of such abreactions, large quantities of repressed affects would obtain recognition in conscious emotional life and would soon put an end to symptom formation, all the more since the superstructure of the affects had been sufficiently loosened through analytical work. Unfortunately, this hope was realized only very imperfectly and some of the cases even put me in a great dilemma. The repetition in which patients were encouraged by analysis succeeded *only too well*. To be sure, noticeable improvement of certain symptoms could be seen, but patients began to suffer from nocturnal anxiety states, frequently even from severe nightmares, and the analytic session degenerated again and again into an attack of anxiety hysteria. Even though we subjected the often seemingly dangerous symptoms of these [attacks] to a meticulous analysis, which apparently convinced and reassured the patient, the expected permanent cure did not come about. The next morning brought with it the same complaints about a terrible night and the same trauma was once again repeated in the analytic session. In this dilemma I was satisfied for quite a while in the usual manner with the thought that the patient was too resistant or suffered from repressions, which could be discharged and made conscious only in stages. But since no substantial change occurred even after quite some time, once again I had to give free rein to self-criticism. I began to pay careful attention when patients, during their attacks, called me unfeeling, cold, even brutal and cruel, when they reproached me with selfishness, heartlessness, and conceit, when they shouted: "For God's sake, help me! Quick! Don't let me perish without help!" I began to examine my conscience to see if in spite of my best conscious intention there was not some truth in these accusations. As an aside, I should note that such outbursts of anger and rage were exceptional. Very frequently the hour ended with a peculiar, almost helpless docility and a willingness to accept our interpretations. However, the superficiality of this impression allowed me to suspect that even these compliant patients secretly felt hate and rage, and I began to urge them to disregard my feelings. Even this encouragement met with little success; most patients resolutely refused what to them was an unreasonable expectation on my part, although it was sufficiently supported by the analytic material.

Gradually I came to the conviction that patients have an extremely refined feeling for the wishes, tendencies, moods, likes and dislikes of the analyst, even should these feelings remain totally unconscious to the analyst himself. Instead of contradicting the analyst, instead of accusing him of certain misdemeanors or blunders, patients *identify with him*; only in certain exceptional moments of a hysteroid excitement, that is, when they are in a condition of near-unconsciousness, can they bring themselves to protest. Generally they permit themselves no criticism of us; such criticism does not even occur to them unless we expressly give them permission to do so, in fact directly encourage them to make such criticisms. Therefore we must, from the associations of patients, discern the existence not only of unpleasant things from their past; we must also, more than we have done until now, look for the existence of repressed or suppressed criticism of us.

But here we come up against not inconsiderable resistances, and this time resistances in us, not in our patients. Above all, we must be more than well analyzed, right down to "rock bottom." We must recognize all our own disagreeable external and internal character traits so that we can be prepared for just about anything in the way of hidden hate, and disdain contained in the patient's associations.

This leads to the tangential problem relating to the analyst's own analysis, whose importance increases more and more. Let us not forget that the in-depth analysis of a neurosis generally takes many years, whereas the usual training analysis frequently lasts only a few months or at the most a year or a year and a half. This may lead to the impossible situation in which little by little our patients become better analyzed than we ourselves. That is, they show signs of such superiority, but are incapable of giving expression to it; in fact they often become extremely subservient, clearly because they are incapable or afraid of displeasing us with their criticism.

A good part of the repressed criticism of our patients concerns what might be called "professional hypocrisy." We politely greet the patient as he enters our room, request that he begin associating and thus promise him to listen attentively, to devote all our interest to his well-being and to the task of interpretation. In reality, however, we might find certain external or internal characteristics of the patient difficult to bear. Or perhaps we feel the analytic hour was an unwelcome interruption of a professional or personal, private matter which was more important to us. Here too I see no solution other than to seek the cause of the interruption in ourselves and to discuss it with the patient, to recognize it not only as a possibility but also as a fact.

It is remarkable that giving up the "professional hypocrisy," which until now was thought to be unavoidable, gives the patient a noticeable sense of relief instead of hurting his feelings. The traumatic-hysterical attack, if it came on at all, turned out to be much milder; past tragic events all of a sudden could be reproduced *in thought* without leading once again to the loss of emotional equilibrium; in fact the level of the patient's personality seemed to be considerably raised.

What brought about this state of affairs? In the doctor-patient relationship there was something unspoken, insincere, and discussing it loosened, so to speak, the tongue of the patient. The analyst's admission of error earned him the trust of the patient. It almost seems as though there is an advantage to making mistakes occasionally so that we can confess them to the patient. This advice, though, is surely superfluous; we make errors enough in any event. A most intelligent woman patient indignantly and justifiably said to me: "It would have been even better if you had avoided making mistakes altogether. You are so vain, Doctor, that you want to turn your very errors to your advantage."

The discovery and solution of this purely technical problem provided me with access to previously hidden or little noticed material. The analytic situation, with its reserve and coldness, professional hypocrisy and the dislike of the patient it masks, which the patient could feel in his bones, was essentially no different from what had led to the illness in his childhood. Since in addition we urged the patient to reproduce his trauma in an analytic setting of this sort, we created an unbearable situation; no wonder that it could have no other and no better consequences than the original trauma itself. However, the setting free of [the patient's] criticism, the capacity to recognize our mistakes and to avoid them, bring us the patient's trust. *That trust is a certain something that establishes the contrast between the present and the unbearable, traumatogenic past*, a contrast therefore which is indispensable to bringing the past to life, no longer as a hallucinatory reproduction, but as an objective memory. [Previously] hidden criticisms on the part of my patients, for instance, uncovered with keen perception the aggressive features of my "active therapy," the professional hypocrisy in forcing the relaxation [technique], and taught me to recognize and master exaggerations in both respects. I am no less grateful to those patients who taught me that we are much too inclined to insist on certain theoretical constructs and frequently ignore facts that would weaken our self-assurance and authority. In any event, I learned the reason why it was impossible to influence the hysterical outbursts and what then made possible the eventual success. I found myself in a position similar to that of the ingenious lady whose neurotic friend could not be roused from her narcoleptic condition by any amount of shaking and shouting. She suddenly hit on the idea to call out to her in a childish-playful manner: "Roll about, jump about, little baby,"[3]

---

[3] *"Roll Dich, toll Dich, Baby."* Undoubtedly a childhood rhyme, used for awakening a child or encouraging him to play. [JMM]

whereupon the patient began doing everything that was asked of her. In analysis we often speak of regression to childishness, but clearly we ourselves do not realize how right we are; we often speak of a split personality, but do not seem to appreciate sufficiently the depth of this split. If we maintain our pedagogical and cold attitude even in the case of an opisthotonic[4] patient, we thereby sever the last link to him. The unconscious patient is in his trance *really* a child that can no longer respond to intelligent clarification, but at most can respond to maternal warmth; without this he feels alone and abandoned in his great distress. He is in precisely the identical unbearable situation which at some point led to psychical splitting and finally to illness. No wonder that now he can act in no other way than he would during the illness proper, that is, repeat symptom formation by means of this shock. [*Erschütterung*?]

At this point I must not fail to mention that patients do not react to theatrical phrases expressing compassion but only to genuine sympathy. I do not know whether they can tell the difference by the sound of our voice, by the choice of our words, or in some other way. In any event, they display a strange, almost clairvoyant knowledge of the thoughts and emotions of the analyst. In this situation it seems hardly possible to deceive the patient and if such deceit is attempted, it can only lead to bad consequences.

Now let me tell you of some insights I gained through this more intimate relationship with patients.

Above all, my previously communicated[5] assumption, that trauma, specifically sexual trauma, cannot be stressed enough as a pathogenic agent, was confirmed anew. Even children of respected, high-minded puritanical families fall victim to real

[4] "A form of tetanic spasm in which the head and the heels are bent backward and the body bowed forward" (*Dorland's Medical Dictionary*). [JMM]

[5] No doubt a reference to "The Principle of Relaxation and Neocatharsis" (1929) and to "Child Analysis in the Analysis of Adults" (1931), both published in *Bausteine,* vol. 3, and *Final Contributions* (see notes 3 and 7, chapter 5). [JMM]

rape much more frequently than one had dared to suspect. Either the parents themselves seek substitution for their lack of [sexual] satisfaction in this pathological manner, or else trusted persons such as relatives (uncles, aunts, grandparents), tutors, servants, abuse the ignorance and innocence of children. The obvious objection that we are dealing with sexual fantasies of the child himself, that is, with hysterical lies, unfortunately is weakened by the multitude of confessions of this kind, on the part of patients in analysis, to assaults on children. Thus I was not surprised when a short time ago an educator known for his high-minded philanthropy came to see me in a state of veritable despair to tell me that thus far he had been unfortunate enough to discover five families of good society in which the governesses lived in a regular conjugal state with nine- to eleven-year-old boys.

The following is a typical manner in which incestuous seductions come about:

An adult and a child love each other; the child has the playful fantasy that he will assume the role of the mother to the adult. This game may also take on erotic forms, but always remains on the level of tenderness. This is not true of adults with a pathological predisposition, particularly when their equilibrium and their self-control have been upset by some misfortune or by the consumption of intoxicating substances. They confuse the playfulness of the child with the wishes of a sexually mature person or let themselves be carried away to engage in sexual acts without consideration of the consequences. Actual rape of girls barely beyond infancy, similar sexual acts of grown women with boys, even sexual acts of a homosexual character by force are commonplace.

It is difficult to fathom the behavior and the feelings of children following such acts of violence. Their first impulse would be: rejection, hatred, disgust, forceful resistance. "No, no, I don't want this, it is too strong for me, that hurts me. Leave me be." This or something like it would be the immediate reaction, were it not paralyzed by tremendous fear. The children feel physically and morally helpless, their personality is still too insufficiently consolidated for them to be able to protest even if only in thought. The overwhelming power and authority of the adults renders them silent; often they are deprived of their senses. *Yet that very fear, when it reaches its zenith, forces them automatically to surrender to the will of the aggressor, to anticipate each of his wishes and to submit to them; forgetting themselves entirely, to identify totally with the aggressor.* As a result of the identification with the aggressor, let us call it introjection, the aggressor disappears as external reality and becomes intrapsychic instead of extrapsychic; however, the intrapsychic is subjected to the primary process in a dreamlike state, as is the traumatic trance, that is, in accordance with the pleasure principle, it can be shaped and transformed into a positive as well as negative hallucination. In any event, the assault ceases to exist as an inflexible external reality, and the child, in his traumatic trance, succeeds in maintaining the former situation of tenderness.

Yet the most important transformation in the emotional life of the child, which his identification with the adult partner, an identification based on fear, calls forth, *is the introjection of the guilt feeling of the adult*, which gives hitherto innocent play the appearance of a punishable act.

When the child recovers after such an attack, he feels extremely confused, in fact already split, innocent and guilty at the same time; indeed his confidence in the testimony of his own senses has been destroyed. In addition to this, the behavior of the adult partner has become harsh, for he is now more than ever plagued and angered by remorse, which makes the child feel even deeper guilt and shame. Almost always the perpetrator acts as though nothing had happened, comforting himself with the thought: "After all, this is only a child, who still knows nothing, and will soon forget everything again." Not infrequently the seducer becomes overly moralistic or religious after such an event and seeks to save the soul of the child by means of such severity as well.

Usually the relationship to a second person of trust, in the chosen example the mother, is not intimate enough either to provide help. Timid attempts of this kind [on the part of the child] are rejected by the mother as nonsense. The abused child turns into a mechanically obedient being or becomes defiant, but can no longer account for the reason for the defiance, even to himself; his sexual life remains undeveloped or takes on perverse forms; I will not mention at this time the neuroses and psychoses that could result from such a situation. The scientific importance of this observation is the assumption that *the still not well-developed personality [of the child] responds to sudden unpleasure, not with defense, but with identification and introjection of the menacing person or aggressor, an identification based on fear.* Only now do I understand why patients so stubbornly refused to follow my suggestion to react to misfortunes they suffered with unpleasure, perhaps with hatred and defense, as I would have expected. A part of their personality, indeed its core, at some point got stuck on a level where one is still unable to react in an *alloplastic* manner: one does so *autoplastically*, as it were with a kind of mimicry. Thus we reach a form of personality consisting only of id and superego, which therefore lacks the ability to maintain itself even in unpleasure. This parallels the fact that for the not fully developed child,[6] being alone, without motherly or other care, and without a considerable measure of tenderness, is unbearable. Here we must revert to ideas long ago developed by Freud, who even then pointed out that the capacity for object-love is preceded by a stage of identification.

I would like to call this the stage of passive object-love or tenderness. Traces of object-love already surface here, but only in fantasy, in a playful manner. Thus children also, almost without exception, play with the idea of taking the part of the parent of the same sex, to become the spouse of the parent of the opposite sex. But, it must be stressed, only in fantasy; in reality they do not wish, nor are they able, to do without tenderness,

[6] In the German text as published in *Internationale Zeitschrift für Psychoanalyse* (1933), this reads: *"das ganz entwickelte Kind"* (the completely developed child). Our translation follows *Bausteine*, 3, p. 520: *"das nicht ganz entwickelte Kind"* (the not fully developed child). [JMM]

especially the mother's tenderness. If during this phase of tenderness *more love* is forced on a child or love of a kind other than what the child desired, this will lead to the same pathogenic consequences as *lack of love*, in which heretofore the cause [of illness] has almost always been sought. It would take us too far afield to point here to all the neuroses and all the characterological consequences brought about by premature grafting of forms of passionate sexual love riddled with guilt onto a still immature, innocent being. The consequence can only be that confusion of tongues to which I allude in the title of this lecture.

Parents and adults, as much as we analysts during analysis, must learn to accept that the desperate wish to free oneself from an all too oppressive love lies behind the submissiveness, indeed adoration, as well as behind the transference love of our children, patients, and students. If we can help the child, patient, or student to give up the reaction of identification and to ward off the burdensome transferences we can say that we succeeded in lifting his personality to a higher level.

Only briefly do I wish to point to a few additional insights to which this series of observations promises access. We have known for the longest time that not only forced love but also unbearable punishments can have a fixating effect. Perhaps the preceding observations will facilitate understanding of this seemingly senseless reaction. The child's playful offenses are lifted to the level of reality only upon administration of passionate, often enraged punitive sanctions, with all their depressive consequences for the child, who had, until then, felt free of guilt.

The more detailed examination of these processes during the analytic trance also teaches us that there can be no shock, no fright, without traces of a personality split. It will not surprise any psychoanalyst that one part of the person regresses to pretraumatic bliss and seeks to undo the trauma. It is more surprising that in the course of identification one sees a second mechanism at work. I, at any rate, knew little of it. I am referring to the sudden, surprising blossoming, as if by magic, of new faculties following violent shock. One is almost reminded of the magic skills of the fakirs who, it is said, can cause stems and flowers to grow from a seed before our very eyes. Extreme adversity, especially fear of death, seems to have the power suddenly to awaken latent, still uncathected predispositions, which awaited their ripening in deepest tranquillity, and stimulate them to action. The sexually violated child can suddenly bring to fruition under the pressure of traumatic exigency all future faculties which are virtually preformed in him and are necessary for marriage, motherhood and fatherhood, as well as all feelings of a mature person. Here one can confidently speak of *traumatic* (pathologic) *progression or precocity* in contrast to the familiar concept of regression. It is only natural to think of fruit that ripens or becomes sweet prematurely when injured by the beak of a bird, or of the premature ripening of wormy fruit. Shock can cause a part of the person to mature suddenly, not only emotionally *but intellectually as well.* I remind you of the typical "dream of the wise baby" singled out by me so many years ago, in which a newborn child or infant in its cradle suddenly begins to talk, indeed teaches wisdom to all the family. Fear of the uninhibited and therefore as good as crazy adult turns the child into a psychiatrist, as it were. In order to do so and to protect himself from the dangers coming from people without self-control, he must first know how to identify himself completely with them. It is unbelievable how much we can learn in reality from our wise children, the neurotics.

If traumatic events accumulate during the life of the growing person, the number and variety of personality splits increase, and soon it will be rather difficult to maintain contact without confusion with all the fragments, which all act as separate personalities but mostly do not know each other. In the end one might reach a state which one need not hesitate to call *atomization*, to continue the metaphor of *fragmentation*. It takes much optimism not to lose one's courage in the face of this condition either and yet I hope that even here connecting paths can be found. In addition to passionate love and passionate punishments there is a third way of binding the child to oneself and that is *the terrorism of suffering*. Children have the compulsion to smooth over all kinds of disorders in the family, that is to say, to take onto their tender shoulders the burdens of all others; naturally, in the final analysis, not out of pure unselfishness but to regain the lost peace and the tenderness that is part of it. A mother can make a lifelong nurse, in fact a substitute mother, out of the child by bewailing her suffering, totally disregarding the interests of the child.

I believe, should all this prove true, that we shall be obliged to revise certain chapters of the [psychoanalytic] theory of sexuality and of genitality. Perversions, for example, are perhaps only infantile at the level of tenderness. When perversions [are accompanied] by passion and a sense of guilt, they perhaps bear witness to their [origin in] exogenous stimulation, that is, in secondary, neurotic exaggeration. My theory of genitality as well failed to take into account this distinction between the phase of tenderness and that of passion. How much sadomasochism in the sexuality of our time is determined by culture (that is, derived exclusively from introjected feelings of guilt), and how much develops autochthonously and spontaneously as an independent phase of organization, is reserved for further investigations.

It would please me if you would take the trouble to examine, in practice and in theory, what I have communicated here, and especially if you would follow my advice to pay closer attention than you have in the past to the strange, much veiled, yet critical manner of thinking and speaking of your children, patients, and students, and, so to speak, loosen their tongues. You will hear much that is instructive.

APPENDIX

This train of thought calls attention to the [distinction between] tenderness in the erotic life of the' child and passionate [sexuality] in the erotic life of the adult from a purely descriptive point of view, but leaves open the question of the real nature of the difference between the two. Psychoanalysis can approve the Cartesian idea that passion [*Leidenschaft*] is caused by suffering [*Leiden*]. But perhaps it will at the same time discover an answer to the question of what it is in the playful satisfaction of tenderness that introduces the element of suffering and thereby of sadomasochism. The above considerations allow us to surmise that, among other things, it is the *sense of guilt*, which in the erotic life of the adult turns the love object into the recipient of *ambivalent* feelings of both love *and* hate, whereas this split is still foreign to the tenderness of children. It is the hate [the adult feels for the child] that traumatically surprises and terrifies the child who is seduced by an adult, and transforms him from a spontaneous and innocently playing being into a guilt-ridden love-automaton, anxiously and, so to speak, self-effacingly imitating the adult. His own guilt feelings and the hatred toward the seductive [child] partner shape the sexual intercourse of the adult into a battle (primal scene) which terrifies the child. For the adult this terminates with the moment of orgasm, whereas the erotic life of the child, in the absence of the "struggle of the sexes," remains at the level of foreplay, or knows satisfaction only in the sense of "satiety" but not the feelings of annihilation that accompany an orgasm. The "theory of genitality,"[7] which seeks the origin of the struggle between the sexes in phylogeny, will have to acknowledge this distinction between the erotic gratifications of children and the love during the intercourse [of adults] which is saturated with hatred.

[7] See S. Ferenczi, *Thalassa: A Theory of Genitality* (Albany, N.Y.: The Psychoanalytic Quarterly, Inc., 1938).

INDEX